Choosing Books for Children

THIRD EDITION

Choosing Books for Children

A Commonsense Guide

BETSY HEARNE

with Deborah Stevenson

University of Illinois Press

URBANA AND CHICAGO

First paperback edition, 2000

Manufactured in the United States of America
♾ This book is printed on acid-free paper.

Library of Congress Cataloging-in-Publication Data
Hearne, Betsy Gould.
Choosing books for children : a commonsense
guide / Betsy Hearne ; with Deborah Stevenson.
— 3rd ed.
p. cm.
ISBN 0-252-02516-4 (cl. : alk. paper)/ISBN 978-0-252-02516-7
ISBN 0-252-06928-5 (pbk. : alk. paper)/ISBN 978-0-252-06928-4
1. Children—United States—Books and reading.
2. Children's literature, English Bibliography.
I. Stevenson, Deborah. II. Title.
Z1037.A1H42 1999
011.62—dc21 99-6144
CIP

3 4 5 6 7 C P 7 6 5 4 3

Contents

Acknowledgments

Permission to reprint the following material is gratefully acknowledged:

"Beavers in November" by Marilyn Singer: From *Turtle in July* by Marilyn Singer (Atheneum, 1989); illustrations © 1989 by Jerry Pinkney. Reprinted courtesy of Atheneum Books for Young Readers, an imprint of Simon & Schuster Children's Publishing Division.

"Cake Mistake" and "Commas" by Douglas Florian: From *Bing Bang Boing* by Douglas Florian (Harcourt, 1994). © 1994. Reprinted by permission of Harcourt Brace & Company.

"Christmas Tree" by J. Patrick Lewis: From *Riddle-icious* by J. Patrick Lewis (Knopf, 1993). © 1993. Reprinted by permission of Alfred A. Knopf.

"Early Bird" and "Where the Sidewalk Ends" by Shel Silverstein: From *Where the Sidewalk Ends: The Poems and Drawings of Shel Silverstein* by Shel Silverstein (Harper, 1974). © 1974 by Evil Eye Music, Inc. Reprinted by permission of HarperCollins Publishers.

"Toad" by Valerie Worth: From *All the Small Poems* by Valerie Worth (Farrar, 1987). © 1987. Reprinted by permission of Farrar, Straus & Giroux, Inc.

Introduction

Jacket illustration by Maurice Sendak for *Celebrating Children's Books: Essays on Children's Literature in Honor of Zena Sutherland,* ed. Betsy Hearne and Marilyn Kaye (Lothrop, 1981). © 1981. Reprinted by permission of Lothrop, Lee & Shepard Books.

Chapter 1

Illustration by Dorothy Donohue for *Turkey Pox,* by Laurie Halse (Whitman, 1996). © 1996. Reprinted by permission of Albert Whitman & Company.

Chapter 2

Jacket illustration by Rosemary Wells for *My Very First Mother Goose,* ed. Iona Opie (Candlewick, 1996). © 1996. Reprinted by permission of Candlewick Press, Inc.

Chapter 3
Illustration by David Small for *The Gardener,* by Sarah Stewart (Farrar, 1997). © 1997. Reprinted by permission of Farrar, Straus & Giroux, Inc.

Chapter 4
Illustration by James Marshall for *Fox on Stage,* by James Marshall (Dial, 1993). © 1993. Reprinted by permission of Dial Books for Young Readers, a division of Penguin Putnam, Inc.

Chapter 5
Jacket illustration by Trina Schart Hyman for *Catherine Called Birdy,* by Karen Cushman (Clarion, 1994). © 1994. Reprinted by permission of Clarion Books.

Chapter 6
Jacket illustration by Elly Simmons for *Go and Come Back,* by Joan Abelove (Jackson/DK Ink, 1998). © 1998. Reprinted by permission of DK Publishing, Inc.

Chapter 7
Illustration by Douglas Florian for *Bing Bang Boing,* by Douglas Florian (Harcourt, 1994). © 1994. Reprinted by permission of Harcourt Brace & Company.

Chapter 8
Illustration by David Wiesner for *From Sea to Shining Sea: A Treasury of American Folklore and Folk Songs,* comp. Amy L. Cohn (Scholastic, 1993). © 1993. Reprinted by permission of Scholastic, Inc.

Chapter 9
Photograph by Bruce Macmillan for *Nights of the Pufflings,* by Bruce Macmillan (Houghton, 1995). © 1995. Reprinted by permission of Houghton Mifflin Company.

Chapter 10
Illustration by Michael Emberley for *It's Perfectly Normal,* by Robie Harris (Candlewick, 1994). © 1994. Reprinted by permission of Candlewick Press, Inc.

Chapter 11
Jacket illustration by Robert Lawson for *The Story of Ferdinand,* by Munro Leaf (Viking, 1936). © 1936. Reprinted by permission of Viking Children's books, a division of Penguin Putnam, Inc.

Chapter 12
Jacket illustration by David Macaulay for *The Zena Sutherland Lectures, 1983–1992,* ed. Betsy Hearne (Clarion, 1993). © 1993. Reprinted by permission of Clarion Books.

Afterword
Gryphon by Trina Schart Hyman for *The Bulletin of the Center for Children's Books.* © 1986. Reprinted by permission of the Center for Children's Books.

Preface

The process of revising this guide to children's books provoked mixed emotions: a sense of loss over great books that have gone out of print and a sense of wonder at the ongoing energy that generates great new books. Despite the creativity of its "products," publishing is a business and editors must abide by the bottom line. In the afterword I discuss some of the pressures determining whether a book stays in print or drifts toward that ominous condition called "out of stock indefinitely"—usually a precursor to the fatal state, "out of print."

Generally speaking, I was surprised to see how stable some genres are compared to others. Beginner and easy-to-read books, for instance, seem to stay in print for a long time, probably because of the educational market, and except for a few sparkling new additions (often to a longstanding series), that chapter took very little revision. General picture book production, on the other hand, has exploded with activity, although pop-up and board books rarely last for more than a few seasons. Nonfiction tends to date and disappear quickly, but poetry, which rarely dates, vaporizes with equal speed.

There was another surprise in store for me during the revision process. I discovered that people can date as much as books can. I wrote the first edition of this book almost twenty years ago and revised it completely ten years later. In both cases, I was a children's book review editor (first of *Booklist* and later of *The Bulletin of the Center for Children's Books*) overseeing the evaluation of nearly all the juvenile books published annually. I was also continually hurled headlong into popular culture through my own children's participation in it. Now, as a professor with grown children, I find myself involved with longer, slower looks at literature, and this third edition, when I finished it, seemed slightly out of sync with the volume and tone of the newest children's books. I asked Deborah Stevenson, associate editor of *The Bulletin of the Center for Children's Books,* to gloss the text, which she did with energetic efficiency and encyclopedic currency, adding titles and commentary that make this a collaborative project. Ultimately, of course, I take responsibility for the content and balance of a book that Deborah did nothing but improve.

Contemporary children's literature is a rich and diverse field, with good books on a multitude of topics from a multitude of talented voices about a multitude of cultures. The annotated lists of books at the ends of chapters reflect this broad range, but they also include personal favorites and are purposely limited because long bibliographies seem overwhelming. While other guides are devoted to comprehensive coverage, the primary purpose here is to discuss children's literature and its uses, with a few pertinent examples. There's a list of "classics," or old favorites, in chapter 11 (along with a few in chapters 2, 3, and 5), but most of this book emphasizes titles published since 1950. Because paperback editions come and go with some frequency, I have listed the title's original publisher and date—but check with your bookstore dealer for the latest edition. In updating the text and the book lists, I sometimes retained or selected less-recent titles over newer ones, as long as the older titles were still in print in either hardcover or paperback, because I liked them better.

Good books cannot be confined to one category or age group, and there's plenty of overlap in the discussions and the lists—a five-year-old may enjoy a toddler book and vice versa. In general, poetry for both children and young adults is included in the poetry chapter, as is nonfiction in the chapter on factual books. The chapter on young adult literature highlights fiction for adolescents. The lists at the ends of chapters offer a good starting point for anyone interested in exploring books for youth, but, like all selection guides, this one is subjective and should be altered by readers to fit their own tastes. The process of tracking down—in bookstores or libraries—the prime choices that are included here will also enrich the reader with exposure to other books not mentioned because of limited space.

I would like to thank the Graduate School of Library and Information Science at the University of Illinois at Urbana-Champaign, publisher of *The Bulletin of the Center for Children's Books,* for so generously allowing me to quote from reviews I have written as an editor and, presently, as a consulting editor. Special thanks to Janice Del Negro, the *Bulletin*'s editor-in-chief, and of course to Deborah Stevenson, associate editor, both of whose reviews I have plundered along with my own and others' and who have provided intelligent, knowledgeable, and friendly support for this and all my other projects. My royalties from this book will go to *The Bulletin,* along with my gratitude; and Deborah Stevenson has contributed her own weeks of concentrated pro bono work to the same worthy cause. With enthusiastic generosity Rosemary Wells provided a smashing jacket illustration in exchange for the purchase of copies of her book *Read to Your Bunny,* to be given away by the University of Illinois Press at various meetings of book buyers and librarians.

Finally, let me express appreciation to the parents, librarians, teachers, professors, critics, and bookstore professionals who have urged me to revise *Choosing Books for Children*—Hazel Rochman was especially persistent. Roger Sutton, as always, made me laugh—an ingredient essential to thinking. And my family, once again, brought me up for air during the submersion necessary for working on a book.

Choosing Books for Children

Maurice Sendak

Introduction

The child is the beginning of life. The story is the beginning of literature. In the beginning, children and stories are deeply connected. The three decades I have spent evaluating children's books as a parent, teacher, librarian, reviewer, and writer have taught me one sure thing: storytelling, reading, and caring for children flow together in a natural way. Children's books can offer any family a humane counterbalance to time-clock living, a chance to pause and take a fresh look at each other.

Think, for example, of the classic five o'clock conversation:

"How was school today?"

"OK . . ." (child kicking table)

"Don't kick the table, dear. . . . What did you do?"

"Oh, nothing."

Can you hear the long awkward pauses and communication breakdown? There is another possibility.

"How're you doing?"

"OK . . ."

"I like that weird poster you put up in your room yesterday."

"It's not weird."

"Well, wild. Stop kicking the table, dear. Anyway, it reminded me of some of the science fiction *I* like. In fact, I bought a great book today. Listen to this . . . "

Few children will turn down an invitation to do something with an enthusiastic parent.

The first conversation is a dead end, but the second one crosses a bridge toward a shared world. The child can be teething on the table or drinking a first cup of coffee. Books can bridge any age or interest. And this goes beyond the family circle. Books loved and shared can build a bridge where all the standard question-and-answer exchanges fail. Is there any real reply to "My, how you've grown"? Try it at a cocktail party; it's another true conversation stopper. Most adults talk to children as if they were a breed apart, and many feel at a loss in talking with children at all. This situation tends to get worse as adult and child separate daily into their own worlds. We trust the education of our children to a school. If our heirs can't read, we logically blame the school system. Too few of us know how to get involved in reading with kids. If we try, it often turns out to be either a chore (boring book) or a concession (cute book), but often it's not a pleasure. Even the best of intentions can lead to picking a book at random, like picking a trail through the wilderness without a guide.

Traditionally, children's librarians, with their historic commitment to bringing children together with books, have offered guidance. If you've got access to a good children's librarian, make use of him or her; you and your child will benefit from such a valuable resource. Knowledgeable bookstore personnel can also be a tremendous asset when you're plunging into the world of children's literature. But in a world apparently overstuffed with experts of all stripes, it seems to be getting harder to sift out the expertise and information that you want from all of it that you don't. Sometimes you don't have access to the kind of bookstore or library resources that you'd like; sometimes even if you do you'd like to be able to bring some knowledge of your own to bear on the situation. This book's objective is to provide you with that knowledge, to give you a little portable guidance in choosing successful books for your children from the dizzying array of brightly colored titles. Choosing books can be a daunting journey, an enlightening journey, even, I hope, an enjoyable journey. It's always an important one.

Literature is vital to children's reading and learning. But children's books are crucial to more than children. Children's books are a matter of adult self-interest as well. There is a child in every adult and an adult in every child, and it is a tragic thing to see them separated. Adults and children can both get a lot out of children's books, just as their ancestors did out of myths and folktales. The power of story is not to be denied. In prehistoric caves, during

Irish famines, in Nazi concentration camps, stories were as important as food. They were sometimes served instead, and they nourished starving hearts.

Children's literature is the inheritance of this tradition. It can be as good or as bad as adult literature. The good is inspired and inspiring. The mediocre is unmemorably entertaining. The bad may be obscene and dull or merely cute and dull. There are best-sellers, literary award winners, unrecognized works of lasting merit, classics, and escape reading.

Today's children are tomorrow's reading adults. If today's adults don't care about children's imaginations or their books, if they don't sense the strong connection, children certainly won't. Today's adults will lose a golden opportunity for pleasure, and tomorrow's adults may lose the passion for literature and learning. It doesn't take an educational study to show that children do what you do, not what you tell them to do. And it doesn't take a market survey to show that you do what you like to do, not what you ought to do. If you like to read to yourself and your children, they will probably like reading to themselves and their children. What really hooks anyone on children's books is liking them—not their theoretical importance, but their artistry and appeal. Children's literature is born of an art that has roots in storytelling older than telling time. It casts a spell that will work by itself if given the chance. The reading relationship between you and your children can shape their feelings and reshape your own.

Childhood is the time and children's books are the place for powerful emotions, powerful language, powerful art. If the book you're reading seems boring, toss it aside. The book probably *is* boring, and there are thousands that aren't. The trick is to find those that cast a spell over you both. There is no room for cutesy books, dull books, or books that talk down. Children are not inferior. They may be small in stature but not in what they feel, think, listen, and see. Whatever the sensitivity ratio between child and adult, there are books that can hold the attention of both. The last several decades have seen a renaissance in children's literature, but most people don't know about it. There are approximately 5,000 new juvenile trade books (not textbooks) published each year. Since 1950 the number has been as low as 2,500—a stable figure through several decades—and as high as 6,000 during boom periods. There are some 126,600 children's books in print (*Children's Books in Print 1998*, 29th ed.), and they range from bad to glorious.

Feeding a child strained bananas, hamburgers, or eventually filet mignon can't beat sharing books like Ezra Keats's *Snowy Day* or Louise Fitzhugh's *Harriet the Spy.* Feeding minds, your own and your children's, is tantalizing. The best menu includes the kind of book that nourishes you both. Obligation will get you nowhere—it's pleasure that counts. The bedtime story that does not bore a parent leads to a book discussion that does not bore an adolescent. Books do not make you fat, do not lead to drunken disorder, and do not cause cancer. That in itself makes them a rare treat.

It's amazing that children's learning to read is considered important but children's *books* often are not. Plastic toys sell better than books. Yet if children's minds are important, so are their books. And there is a literature good enough to match any child's freshness, interest, and honesty. Mother Goose is still one of the best sources of nursery rhymes, but her offspring have flown the coop and multiplied into thousands of picture books, novels, and works of nonfiction. Unfortunately, there are many readers, both child and adult, who haven't had the chance to know or enjoy them.

The gap between books and readers comes from a basic problem in our society. Children are loved in their place, but their place is too far from what "really counts"—money, power, and prestige. Their books, too, are held at arm's length from the literature that "really counts"—adult literature. This isn't because of quality—adult best-sellers rarely approach the level of Shakespeare—but because in most cases children aren't considered a real part of adult work and play. It's easy for children and adults to become strangers to each other's minds.

It doesn't have to be that way. A parent preoccupied by work can take a break reading Maurice Sendak's *Where the Wild Things Are* to a child at bedtime. An aunt, uncle, or friend can spark or rekindle acquaintance just by sitting on the couch with a child and reading a chapter of E. B. White's *Charlotte's Web.* Grandparents can share *The Lord of the Rings* with a high school student. There's no better way to relate to the young than over a bridge of books.

Choosing Books for Children tells how, what, when, and where. You may want to skip around, or you may want to see how the literature grows with the child. There's a chapter for every age group. There's a book for every situation. There's a world waiting for you and the children you love.

Dorothy Donohue

1

Choosing Books for Children

Whether you're a parent or a friend of one, it's going to happen: you're going to be standing amid the children's books in the library or bookstore wondering where on earth to start. Maybe you're at the bookstore because you've decided it's time to expand your home collection beyond books picked up in the checkout lane of the local supermarket. Or maybe a special child's birthday has snuck up on you, providing a golden opportunity to invest in the future, since a good book given as a gift will (1) last a long time and (2) be enjoyed over and over again. Or maybe you're at the library hoping to find some likely choices for a bedtime story.

Whatever the reason, there you are among the shelves, surrounded with books, *lost* among books. If you're in the library, you can console yourself with the thought that they are free (relatively speaking), but you still don't want to spend your time or your child's on a bad book. If you're in a bookstore, you're probably thinking that the books all seem expensive, even though you know that quality costs money and a book can last a long time. Still, whether you're taking a book home for a week, making it part of your permanent family library, or sending it across the country as a token of love you have the same question: How do you tell a good children's book from a bad one?

I used to buy a copy of *Winnie the Pooh* every time I got a birth announcement. There's nothing wrong with *Winnie the Pooh,* but sometimes I wanted a little variation, especially if I was going to be the visitor who read bedtime stories in a couple of years. Later, as a parent who was going to read bedtime stories every night, I wanted more than a little variation.

The same old question haunts the aisles of every children's book department: What's a good book for young Hermione or Herbert going on *x* years old? In libraries, there are often good children's librarians to help you, but bookstore salespeople aren't as likely to be able to lay the question to rest. They sometimes don't know where to start any more than consumers do. They also don't know the child, and they may not be familiar in any meaningful way with children's books—unless you're lucky enough to encounter one of those dedicated booksellers who reads widely and makes it her or his business to know both books and customers.

Too often booksellers and book buyers are stuck in the myth that children and their books are a breed apart. Take heart and remember rule number one: Don't panic and grab a copy of *Black Beauty* because your grandmother recommended it to you in your youth. Stand there and calmly ask yourself how you pick out a good coat. Color? Cut? Fabric? Warmth? Is it going to wear well? Do you just like the way it looks? Does it make you happier than the others? Think carefully and react honestly. Picking a good children's book isn't that different from making any other purchase. Actually, it's more like deciding what interests you in a movie. Is it the plot, the characters, the scenery, the script? Did you like the last movie these same people created?

Pick up the book. If it's a picture book, read it. If it's longer, read the beginning, leaf through a few pages in the middle, investigate the illustrations, if it's got any, and check out the ending. Don't rely solely on the front cover (even if it's got an award medal on it) or on the blurbs. Just as when you browse through a book rack at the airport, something may catch your attention—a suspenseful opening, a poetic sentence, a funny scene. If you're looking for something informational, pick a topic that interests you as well as the child. Ask for a book on bugs or ballet and then read some of it. The text and illustrations should seem clear, accurate, and interesting *to you.* Ask yourself, Is the text clever or cloying? Engaging or boring? Original or clichéd? Does it make sense to you? Do you wish you didn't have to read more? Look at the illustrations slowly, carefully. *Stare* at them. That's the way a child will do it. Can you live with them? Are the images fresh enough to absorb your attention? Do they entertain you or do they look like "kid stuff," filler pictures anyone could do with ten toes rather than a nimble wit? You're the key here, because if you enjoy the book, your children will soak it up. They won't get half as much pleasure stuck off alone with something you don't like well enough to share, and you really won't want to be left out of the fun either. Trust your own reactions.

Of course, tastes and interests vary as much for children's books as they do for adult books. It's useful to remember that every book doesn't have to do everything, and it's not the end of the world if a promising title flops. Maybe you can figure out why—and in the process learn more about your child's developing tastes—or maybe the book will be better received later. There are always other books to be shared, and there's always more to learn in the process. Reading can be the same kind of shared activity as fishing, playing cards, or going to a concert. Your response to a children's book, linked with your involvement with the child, is as important as any expert's recommendation.

The question of what age child can understand and enjoy what book is not as big a mystery as it may seem. You can sense when a child is ready to try solid food, to play alone outside, to start piano lessons, to ride the bus or subway unattended, or to take the car for the evening. Similarly, when a child is ready for a particular book depends on the child's skills, knowledge, interest, and experience.

One difference between shopping for a coat and shopping for a children's book is that the size of a child's mind is more adjustable than sleeve length, especially when an adult plans to adjust the fit by sharing the book. Here are some general guidelines:

- From birth to age six, picture books should have illustrations on every page and very little text. The plot and progression should be accessible to young listeners, and the illustrations should be understandable as well as enticing. These picture books are meant to be read aloud while the listener pores over the pictures. (See chapters 2 and 3.)
- For ages six to nine, beginner and easy-to-read books require short episodic chapters, scattered illustrations, simple vocabulary, slightly enlarged type, an open, friendly format, and a plot and cast of characters without too many complications. Beginner books especially require pictures to ease the transition to reading and to provide content clues. They can be read aloud to youngsters and/or alone by the child as reading skills start to develop. (See chapter 4.)
- For ages nine to twelve, there is a wide range of fiction and nonfiction, depending on a child's interests, motivation, and reading ease. This "middle-grade" audience has a variety to choose from: comedy, tragedy, mys-

tery, romance, adventure, fantasy, and realism. Though longer than the easy-to-read level, these books are generally shorter than those for young adults and adults. (See chapters 5, 7, 8, and 9.)

- For teenagers, books range from titles nearly indistinguishable from adult works (some of the readers in this age bracket will be reading adult literature with relish) to books dealing, in fiction and nonfiction, with specifically adolescent issues, to books offering a respite from the more serious fare without being condescendingly childish. (See chapter 6.)

Nonfiction, poetry, and folklore titles are also available for a wide range of readers, from preschool to high school and beyond.

If you know someone's hobbies or interests, you probably know their abilities, especially if you take the opportunity to talk books or read together. Your own involvement is the key. Sometimes having the child along helps—a trip to the library or bookstore can turn into a browsing party, and you'll learn a lot about each other by swapping tastes. But evaluating children's books is a matter of practice as well as taste. The best way to start is with a few touchstone titles, surefire suggestions that rarely miss. Once you've experienced something really good, it will be hard to grab any old thing off the shelf. Having the background on what's happened lately in children's literature may help.

The social and political upsets of the 1960s were reflected in children's books as well as in protest movements. Maurice Sendak's *Where the Wild Things Are* (1963) was a turning-point title for young children, as was Louise Fitzhugh's *Harriet the Spy* (1964) for middle-grade readers and S. E. Hinton's *The Outsiders* (1967) for junior high and high school readers. These three books represented a trend of tackling children's emotional reality head-on. At first they were mightily protested because they touched some "negative" aspects of childhood or society that adults didn't particularly want to deal with openly and in front of their children. Their children, of course, were already dealing with them.

In *Where the Wild Things Are,* which has become a U.S. cultural icon, a little boy named Max gets mad when his mother punishes him for misbehaving. He dreams of running wild with monsters, as their lord and master, empowered by the trick of "staring into all their yellow eyes." What seemed initially to alarm people about the book was the terror those monsters might strike into the heart of any child who beheld them.

The book does, in fact, deal with primal emotions, but children have always been able to sense that neither Max's anger nor his monsters are ever out of control. They love his freewheeling fantasy, set as it is in a secure framework. Not only does Max tame the monsters, but when he wakes up his mother has brought him supper—and it's still hot! The artwork, in contrast, is cool: cool blues, dexterous crosshatch line work, rhythmic compositions that dance across the page in varied frames. Even translated into another medium, these images captivate children's attention. The opera of *Where the Wild Things Are* is a spellbinder. Max's inner journey has the mythical dimension of a hero's quest.

Fitzhugh's novel *Harriet the Spy* meets as high a standard for writing as Sendak's picture book does for art, but it has faced an even more serious charge than that of frightening children: many adults feared that it would motivate kids to misbehave! Harriet is not a traditional innocent heroine, nor are her parents the traditionally wise and attentive sort. Initially, some educators were sure that juvenile spy clubs would spring up all over the country under Harriet's influence. As it turned out, children simply recognize that Harriet is one of them, imperfect but surviving the odds of growing up in the best way she can. Kids love her.

A similar fear of rebellion inspired protest against the teenage novel *The Outsiders,* which deals with gang warfare, death, and adolescent alienation. In presenting characters faced with a harsh reality far removed from traditional notions of idyllic childhood, Hinton threw down the gauntlet and helped move young adult literature into a new age.

All three books became wildly popular not long after publication and have achieved the status of contemporary classics. They now appear mild in view of later developments but certainly serve to update the newcomer whose hand wavers uncertainly toward *Black Beauty* or *The Swiss Family Robinson.*

Classic choices such as *The Hobbit* and *Little House in the Big Woods* (there's a list at the end of chapter 11) don't need much advertisement. They've already been discovered by adults. These well-known titles are a good starting point, but many recent children's books are just as appealing as the Laura Ingalls Wilder series. Patricia MacLachlan's *Sarah, Plain and Tall,* a near-perfect miniature novel that fulfills the ideal of different levels of meaning for children and adults, may be familar to adults from its television adaption; the book deserves to be at least as well known. Readers who love Laura and Sarah may find similar satisfaction in Jennifer Armstrong's *Black-Eyed Susan,* an evocative story of a pioneer girl who is afraid that her mother's longing for civilized life in Ohio will force the family to leave the plains she herself has come to love. The parent who grew up loving *The Outsiders* may find his or her adolescent wrapped up in Chris Lynch's *Slot Machine,* a funny, sharp-edged story about outsider kids bonding at an athletic camp. For every classic you know about, there is a shelfful of similarly wonderful but less famous books waiting to be found and united with a reading child.

If you wait for recommendations to come to you, you may wait for awhile. Children's literature suffers from irregular mainstream attention. There are two well-known annual children's book awards, the Newbery Medal for writing and the Caldecott Medal for illustration, but the annual winners are simply two of scores of good books published each year. The National Book Award reopened their children's category, but their selections lean toward titles for older readers. The handful of children's best-sellers (rarely award winners), including the picture books of Richard Scarry or Dr. Seuss and the novels of Judy Blume, also don't begin to represent the wide range of books available. Bookstore shelves are packed with mass market series such as Animorphs and Goosebumps and with television tie-in titles. These are wildly popular in cycles, but where do you find individual titles that stand out in the crowd and last beyond the current trend? While children's books are making some headway in finding review space in newspapers, such reviews are often simply holiday roundups and rarely indicate what's really available. We just don't consider books for children in the same league as books for adults when it comes to space for reviews.

Yet they *are* in the same league in terms of quality. That doesn't have to mean they're "just like books for adults"; but it does means that the creators of these books demonstrate craft and imagination that result in books of merit for their intended audience. Some individuals have met that standard for both adults and children: a case in point is the work of the picture book illustrator William Steig, who won the Caldecott Medal for *Sylvester and the Magic Pebble.* Steig is a cartoonist for *The New Yorker,* and many people know his drawings if not his name. Equally ingenious, however, are his picture books for children. *The Amazing Bone* is my favorite. In it, Pearl, a lovely young pig, is appreciating the first day of spring when she has the good fortune to run into a talking bone and, shortly thereafter, the misfortune of meeting a hungry fox. Perhaps there are only four plots in the world, and this one certainly isn't unusual. But among a rainbow of variations, this version is one of the brightest.

Just as Beatrix Potter does in *Peter Rabbit,* Steig uses the choicest words without worrying whether or not children can understand them. The truth is that children understand much more than we give them credit for, especially in the context of a story. "It was a brilliant day, and instead of going straight home from school, Pearl dawdled." What a wonderful word, "dawdled." What an appropriate word for children. We're treated to a picture of a succulent young porker dressed in romantic pink and dreaming of exciting things to come.

It's the little details that count. Pearl expects to be eaten soon. Readers know this isn't going to happen, if for no other reason than the irrepressibly cheerful colors, but the suspense is heightened by Steig's straight-faced wit. "'I hope it won't all take too long,' said Pearl. She could smell vinegar and oil. The fox was preparing a salad to go with his meal." What brings about Pearl's escape is a suddenly remembered incantation from the bone.

> "Yibbam!" said the bone suddenly, without knowing why he said it.
>
> "What was that?" said the fox, standing stock-still.
>
> "Yibbam sibibble!" the bone intoned. "Jibrakken sibibble digray!" And something quite unexpected took place. The fox grew several inches shorter.
>
> "Alabam chinook beboppit gebozzle!" the bone continued, and miraculously the fox was the size of a rabbit. No one could believe what was happening, not Pearl, not the fox, not even the bone, whose words were making it happen.
>
> "Adoonis ishgoolak keebokkin yibapp!" it went on. The fox, clothes and all, was now the size of a mouse.
>
> "Scrabboonit!" the bone ordered, and the mouse—that is, the minuscule fox—scurried away and into a hole.

When parent and child say that incantation together, villains shrink away.

Steig's work is a standard against which to compare the many offerings on the shelves devoted to preschool and primary-grade children's books. His *Dr. DeSoto,* another favorite, has to be the greatest dental fantasy in the history of literature. These and other picture books for children open up a whole unexpected world to explore.

As for touchstone titles for older children, Natalie Babbitt deserves a place in every heart for crafting the novel *Tuck Everlasting.* In *Tuck* an eleven-year-old girl discovers a secret stream that makes anyone who drinks from it live forever. Babbitt's words are chosen with care and humor. The first sentence of the book is a perfect example: "The road that led to Treegap had been trod out long before by a herd of cows who were, to say the least, relaxed." Anyone who knows cows can spot them in that sentence, and anyone who doesn't know cows can find out about them right there in the word "relaxed." In fact, the whole first paragraph of the prologue makes a reader see sharply and clearly:

> The first week of August hangs at the very top of summer, the top of the live-long year, like the highest seat of a Ferris wheel when it pauses in its turning. The weeks that come before are only a climb from balmy spring, and those that follow a drop to the chill of autumn, but the first week in August is motionless, and hot. It is curiously silent, too, with blank white

> dawns and glaring noons, and sunsets smeared with too much color. Often at night there is lightning, but it quivers all alone. There is no thunder, no relieving rain. These are strange and breathless days, the dog days, when people are led to do things they are sure to be sorry for after.

The same kind of superb writing that gives *Tuck Everlasting* its tightly wound plot and hauntingly real setting can be found in a number of novels for junior high readers. The whole area of young adult literature is fast growing—and growing richer—since its genesis in problem novels of the 1960s. One of the finest contributions to contemporary literature for young teens is Brock Cole's *The Goats.* In it, two outcasts, a boy and a girl, are left by their fellow campers on an island with no food or clothes. In a much larger sense, these two are social misfits, already marooned from their families and peers. They know it and, in an urgent but steadily credible story, they create a relationship that is unique, yet puts them back in touch with the rest of the world.

The story operates on many levels. The action of survival and evasion of authority when the children run away holds readers' attention. The main characters' vulnerability, desperate connection, and eventual expansion into trust of some African-American, inner-city, fresh air camp kids create a different kind of suspense that climaxes in a triumphant commitment after their success almost tears the two characters apart. Finally, their progress is marked by the emergence of each from an almost nameless anonymity to comfortable familiarity with each other and themselves.

The style does not miss a beat, either in narrative or dialogue, asserting itself without ostentation. Cole hints at sacrificial myth in the boy's story of a haunting experience in a Greek cave, supposedly inhabited by a god to whom worshipers sacrificed goats. Yet the symbolic allusions here and elsewhere reflect rather than obtrude, even when reinforced by references to a deputy sheriff trapping them in his goat farm jeepster. Several complex thematic questions of social cruelty and moral obligation arise subtly and are developed concretely. This is an unflinching book, and there is a quality of raw emotion that may score some discomfort among adults. Yet such a novel restores faith in the continuing cultivation of children's literature. The bookmaking is meticulous, highlighted by Cole's watercolor cover and pen-and-ink chapter heading sketches.

Tuck Everlasting and *The Goats* are for a more advanced reader, and some children's books are quite complicated indeed, but simple books can be just as good. Simple does not mean simplistic; witness some of the wonderful writing that has found its way into beginning readers such as Arnold Lobel's Frog and Toad books. If there's an underlying principle in children's literature, it's that simplicity should not lessen a story book but add depth to it—a standard of high quality plus fresh perspective that applies to nonfiction illustration, and poetry as well.

In nonfiction, Milton Meltzer pioneered the use of primary sources in writing history for children. One of the most extensive, thoughtful studies ever published for young people, his *Never to Forget: The Jews of the Holocaust* is a well-organized history supported by first-person accounts of survivors and by the recovered documents of victims. Along with later books, such as Barbara Rogasky's *Smoke and Ashes: The Story of the Holocaust* and Schoschana Rabinovici's autobiographical *Thanks to My Mother, Never to Forget* informs (without overwhelming) older readers in junior and senior high school of the worst horrors of a historical nightmare.

On a lighter note, the same kind of accuracy and involvement has been demonstrated in pictorial nonfiction books, such as *Cathedral, City, Pyramid, Underground,* and *Castle,* five titles in David Macaulay's architectural history series. Each combines sweeping black-and-white drawings and diagrams with carefully researched facts. The books attract fourth graders, college students, and anyone with a sense of curiosity because they're *well done and accessible*—a combination that is difficult to achieve but is the key to pleasing children and adults alike. *The Way Things Work,* which he has since updated as *The New Way Things Work,* was reviewed as an adult *and* a children's book and in both cases was heralded as an unprecedented introduction to basic principles of machinery and technology. The bottom line is that Macaulay's books are just plain interesting to everybody, and you won't find a better introduction to his subjects anywhere.

On the very simplest level, Joanna Cole and Jerome Wexler do the same thing in their scientific presentation for preschool and primary school children, *A Chick Hatches.* Step by step, with photographs that are almost translucent and terms that are exact but always understandable, the writer and the photographer together show an everyday event for the miracle it really is. Cole also knows how to have fun with facts. Her Magic School Bus series, illustrated by Bruce Degen, is an experience in cartoon hypertext. Chapter 9 on factual books for children has a full introduction to Joanna Cole and to other writers with a special gift for clarifying and enlivening information at an easy-reading level.

The combination of high quality and accessibility exists for illustration as well. Nancy Ekholm Burkert is a highly respected artist. Her paintings for *Snow White and the Seven Dwarfs* (translated by Randall Jarrell) raise book illustration to a fine art and demand the reader's attention. Each double-spread picture follows a double spread of text, so that you first read the story in words and then absorb it visually in the paintings. This is the kind of book that adults shouldn't rush through—for their own sake as well as their children's. It's the kind of book adults and children can—and should—take the time to enjoy together.

For the especially wiggly five-year-old, or any other child with a short attention span who might not be able to handle long stretches of reading between illustrations, I recommend the edition of *Snow White* that includes paintings by Trina Schart Hyman. The illustrations are more numerous and they quickly and dramatically move the story along. Or, for a *real* change of pace, try *Snow White in New York,* Fiona French's Art Deco spoof of the traditional tale. It's fascinating to see children respond to utterly different variations of the same story. Between multiple versions and the new wave of postmodern takeoffs, such as Jon Scieszka's *Stinky Cheese Man and Other Fairly Stupid Tales,* illustrated by Lane Smith, the possibilities for enjoying fairy tales and folktales are endless.

Poems for the young are just as rich. Nursery rhymes are the cradle of poetry, and those verses sometimes make more sense than nonsense. It's worth looking carefully at the multitude of Mother Goose books available before picking one out. Some of them are guaranteed to make you smile as surely as they do the child. *My Very First Mother Goose,* edited by Iona Opie and illustrated by Rosemary Wells, is a big book with a tiny first verse that sets off an immediate humor of contrast. Down in the corner of a full-page red-checked-tablecloth is the miniature scene of a minuscule cat with a toothy rat looming over his chair:

Jerry Hall,
He is so small,
A rat could eat him,
Hat and all.

And don't we all feel that small, not to mention endangered, sometimes—but especially at the age of one? Later on, a double spread dominated by pastel shades of cream and pink depicts mother and child rabbits in a cheery kitchen scene that's much more reassuring:

Wash the dishes,
Wipe the dishes,
Ring the bell for tea;
Three good wishes,
Three good kisses,
I will give to thee.

For preschoolers, the offhand hues, squiggly lines, and comic-satiric view of Wallace Tripp in *A Great Big Ugly Man Came Up and Tied His Horse to Me: A Book of Nonsense Verse* approaches story art at its funniest. A picture of an elite dinner party goes with this rhyme:

Hannah Bantry, in the pantry,
Gnawing at a mutton bone;
How she gnawed it,
How she clawed it,
When she found herself alone.

While Hannah cowers, chewing greedily, the guests sit under a picture of several lions crossing in front of a stream. The picture is labeled "Pride Goeth Before a Fall"—far from the main focus of the illustration, but a side joke for the sharp-eyed. Tripp's characters are often political figures, as were those in many of the original Mother Goose rhymes.

The titles mentioned here, like the bibliographies following each chapter, are merely starting places and examples. A well-stocked bookstore will have many touchstone titles to browse through. A good library can offer hours of browsing for you and your child. A book you really love may persuade you to start your own permanent collection. The bookstore and the library can use your full support, just as you can use their full resources. They offer the same kind of service that a fine restaurant does—and for less money!—in that they have an assortment of goodies from which to choose and ideas for your own home cooking. The answer to that question of how to tell a good children's book from a bad one is the same as telling a good recipe from a bad one: taste it. Looking and reading are the test. With a little time and interest, anyone can be a first-class, four-star, triple-A children's book connoisseur, and glad of the experience.

❧

The best year-round gift is any great book—picture, fact, or fiction—of the kinds suggested in the next several chapters. Sometimes, though, you want something tailored to the time—a birthday, for instance. Every child dreams of birthday surprises, but in Anthony Browne's *Gorilla,* Hannah's dream comes true when she imagines a trip to the zoo with a friendly gorilla, only to discover her busy father has planned just such an outing for her birthday. The illustrations are full of sly visual surprises, and children will pore over them long after the birthday is over.

One of the best ways to celebrate Christmas is by sharing Julie Vivas's book

The Nativity. Accompanying a minimal text excerpted from the King James version of Luke are blissfully exuberant watercolors of the Annunciation and birth of Christ. There are tattered angels and poor folk who keep chickens along with their naïve senses of humor. Each spread is a scenario for visual exploration: Mary's expression as she watches her belly grow enormous; her attempts to mount the donkey; the donkey's angle of reluctance in proceeding along a rocky trail; Joseph's cuddling of the baby; the townsfolk crowded onto perches of roof and tree; the shepherd ordering his sheep back to the flock. The compositions are fresh enough to make other nativity book illustrations look like greeting card art. "And she brought forth her firstborn son" shows on one page the baby's head and hands peeking into a dark square of night and on the next page the baby tumbling naked into the world. In the end, a mottled angel, his workboots still untied, holds the baby while Joseph helps Mary heave herself back up onto the donkey. This is a book that summons the familial joy of any birth—rainbow colors replace the traditional red and green—with no less reverence for the birth celebrated at Christmas.

If you're looking for an Easter treat, you should know that Ruby and Max, of board book fame, also appear in picture books for slightly older children. In *Max's Chocolate Chicken* by Rosemary Wells, it's superego versus id, with Ruby telling Max what to do and Max eating the chocolate chicken anyway. What cares he about finding the stupid eggs? A mudpuddle he finds, acorns, a spoon, ants even. ("Pull yourself together," says Ruby. "Otherwise you'll never get the chocolate chicken.") While Ruby counts her gold egg with purple stripes and her turquoise egg with silver swirls and her lavender egg with orange polka dots, Max makes ant-and-acorn pancakes in the mud. While Ruby declares herself the winner of the egg hunt, Max claims the prize and hides with it in a convenient hole under the tree. While Ruby offers to share it if he will come out, he nibbles it all, tail first, head next, wings last. Thoughtfully, a benign Easter Rabbit (not unlike Max in appearance) provides a chocolate duck as well—perhaps with Ruby in mind—but Max is closing in on that by the concluding picture. Bright in color and concept, this book is as fresh as the spring-green grass that dominates every spread.

One of the best gifts for almost any holiday in the Jewish tradition is Isaac Bashevis Singer's *Stories for Children,* an assortment of tales so rich with remembering that the past comes to life in the present. Whatever the religious or ethnic tradition, ritual is basic to all of us, and holidays have a tangible magic in childhood. This list includes a few samples so good they'll inspire requests all year round. Remember, buying or borrowing is only the beginning. It's reading together that makes an occasion special.

Holiday Books for Children

BIRTHDAYS

Browne, Anthony. *Gorilla* (5–8). Knopf, 1985.

Browne's masterly drafting and composition have never carried keener glints of irony than in this picture book about a girl who imagines a trip to the zoo with a gorilla, only to find her usually preoccupied father proposing just such a trip for her birthday.

Hershenhorn, Esther. *There Goes Lowell's Party,* illustrated by Jacqueline Rogers (4–7). Holiday, 1998.

Lowell's relatives defy a huge Ozark mountain rainstorm and flooded creek to mudslide right on home in time for the big party, with sprightly watercolors catching all the suspense and happiness involved as a small boy waits for his birthday bash.

Hoban, Russell. *A Birthday for Frances,* illustrated by Lillian Hoban (4–7). Harper, 1968.

Alas, it's not Frances's birthday but her baby sister's—and it's hard to *give* presents and not *get* them, even for a young badger! The authentic tone and reassuring humor of the Frances series, with its softly drafted drawings, makes every one of them a perennial pick. Whether it's *Bedtime for Frances* or *Bread and Jam for Frances,* it's always time for Frances.

Hughes, Shirley. *Alfie Gives a Hand* (3–5). Lothrop, 1984.

Alfie is one of many satisfyingly scruffy children who romp through the cheerfully hued, realistically detailed pictures, but he's the only one with a security blanket—and he learns, by the end of the birthday party he's attending, that he can give it up to help a friend.

Hurwitz, Johanna, ed. *Birthday Surprises: Ten Great Stories to Unwrap* (9–12). Morrow, 1995.

Ten children's authors create stories based on the premise that a child receives, along with other presents on his or her birthday, one beautifully wrapped box that's empty. The resulting variety of characters, action, and tone makes this an inventive surprise package itself!

Rice, Eve. *Benny Bakes a Cake* (3–5). Greenwillow, 1981.

Benny and his dog each have an eye on the birthday cake, but Benny's dog gets to it first in this roundly illustrated narrative of anticipation dashed and happiness restored.

Rylant, Cynthia. *Henry and Mudge and the Best Day of All,* illustrated by Suçie Stevenson (6–8). Macmillan, 1995.

A piñata with crackers? Well, even if it's Henry's birthday, his dog Mudge has to be in on the fun, and Mudge LOVES crackers. Breezy watercolor drawings help both listeners and beginning readers enjoy Henry's party as much as he does.

Wells, Rosemary. *Bunny Cakes* (3–6). Dial, 1997.
Ummm! An earthworm birthday cake with caterpillar icing and Red-Hot Marshmallow Squirters!! Max knows what Grandma really wants for her birthday, even if Ruby insists on angel surprise cake with raspberry-fluff frosting, silver stars, sugar hearts, and buttercream roses. And once again Max somehow wins the day, sort of, while every young listener wins with these richly goofy pictures.

VALENTINE'S DAY

Adoff, Arnold. *Love Letters,* illustrated by Lisa Desimini (8–12). Scholastic, 1997.
Eye-catching graphics and book design support a variety of upbeat, offbeat love poems—the operative word here is *beat,* and these are really fun to read aloud as well as look at alone.

deGroat, Diane. *Roses Are Pink, Your Feet Really Stink* (5–8). Morrow, 1996.
Caught in the act of uncomplimentary Valentine verses to two classmates he dislikes, Gilbert the opossum exhibits some truly human behavior, cleverly reflected in friendly scenes of too-true school life.

Lexau, Joan M. *Don't Be My Valentine* (6–8). Harper, 1985.
An easy-to-read comedy of errors in which Sam's unloving valentine gets delivered to his teacher instead of the girl who's always giving him unwanted advice.

London, Jonathan. *Froggy's First Kiss,* illustrated by Frank Remkiewicz (4–7). Viking, 1998.
True love comes too soon for Froggy, who responds to his first kiss with a heartfelt "BLAAAAAAH!" Colorful, comical, and anything but sentimental.

Stevenson, James. *A Village Full of Valentines* (6–8). Greenwillow, 1995.
Illustrated with the cartoonist's gleeful watercolors, these seven quick stories depict Valentine's Day in a village populated by a variety of animals, including Clifford the turtle, who hasn't gotten a valentine for fifty-six years!

HALLOWEEN

Bunting, Eve. *Ghost's Hour, Spook's Hour* (4–7). Clarion, 1987.
The young narrator's search for his parents through a house filled with nighttime noises will find a sympathetic hearing among listeners who will identify with the fears reflected in these suspenseful pictures and cheer as the hero overcomes his anxieties.

Del Negro, Janice. *Lucy Dove,* illustrated by Leonid Gore (7–9). Kroupa/DK Ink, 1998.
A stunning example of the many eerie folktales adapted into picture-book format for prime-time (or any other time) Halloween read-alouds, this one will send chills up the spine as a brave seamstress outwits and outruns a graveyard ghost and thereby makes her fortune. Powerful illustrations, deep-blue screened with bone-white, sharpen the suspense.

Martin, Bill, Jr., and John Archambault. *The Ghost Eye Tree* (5–8). Henry Holt, 1985.
Shadowy watercolor paintings and a poetic story of two children walking past a "haunted" old oak tree in the dark make a top-notch Halloween hair-raiser.

Merriam, Eve. *Halloween ABC* (8–10). Macmillan, 1987.
Delicately surrealistic art heightens the spooky mood of sophisticated poetry that's arranged alphabetically by title: "Apple," "Bat," "Crawler," "Demon," "Elf," "Fiend," and so on.

O'Malley, Kevin. *Velcome* (7–9). Walker, 1997.
Ghoul humor at its goofiest, this cornball spoof on scary stuff will leave kids laughing out loud, grownups smiling sheepishly, and both going back for a second look at the bountiful visual jokes.

Sierra, Judy. *The House That Drac Built,* illustrated by Will Hillenbrand (6–8). Gulliver/Harcourt, 1995.
Trick-or-treaters are in for a shock when they knock at Drac's door, since the occupants don't need costumes to look scary! The rhyme and pictures, though, are strictly for fun and surely healthier for young listeners than a bag full of candy.

Silverman, Erica. *The Halloween House,* illustrated by Jon Agee (4–8). Farrar, 1997.
Two escaped convicts are glad to get back to prison after a stint in the haunted house, where they encounter the characters of an old counting rhyme gone awry: "In the Halloween house, on a bed made of pine, a mama vampire woke with her little ones, nine." The watercolor illustrations make this more funny than spooky.

Titherington, Jeanne. *Pumpkin Pumpkin* (2–4). Greenwillow, 1986.
In this book, tailored for Halloween and gardening activities with nursery school children, finely shaded, subtly colored spacious drawings show a little boy planting his pumpkin seed and watching it grow, flower, and produce a ripe pumpkin, which he turns into a jack-o'-lantern with seeds left over to plant in the spring.

Winters, Kay. *The Teeny Tiny Ghost,* illustrated by Lynn Munsinger (4–7). HarperCollins, 1997.
This teeny tiny takeoff on a teeny tiny folktale makes rhythmic reading aloud—with reassuring watercolor art.

THANKSGIVING

Anderson, Laurie Halse. *Turkey Pox,* illustrated by Dorothy Donohue (5–8). Whitman, 1996.
Everybody's too busy getting ready for the big dinner to notice that Charity has broken out with chicken pox. Nana produces if not a cure then at least a comfort. Nothing's perfect compared to holiday expectations, but these watercolor and colored pencil pictures come close.

Brown, Marc. *Arthur's Thanksgiving* (6–8). Little, 1984.
A classroom play proves Arthur's prowess as a director—and a turkey—in a picture book children will find funny whether read aloud or alone.

Child, Lydia Maria. *Over the River and through the Wood,* illustrated by David Catrow (5–8). Henry Holt, 1996.
Never did such a traditional song get such untraditional treatment in this surrealistically riotous car ride to Grandma's house.

Cowley, Joy. *Gracias: The Thanksgiving Turkey* (5–8). Scholastic, 1996.
Miguel's truck-driving father gives him a live turkey for Thanksgiving, but who's going to eat a pet that comes gobbling after Miguel in church, especially after the priest blesses it? Warm colors enliven this cheerful urban story.

Livingston, Myra Cohn, ed. *Thanksgiving Poems* (5–8). Holiday, 1985.
Softly colored pencil drawings accompany verses by noted poets including David McCord, Valerie Worth, X. J. Kennedy, and Eve Merriam, along with several Native American songs.

CHRISTMAS

Briggs, Raymond. *Father Christmas* (4–8). Random, 1997.
Delicately lined watercolor cartoons depict a grumpy Father Christmas going about his domestic chores and grand tour, reindeer and all. This book is intimate and inclusive of a broad age range—children are attracted by the comic-book format and can "read" the pictures on their own.

Bunting, Eve. *December,* illustrated by David Diaz (8–10). Harcourt, 1997.
A homeless boy and his mother welcome a poor stranger into their cardboard-box shelter, sharing their meager Christmas fare of two cookies and discovering afterward that an angel has left them with a change of luck. The heavily outlined paintings against collage backgrounds complete the effect of this unusually thoughtful holiday tale.

Collington, Peter. *A Small Miracle* (5–8). Knopf, 1997.
Children can "read" the expressive pictures of this wordless book in which the figures in a church Nativity scene magically save a poor woman who has been robbed.

Paterson, Katherine. *Marvin's Best Christmas Present Ever,* illustrated by Jane Clark Brown (6–8). HarperCollins, 1997.
Even good times must pass, and Marvin comes to understand seasonal cycles when his handmade Christmas wreath becomes a home for springtime's nesting birds. A good choice for beginning readers during the postholiday slump.

Robinson, Barbara. *The Best Christmas Pageant Ever* (9–11). Harper, 1972.
The six dirty, disrespectful Herdman children, "absolutely the worst kids in the history of the world," lend unusual atmosphere to a traditional Christmas Pageant—and are affected by it in ways they didn't expect.

Sabuda, Robert. *The Christmas Alphabet* (4–8). Orchard, 1994.
Surprise is only the beginning of this pop-up book experience. As each flap lifts to reveal a different Christmas figure (angel, bell, candle, etc.), adult and child alike will wonder at the skillful crafting of art in action.

Van Allsburg, Chris. *The Polar Express* (5–8). Houghton, 1985.
Dark colors and rich textures give a mysterious tone to this fantasy about a boy's journey to the North Pole, from which he brings home a magic silver sleigh bell.

Van Leeuwen, Jean. *Oliver and Amanda's Christmas,* illustrated by Ann Schweninger (6–7). Dial, 1989.
Rounded figures and family romps make these pig siblings a welcome source of entertainment for beginning readers in any season.

Vivas, Julie. *The Nativity* (5–8). Harcourt, 1988.
Joyful watercolor paintings depict Mary, Joseph, the baby Jesus, and the angel who announces his birth as naïve, sweet-natured, salt-of-the-earth folk who cope as best they can with the miracle that has been delivered unto them.

Wells, Rosemary. *Morris's Disappearing Bag* (4–6). Dial, 1978.
Morris discovers a way to play with all his older siblings' presents, of which he's been jealous, in this funny picture book that makes the most of expressive (and somehow familiar) rabbits in brightly colored rooms.

HANUKKAH

Adler, David. *Chanukah in Chelm,* illustrated by Kevin O'Malley (5–8). Lothrop, 1997.
Every Chelmite has a special take on confusion, especially Mendel, the caretaker of the synagogue, who looks everywhere—under the table, over the table, and behind the table—for a table on which to put the menorah. Finehatched pen-and-wash art doubles the fun with sly details such as a square-wheeled bicycle and a satirical cat that pokes fun at these lovable folkloric fools.

Chaikin, Miriam. *Light Another Candle: The Story and Meaning of Hanukkah* (8–10). Clarion, 1981.
A well-illustrated history of Hanukkah and its holiday traditions explains customs still celebrated today.

Ehrlich, Amy. *The Story of Hanukkah* (5–8). Dial, 1989.
With inspired simplicity of text and art, this book relates the Jews' recovery of their defiled temple.

Hirsh, Marilyn. *Potato Pancakes All Around: A Hanukkah Tale* (5–7). Bonim Books, 1978.
A European village is the site of a romping picture-book version of "Stone Soup," though here the result is latkes from a crust of bread.

Kimmel, Eric. *Hershel and the Hanukkah Goblins,* illustrated by Trina Schart Hyman (5–8). Holiday, 1989.
A traveler agrees to spend the eight nights of Hanukkah in a haunted old synagogue to rid a village of goblins. Windswept landscapes and imaginatively wicked creatures charge this picture book with energy.

Moss, Marissa. *The Ugly Menorah* (7–9). Farrar, 1996.
During her first Hanukkah visit with Grandma since Grandpa's death, Rachel listens to the story of how he made a tin-and-wood menorah during the Depression, and she begins to understand the true values of her heritage. Homey watercolors comfortably complement the story.

Singer, Isaac Bashevis. *The Power of Light: Eight Stories for Hanukkah,* illustrated by Irene Lieblich (9–11). Farrar, 1980.

Whether the setting is a Polish ghetto or a Brooklyn apartment, whether the tone is realistic or mystical, these eight well-crafted stories convey a warm Hanukkah atmosphere that is beautifully reflected in Lieblich's impressionistic paintings.

SEASONAL

Drucker, Malka. *The Family Treasury of Jewish Holidays,* illustrated by Nancy Patz (all ages). Little, 1994.

Nine holidays of the Jewish year are covered—through literary selections and activities—in this large, well-designed volume, with a final section on the weekly celebration of Shabbat.

Friedrich, Priscilla, and Otto Friedrich. *The Easter Bunny That Overslept* (5–7). Lothrop, 1983.

After sleeping through a rainy Easter, the bunny tries to pass out his eggs on Mother's Day, the Fourth of July, Halloween, and Christmas, with each holiday celebrated in glowing illustrations.

Wood, Audrey. *The Horrible Holidays* (6–8). Dial, 1988.

Three easy-to-read stories, "The No-Thanksgiving," "The Crummy Christmas," and "The Unhappy New Year," show an antihero beleaguered by relatives, all amusingly quirky animal characters.

MY VERY FIRST
MOTHER
GOOSE
edited by
IONA OPIE
illustrated by
ROSEMARY WELLS

Rosemary Wells

2

First Adventures with Picture Books

The best book creators express things to a one-year-old that a one-hundred-year-old can also respect. The two ages may not see the *same* thing, but each will see *some*thing. Speaking to differing age levels requires a skillful simplicity in dealing with complex issues, actions, images, and emotions. A large concept can be boiled down to pithy but no less punchy language, to literal but no less skillful art, that means something to all ages.

The ability to say so much with simple language extended by illustration has characterized the best of children's literature from its beginning, but lately there have been some startling advances. As an art form, children's books have been raised to a new level by some of the best writers and illustrators around. Even before the age of one, a baby can see a song or verse translated into art and propped up on a lap in the form of a book. Some of the most beautiful books available are illustrated lullabies, songs, and nursery rhymes (there's a list at the end of this chapter).

Why bother with beautiful? Beautiful is expensive, and this baby can hardly focus her eyes yet—or maybe she's advanced to drawing on the table with a banana. The answer is twofold, the first being yourself. Looking at clichéd, clumsily cartooned pictures is a form of persecution. Reading trite jingles will double the agony, and that agony is unnecessary when there are so many books for the young that have more to offer. So why foist bad stuff on the smallest members of the community? Children are a product of their environment. Their mental capacity will grow with what they hear and see. The price of a book isn't really too much to pay for developing an instinct for quality.

The songs a mother, father, or grandparent sings to a baby, the nursery rhymes they chant, are deeply embedded in literature. When I was nursing my oldest daughter, Bob Dylan happened to be one of my favorite songwriters. In fact, I had named my baby Joanna, after Dylan's "Visions of Johanna." The song I sang her most often was "Just like Tom Thumb's Blues," which is a musically soothing but lyrically morbid number that fits in well to the rocking chair motion. Through long, tired nights of infant colic and crying, I can remember singing. I don't know whether I sang for me or for her, but it always put both of us to sleep. Long after I had stopped nursing and stopped rocking and even stopped singing lullabies, I happened to hum "Just like Tom Thumb's Blues," and the same baby who was now six stood transfixed in the middle of the kitchen and begged to hear the song again. She still loved that song at ages sixteen and twenty-six.

The point is that whatever you do counts. It all enters into the child's consciousness at an unconscious level. You can quote Shakespeare, sing Dylan, push Disney videos, or read a children's book. The sights and sounds surrounding a very young child, even a newborn, may not be understood, but they will be imprinted.

Infancy is a logical starting point for everything, including literature. And what comes first? There is nothing more satisfying than putting something in the mouth. What goes into the mouth goes into the mind. Let it be literature as well as plastic. Songs and sucking; cardboard, cloth, and chewing; paper, pictures, and pointing; language and listening—it's such a natural progression of events. You and your child can begin sharing the pleasures of reading as soon as you can prop the baby and the book in your lap without dropping either one. The formula is simple: the key to choosing the right book is your own enjoyment of it. Any child from birth on will respond to that. While you and your baby are regularly relishing lap-sitting sessions of singing a book or saying nursery rhymes and perusing their illustrations, your baby will, some bright and unexpected day, try to grab the book and eat it.

Well, why not? How often have you chewed on a thought? Give a child the same chance. There is nothing wrong with familiarity, with the book as a physical companion. The things dearest to us always get the most wear, whether they are teddy bears or blue jeans. I have seen children hug books they love.

For crawlers and toddlers, "physical" and "mental" are one and the same—the exploration of an unknown world through taste, sound, touch, sight, smell. *Every* book is a scratch-and-sniff book for children, or more likely a scratch-sniff-and-chew book. They are getting comfortable with the book as part of living. Soon they'll be ready to yell "DOG" when they see one in the book. Language is a magical bridge from physical to conceptual. Finally, they'll be ready to hear that word magically transformed into a dog story with a beginning, middle, and end. "Once upon a time there was a dog that loved to chase rabbits . . ."

Along with even the very youngest, you can enjoy nursery rhymes and singing books, ABC and I.D. (identify the object) books, concept books, and counting books (lots of these are listed at the end of this chapter), not to mention the simplest tales. As far as I'm concerned, Rosemary Wells should be crowned queen of books for the very young. She has illustrated board books for toddlers that tell stories about two rabbit siblings, Max and Ruby, with just a few words and slyly expressive, bright shapes on each page. In *Max's Breakfast,* Ruby tries to bully Max into eating his egg. Max hides it, hides *from* it, and finally tricks his older sister into eating the disgusting object herself. Reading these books out loud certainly beats mopping the kitchen floor while your children are in the next room overturning wastebaskets, exploring the contents for edible objects, and fighting over what they find. If you read to or with them, the kitchen floor will stay dirty but everyone will be in a better frame of mind, not to mention artistically enriched.

Sturdy, resilient, and fairly chew-resistant board books, with their thick cardboard pages and rounded corners, are a wonderfully useful format for the youngest audiences. Many old (and some not so old) favorites are available in this form as well as in the traditional larger binding, so if you're hoping for a more travel-safe edition of *Goodnight Moon* you're in luck. Don't be misled by format, however: books designed for a larger format don't always work as well in the confines of a board book's smaller pages, and the fact that the format appeals more to toddlers and infants doesn't guarantee that the *book* will. There's no reason why all of a two-year-old's books have to be board books, so get the regular version if it's likely to offer both of you more pleasure.

Pop-up and lift-the-flap books are also a favorite format for this age group. Of the spate of pop-up books popping up on the market, few last longer than it takes to wear out their paper parts, but they're fun while they last, and some score higher than others for invention, information, and amusement. Eric Hill's *Where's Spot* is one of the most enduring and successful, offering listeners a game of hide and seek right along with a mother dog who's looking for her puppy. The flaps are simple and can be reglued. Most important, the paper engineering is a crucial part of the text—there's a *reason* for the three-dimensional book design other than just to have things fly off flat pages to surprise a viewer.

Just as entertaining is *What's in My Pocket? A Pop-Up and Peek-In Book* by David Carter. The heads of a series of animals pop up on every page, while flaps form pockets revealing each animal's favorite food (an enticing search-and-find game). These are age-appropriate toy books where the paper engineering, instead of limiting the books to gimmickry, adds a new dimension to story and art.

Toddlers can find rainy afternoon relief looking at Aliki's rustic paintings for *Hush Little Baby* while you sing the song—on-key or off-key, but sing no matter what. At first you might feel foolish playing "This Little Pig Went to Market" and "Peek-a-Boo," but once you get involved, you'll find it's not any worse than some of the television shows you expose your mind to, and it can be considerably more lively, given a few creative variations. Marc Brown's *Finger Rhymes* and *Hand Rhymes* will give you a boost when it comes to refocusing squirmy toddlers who, for reasons mysterious to them, have to sit still in tight places such as airplanes or doctor's offices. Learning the games while using the books will foster playing the games—even without the books—in times of great need. Familiar routines often help settle children down in unfamiliar settings, and actions of diversion are far more effective than threats of punishment.

Action is important in the development of young children's first interest in books. Beginners need books that move in some way: dramatic detail, silly sounds, wordplay, games, singing, or just pointing-and-naming possibilities. That's why the picture books of Dr. Seuss and Richard Scarry are so successful: they have a lively cinematic quality. Neither artist varies his style, so a book-after-book reading can get wearisome, but each is an enduring attention-grabber, offering youngsters tidbits like those that tempt an inquisitive adult browsing through the encyclopedia or a favorite magazine. In fact, a picture encyclopedia isn't a bad investment for a child just learning to talk. Or try books like Eve Rice's *Sam Who Never Forgets,* with its warm, simple story about a zookeeper and lots of animals to name. Then move on to Peggy Rathmann's *Good Night, Gorilla,* another tale of a zookeeper and the creatures he cares for (who somehow act exactly like children).

Mother Goose and nursery rhyme books are innumerable. Such rhymes are as old as childhood and seem to multiply like children. They've flourished in jungles, in streets, and now in print. They range from old-fashioned versions like Blanche Wright's *Real Mother Goose* to contemporary ones like Iona Opie and Rosemary Wells's *My Very First Mother Goose* (described in chapter 1) and Arnold Lobel's endlessly entertaining *Random House Book of Mother Goose.* The number of verses will vary, as will the art, from light-toned illustrations to dark-toned, from sensible to nonsensical, from ancient to current.

Illustrations such as Kate Greenaway's from the nineteenth century still flourish alongside contemporary Japanese poster art on the picture-book shelf, a shelf that appears to stretch to every corner of the world in rhyme and prose. U.S., British, East and West European, Russian, Asian, African, South American, and Australian nursery rhymes and tales all have found homes in picture books for the youngest child.

Of course, early reading sessions may not follow a perfect or even predictable pattern. Once, as I was reading to my two-year-old, she seemed to be listening intently to the story while running a pudgy finger around the heavy orange border framing every picture. At the end of a turtle's harrowing escape from a fox, Elizabeth popped the question burning in her mind. "What's this?" she asked, rubbing the orange border. Although she seemed to have completely disregarded my dramatic narrative, I considered the reading session a success. She was absorbing the story art in her own way. It may have been that the tale seemed a little scary to her and she found comfort in the limits set by the formal border.

Most educators, psychologists, librarians, and best-selling authors agree that parents who read to their children early on give them a head start. But the difference between theory and practice in reading to a toddler is left up to the parent to find out. As a professional reviewer of children's books and a veteran mother as well, I can attest that first reading experiences are not so much instant magic as long-range development.

That first golden glow of snuggling together over a book may dim with some typical struggles. For readers in the oral stage, there is the question of whether the book should be eaten or read. In cases of siblings close in age, should the baby be allowed to teeth on the book while the toddler tries to look and listen? Who is going to clutch the book during bedtime sharing? How much force can go into turning a page without tearing it? Can the parent survive the aura of a poopy diaper in face of the charmed toddler's plea to "Read it again"? Is the book drip-dry, in case of carsickness? How far across the floor should the adult reader chase the wiggly toddler in order to finish reading the story? In conflicts of taste between *Carpet Critters™ Get into Yet More Mischief* and *The Very Hungry Caterpillar,* should the parent's age and experience count toward consumer selection? Do a toddler's continual interruptions with comments and questions about his or her belly button mean a parent has failed to convey the full power and expression of *The Three Billy Goats Gruff*?

The answer to any or all of these questions is "Be flexible." Looking and listening take practice. A reasonable attention span is precious and needs to be cultivated—most children today cannot develop one without their parents' help. Some days, especially in the beginning, reading aloud may have to be extradramatic, adapted, improvised, interrupted, or simply dropped. Lots of early reading sessions involve no more than pointing, naming, and relating objects to the child's own experience. Keep the action level high with liberal tickling, face-making, finger play, and physical nonsense. Slow it down with singing, rhyming, and cuddling. Just associating a book with attention and interest is an achievement for you and your baby.

Three- to five-year-olds have mastered more concepts and seem more verbal than toddlers, but their physical interaction with literature is still primal. They'll appreciate bouncy books like Nancy Carlstrom's *Jesse Bear, What Will You Wear?* This is one of those lilting chants that parent and child will find themselves saying with or without the book, although the illustrations certainly offer plenty to pore over in lap-sitting sessions. Little Jesse starts out sensibly enough with a "shirt of red / Pulled over my head" but proceeds to "pants that dance," "a rose in my toes," "sun on the run," and "sand on my hand in the morning." Each time of day offers him more opportunities for silly apparel ("juice from a pear / and rice in my hair") until finally he wears hugs and kisses to bed, along with some dreams in his head. The big, cheerful watercolor paintings show the baby bear in loving relation to his family and his world. Without crossing the line into sentimentality, this book offers a happy, humorous soundfest that will associate reading aloud with a sense of play.

Audrey and Don Wood have a special touch with books for the three- to five-year-old. *The Napping House* is a cumulative tale that starts with an old woman napping on a rainy day. First a child and then a dog, a cat, and a mouse pile on top of her, until a flea bites the mouse and causes an explosion of activity just as the sun comes out. The blues and golds of the illustrations set off the verbal rhythms like a stage backdrop. *King Bidgood's in the Bathtub*, another super-romp by this author-illustrator team, pokes fun at adults (and royalty) for something children often do: refuse to get out of the tub. King Bidgood demands that his whole court join him, and they're all suitably soggy by the time the little page pulls the plug ("Glug, glug, glug"). What better bribe to lure your waterlogged offspring into the towel than promising a bedtime rendition of King Bidgood? Fortunately, most adults find it beguiling too, which always helps through the fiftieth reading.

British author-illustrator Shirley Hughes strikes a cozier note with her books about Alfie and and his little sister, Annie Rose. Her illustrations are affectionately realistic and her gentle texts based on close observation of children's activities. *Alfie and the Birthday Surprise,* for instance, offers Alfie the satisfaction of secreting a kitten until it's time for a neighbor's birthday. The ensuing celebration is warm and joyous without ever becoming cloying, and the cat stalks happily through the pages in a most authentically feline way.

Alphabet, counting, and concept books offer endless inventive variety. There's no need to let the number of possibilities overwhelm you, though—focus instead on the capability of the child in question. Two- to five-year-olds need a clear-flowing arrangement of letters or numbers. *Ben's ABC Day* by Terry Berger, which features friendly color photographs of a boy's activities from morning till night, is a good example, as is *Flora McDonnell's ABC,* with its big bright paintings. Familiar scenes such as those depicted in Rachel Isadora's *City Seen from A to Z* help the youngest in their conceptual leaps between life and literature. Six- and seven-year-olds can handle artistically complex books (included at the end of the next chapter) such as *Anno's Alphabet,* which catches the older eye with illusory twists in every drawing, or *Anno's Counting Book,* which is like a puzzle that unfolds the four seasons. Pages from Bert Kitchen's sophisticated *Animal Alphabet* could be hung in a museum.

Ape in a Cape by artist Fritz Eichenberg was one of the first ABC books with a sense of mischief, and it still works like a charm. Margaret Musgrove's *Ashanti to Zulu,* illustrated by Leo and Diane Dillon, and *Moja Means One: Swahili Counting Book* by Muriel and Tom Feelings offer the opportunity to travel to Africa between the covers of a book. My favorite counting book goes backward: *Ten, Nine, Eight* by Molly Bang is a bedtime countdown by an African-American father and daughter, with highly textured paintings depicting a cozy family snuggle that gently winds down the day. Books such as Tana Hoban's *Opposites,* accompanied by her characteristically fine photographs, set out to teach specific concepts, but any book can be made into a game of identification—the word spoken, the object pointed to—in an ongoing introduction to language, art, and bedtime.

The adult reader often has no clue as to what will grab and hold a particular young listener's attention—or when, or why. Sometimes a child who seems to pay no attention at all to a new book will ask for it again the next day with a vivid description or will incorporate words from it into a potty-chair monologue. But you are the best person to locate a young listener's home on the range of these books. For parents who anticipate some setbacks, or who don't expect too much too soon, regular reading will lead to a time of wonder—and better, a lifetime habit.

The first step involves "storytelling the book"—incorporating the book into the child's experience, establishing a common world of story. After that I-thou relationship has been established, books will be irresistible. Story is suspense, and the power of storytelling runs almost as deep as the power of singing or rhyming. Two-year-olds are ready for stories, in pictures and in words. They are ready for the first great segment of children's literature, the early picture book—which will lead to the older picture book, to longer stories, and then to novels and nonfiction. As for you, the adult—you're just in time. The story is about to begin.

First Adventures with Picture Books

This list is mainly for babies and toddlers, with some "crossover" simple stories thrown in for three- to five-year-olds. Look at the end of the next chapter for picture books for the "older preschooler" and primary-grade reader, ages four to seven.

Ahlberg, Allan, and Janet Ahlberg. *The Baby's Catalogue* (1–3). Joy St./Little, 1983.
Any toddler who has ever pored over a catalog will grab this one, tailored to very young tastes and ranging from all kinds of breakfasts to all kinds of moms and dads. By the author-illustrators of *Peekaboo,* this is another treat for the youngest listeners.

Aliki. *Hush Little Baby* (1–3). Prentice-Hall, 1968.
An old Appalachian lullaby gets fresh, endearing pictures in a version that will help the smallest listeners associate the warm security of singing with turning the pages of a book.

Bang, Molly. *Ten, Nine, Eight* (1–4). Greenwillow, 1983.
Warm, luxuriously patterned paintings thick with color but simply composed provide a counting lesson along with a bedtime story of father-daughter sharing.

Brown, Marc. *Hand Rhymes* (1–3). Dutton, 1985.
Fourteen rhymes culled or adapted from traditional sources and accompanied by miniature pen-and-ink diagrams of hand motions are set into soft watercolor spreads that make this book useful for reading aloud or remembering in situations where distracting entertainment is desperately called for. A fit companion volume for Brown's earlier *Finger Rhymes.*

Brown, Margaret Wise. *Goodnight Moon,* illustrated by Clement Hurd (1–4). Harper, 1947.
"In the great green room there was a telephone and a red balloon." Thus begins a comforting poem of contemporary bedtime ritual.

Burningham, John. *Mr. Gumpy's Outing* (2–4). Henry Holt, 1971.
Animals and children promise to behave if Mr. Gumpy will just let them on his boat. But of course they DON'T behave, and "the boat tipped and into the water they fell" with a gigantic splash. The pen-and-wash drawings make a splash as well.

Carle, Eric. *The Very Hungry Caterpillar* (1–4). Philomel, 1969.
All heroes require sustenance. This one consumes—on consecutive weekdays—one apple, two pears, three plums, four strawberries, five oranges, etc.; on Saturday he gets a stomachache and on Sunday he takes an herbal cure of nice green leaves. Listeners can peek through round holes in the pages as the caterpillar eats his way through the book.

Carlstrom, Nancy W. *Jesse Bear, What Will You Wear?* illustrated by Bruce Degen (2–4). Macmillan, 1986.
The sparkling pictures are as gleeful as the nonsensical text in a rhyming romp that follows Jesse Bear through a day of play.

Chorao, Kay. *The Baby's Lap Book* (1–3). Dutton, 1977.
Soft, gentle drawings in pastel colors illustrate favorite songs, nursery rhymes, and rhyme games from "Patty Cake" to "This Little Piggy."

Cousins, Lucy. *Maisy Goes to Bed* (2–4). Little, 1990.
Little listeners will relate to this wee mouse while lifting flaps and pulling tabs to see aspects of her evening activities, including a tiny book that she reads in bed and a toy clutched under her blanket. There are lots of Maisy books, among them *Maisy Gets Dressed, Maisy Goes to the Playground,* and *Maisy Goes to School.*

Crews, Donald. *Freight Train* (1–3). Greenwillow, 1985.
With its dramatic pictures of trucks in motion, this is a book toddlers find exciting to whiz through, making all the attendant sound effects of speeding up and slowing down.

Gág, Wanda. *Millions of Cats* (3–5). Coward-McCann, 1928.
Young listeners infallibly chant the chorus of this story about the homely kitten that becomes the darling of a lonely old couple. The black-and-white drawings roll the words along with strong lines and rounded shapes.

Galdone, Paul. *The Three Billy Goats Gruff* (3–5). Houghton, 1981.
Dramatic action fills every page of this folkloric confrontation between a hungry troll and three equally hungry goats. Fortunately, the younger two have the good sense to turn the fight over to their oldest brother, who's big enough to handle it—a reassuring message for young listeners in the oral stage of development who may be as afraid of being eaten as they are eager to eat.

Hill, Eric. *Where's Spot?* (1–3). Putnam, 1980.
A toy "action book" that offers children the chance to open doors and peek under the bed in search of a puppy hiding from his mother.

Hoban, Tana. *Red, Blue, Yellow Shoe* (6 mos.–3 yrs.). Greenwillow, 1986.
With clarity of concept and precision of photographic composition, Hoban has

created a board book to equal *1, 2, 3 (A First Book of Numbers)* and her other concept books for the youngest child. Each page contains one object with a large dot in the featured color, along with the name of the object in large block print.

Hughes, Shirley. *Alfie and the Birthday Surprise* (3–7). Lothrop, 1998.
Alfie is responsible for hiding the new kitten until his neighbor's birthday in this tender but never cloying addition to the series of books about Alfie and his sister, Annie Rose.

Johnson, Crockett. *Harold and the Purple Crayon* (3–5). Harper, 1955.
Harold's imagination takes him on a fantastical adventure that children can share by following the purple line he draws with his crayon: from defying a dragon and sailing across the sea all the way back to his own bed. The simplicity of forms against plenty of white space makes the story easy to focus on and follow.

Keats, Ezra Jack. *The Snowy Day* (3–5). Viking, 1962.
A boy shares his delight at seeing the winter's first snowfall in a picture book of rich simplicity and exquisitely patterned artwork.

Leaf, Munro. *The Story of Ferdinand,* illustrated by Robert Lawson (3–5). Viking, 1936.
The original flower child, Ferdinand the bull is mistakenly thought to be ferocious when he sits on a bee and then runs around half-crazed, but he defies his reputation and refuses to fight in the ring. Lawson's pen-and-ink drawings show the power of minimum lines and maximum imagination.

Lester, Alison. *Bibs and Boots; Bumping and Bouncing; Crashing and Splashing; Happy and Sad* (1–3). Allen and Unwin, 1997.
Lively pen-and-wash drawings make these four board books companionable viewing and chewing for babies and their siblings, who can dress with the first, romp with the second, bathe with the third, and laugh at the fourth: "Baby is brave [baby pets dog]. Baby is scared [dog licks baby]. Baby is grumpy. Baby's in bed."

Lindgren, Barbro. *Sam's Cookie,* illustrated by Eva Eriksson (1–3). Morrow, 1982.
Simply composed but very funny watercolor pictures support a straight-faced one-line-per-page text in which a little boy gets in and out of trouble with aplomb. Sam's reading public will also delight in *Sam's Car* and *Sam's Teddy Bear.*

Lionni, Leo. *Inch by Inch* (2–5). Astor-Honor, 1962.
Lionni's spacious paper collage pictures have illustrated many favorites, among them this clever tale of a worm that measures one bird after the other until he inches out of sight to safety while measuring the nightingale's song. *Swimmy,* about a lonely fish whose ingenuity makes him a hero, is equally appealing.

Lobel, Arnold. *Random House Book of Mother Goose* (6 mos.–5 yrs.). Random, 1986.
A comprehensive collection of 306 nursery rhymes, with endlessly inventive illustrations.

Martin, Bill, Jr. *Brown Bear, Brown Bear, What Do You See?* illustrated by Eric Carle (1–4). Harcourt, 1967.
A guessing game with a beat, this book depicts a sequence of brightly colored

animals, each one introducing the next in answer to the question, "What do you see?" This is a cumulative quest that invites choral response to complete the circle.

McDonnell, Flora. *Flora McDonnell's ABC* (3–5). Candlewick, 1997.
Humorous contrasts rule this oversized alphabet book in which large figures clearly reflect the letter they represent, as when a huge gray rhinoceros, whose horn points to "capital R, small r," stares delightedly at a small red radish.

McMillan, Bruce. *One Sun: A Book of Terse Verse* (1–3). Holiday, 1990.
Brilliant color photographs of children at play on the beach are coupled with ingenious rhyming words that describe their activities. This is poetry on the go! After you've experienced the book, see if you and your kids can continue with your own terse verses.

Miller, Margaret. *Where Does It Go?* (1–3). Greenwillow, 1992.
"Where does Tavo put his socks?" begins the first full-page question. "Among the flowers? On his nose? On the dog's paw? In the wading pool?" ask the four funny pictures on the next page, which, when you turn it, declares in boldface print across from a large picture of a delighted little boy, "On his feet!" Just silly enough to help with boring cleanup jobs.

Opie, Iona. *My Very First Mother Goose,* illustrated by Rosemary Wells (6 mos.–5 yrs.). Candlewick, 1996.
Rosemary Wells's exuberant illustrations, inventively varied in style and format from page to page, set off this prime selection of Mother Goose rhymes. Some of the most popular rhymes are also available in a series of handsome, sturdy board books, including *Humpty Dumpty, Wee Willie Winkie, Little Boy Blue,* and *Pussycat Pussycat,* each containing six to eight rhymes.

Ormerod, Jan. *Peek-a-Boo!* (6 mos.–2 yrs.). Dutton, 1998.
Your baby can play peek-a-boo with a multicultural cast of other babies by lifting the flaps on this sturdy board book.

Oxenbury, Helen. *All Fall Down; Clap Hands; Say Goodnight; Tickle, Tickle* (6 mos.–2 yrs.). Aladdin, 1987.
Buoyant action and vibrant colors against open white space distinguish this set of large board books full of bouncing babies and playful, rhythmic chants.

Potter, Beatrix. *The Tale of Peter Rabbit* (3–5). Warne, 1902.
Charming illustrations capture the humor and excitement in this beloved tale of a mischievous rabbit who narrowly escapes disaster.

Prelutsky, Jack. *Read Aloud Rhymes for the Very Young,* illustrated by Marc Brown (1–3). Knopf, 1986.
More than 200 verses cover every conceivable aspect of child life in this lively oversized picture-book poetry collection.

Raschka, Chris. *Can't Sleep* (2–4). Jackson/Orchard, 1995.
This visual lullabye, with its rhythmic night-blue and mellow-yellow watercolor

compositions, reassures little listeners via an equally rhythmic text about a dog-child's nighttime experiences: "When you can't sleep the moon will keep you safe. The moon will stay awake."

Rathmann, Peggy. *Good Night, Gorilla* (2–5). Putnam, 1994.
While the text is mostly a repetition of the phrase "Good night," a *lot* is happening in the pictures as a gorilla steals the zookeeper's keys and releases all the animals to follow him home for a cozy evening. Listeners will love knowing what the main character doesn't.

Rosen, Michael. *We're Going on a Bear Hunt,* illustrated by Helen Oxenbury (2–5). McElderry, 1989.
Big pictures of a family romp with lots of sound effects will channel this traditional story-game toward a climactic choral shout: "IT'S A BEAR!!!!"

Rounds, Glen. *Old MacDonald Had a Farm* (1–4). Holiday, 1989.
From hefty black outlines and richly textured colors are formed an irresistibly ridiculous assortment of cows, roosters, sheep, dogs, turkeys, horse, ducks, cats, hens, crows, geese, guinea hens, and . . . what's this, a skunk? "With a PEE-YOO here, and a PEE-YOO there," this is fun to say, sing, or just laugh at the pictures.

Scarry, Richard. *The Lowly Worm Book* (6 mos.–2 yrs.). Random, 1981.
A tiny board book with a spacious look shows Lowly Worm's house, car, and cuisine in clear and clever detail.

Shannon, David. *No, David!* (2–4). Blue Sky/Scholastic, 1998.
You can imagine what this toddler does to provoke his mother's constant response of "No, David," but these larger-than-life pictures are so fresh and funny in depicting mischief that you'll want to see for yourself—as will your youngest listener, over and over.

Slobodkina, Esphyr. *Caps for Sale* (3–5). Scott, 1947.
When no one will buy the peddler's caps, he lies down under a tree for a nap, only to wake and discover some monkeys have stolen his caps. Little ones who love to imitate will relish the way the tricksters get tricked in this satisfying tale illustrated with effectively literal, old-fashioned pictures.

Van Laan, Nancy. *So Say the Little Monkeys,* illustrated by Yumi Heo (2–5). Schwartz/Atheneum, 1998.
With bountiful sound effects in the text and whooshing action in illustrations that jump all over the page, this Rio Negro Indian folktale from Brazil is a natural read-aloud for young mimics, who can shout with the playful monkeys: "JUMP, JABBA JABBA, / RUN, JABBA JABBA, / SLIDE, JABBA JABBA, / Tiny, tiny monkeys having fun!" The large type and varied images create a rhythmic effect of bed-spring-breaking chants.

Voake, Charlotte. *Ginger* (3–5). Candlewick, 1997.
Big cat is happy till little kitten comes along; then it's jealousy and adjustment (with the help of a cardboard box no feline can resist). Youngsters with a new baby ar-

riving will get the idea and also get a chance to enjoy these humorous, large-scale figures scatting across spacious pages.

Wells, Rosemary. *Max's Breakfast* (1–3). Dial, 1985.
Little rabbit Max and his big sister, Ruby, play and squabble like real children, with very funny and sometimes educational results in these simple but amusing board-book vignettes, which include *Max's First Word, Max's New Suit, Max's Ride, Max's Toys: A Counting Book, Max's Bath, Max's Bedtime,* and *Max's Birthday.* In 1998, these were re-illustrated in a larger board-book format.

Wood, Audrey. *The Napping House,* illustrated by Don Wood (2–5). Harcourt, 1984.
Rhythmic in text and graphics, this book builds from the blues of a rainy day when a granny is napping to a golden explosion when she and the child, dog, cat, and mouse are awakened by a flea.

Wright, Blanche Fisher. *The Real Mother Goose* (6 mos.–5 yrs.). Macmillan/Checkerboard Press, 1987.
Selections from a popular old edition of nursery rhymes appear in two sturdy board books to withstand earliest use and abuse.

Young, Ed. *Seven Blind Mice* (3–5). Philomel, 1992.
Each blind mouse conjectures, by feeling a different body part, about the big strange Something whose identity every young viewer has already guessed: it's an elephant! For counting, identifying colors, naming days of the week, or just watching a story unfold in striking contrasts of shape and hue, this is a winner.

Zion, Gene. *Harry the Dirty Dog,* illustrated by Margaret Bloy Graham (2–5). Harper, 1956.
Once a white dog with black spots, Harry turns black with white spots after he runs away from his bath. Only when he digs up his hidden brush and jumps into the tub does his family finally recognize him in a happy ending that will lead nicely toward tubtime for young listeners.

David Small

3

Further Adventures with Picture Books

Picture books aren't only for the youngest audience, of course. When the toddler's toddle turns to a sturdy walk (or a run sometimes faster than yours), there are a host of books waiting for this more-experienced consumer. The wealth is quite astonishing: ethnic tales, folklore, contemporary short fantasies, entry-level science fiction, funny stories, tearjerkers, tender family sagas, rollicking adventures, and lively nonfiction for five- to eight-year-olds, who will appreciate a shared book experience whether they're ready to read solo or not. Increasingly, in fact, sophisticated picture books—as works of art and as works of literature—are reaching upper elementary-grade, junior high, and even high school readers, so that picture books no longer mean "baby books" and learning to read no longer necessitates leaving art behind. If you're choosing a picture book for an older child, the good news is that there are a lot of wonderful books begging for your consideration.

Analyzing picture books reminds me of a time in freshman biology lab when I was handed a frog in preparation for an anatomy exam and told to dissect it. As faithfully as I had studied the diagram—stomach here, brain there, tubes and muscles everywhere—I couldn't lay out that frog and locate the parts that existed so clearly and neatly in the labeled diagram. So I sneaked it into my pocket and out of the lab for further study in the girls' bathroom (which, thanks to my roommate's protest, was the only spot available in the dormitory for such activity). What I discovered, besides a lot of now-forgotten biology terms and the panic that can strike coeds who stumble upon frog parts in a dimly lit bathroom at midnight, was this: *every frog is different.* Theory and life don't always fit together.

There is no such thing as a theoretically good book. You can talk about what makes a good children's book—or any good book—till you're blue in the face, but the real live book is a one-of-a-kind experience. Which leads me to another major principle I discovered on that bathroom floor: *dead frogs are considerably less appealing than live ones.* A dead book doesn't move you one way or another. It just leaves you cold. A live book is the kind to find for yourself and your children, a fresh breath of life, nothing dead or dull or preserved past its time. Whether it's a picture book, fiction, or nonfiction, it must be alive enough to grab your attention and hold it. That's the main criterion. In every good book the elements of skill and originality will cause a contagious reaction. A good Halloween story, for instance, will be just as ingenious as a good costume—and just as important to the occasion. That's a handy thing to remember for party entertainment.

Picture books are often full of good intentions, but that doesn't make them good books. Indeed, some of the worst books have the best of intentions. Sweet and preachy is a nauseating combination. The child who's preached at will probably turn off or wriggle away. Good picture books entice rather than estrange. They will make their audience want more good picture books. Picture books can move as quickly as an action-packed novel with lots of dramatic potential for reading aloud. Or they can be a cross between painting and poetry, to be savored slowly and looked at leisurely.

These days, adults and children alike are barraged with images and sound. There is so much to see and hear—on television, on the Internet, in life at high modern speed—no one really has much chance to look or listen. Picture books are a chance to slow down and do both. It's important, then, that the words sound smooth and natural, not choppy and artificial like the old Dick and Jane textbooks. It's important that the pictures look distinctive and inventive, not empty and superficial.

Old and young will smile in response to funny pictures, or concentrate on beautiful ones, or feel warm and secure with a cozy bedtime story, or sometimes get caught up in a tale of suspense. Children can teach adults a lot about looking at things because they take their time when they feel like it, whether it's putting on shoes or going to the store, and they allow themselves to get sidetracked by interesting things. Sometimes it's enough to drive you crazy, but in relation to books it's an advantage. A child's only deadline is when he or she has finished exploring the book. And children's instincts are right.

The best way to choose a picture book is to look at it—to really stare at it. Take the approach of the tourist or art gallery gazer. Make your way to the library or bookstore, child in tow, and look at all kinds of children's book illustration—paintings, drawings, collages, cartoons. It will soon be clear that the real trouble with poor quality pictures is that they all look alike. Good illustrators get right into the heart of the story and make it come alive with individualized lines, colors, shapes, textures, and patterns. Book designers enhance those distinctive illustrations with the right paper, white space, print, margins, and endpapers.

In any random selection of books, what you see may be finely detailed or frantically cluttered, profoundly simple or crudely simplistic, absorbing or dull, unusual or stereotyped, original or conventional, careful or sloppy, strong or heavy-handed, deepened or overstuffed. To some extent, what you like will be a matter of taste. People furnish their minds like they furnish their rooms, with words and pictures that simply appeal to them.

One of the things that emerges as important in picture-book art is expressive characters. Characters don't have to be pretty. They can be *quirky;* they can reveal something distinctive about being human or animal. They can offer a change from Hollywood heroes or television-commercial heroines or cutesy-faced creatures that people used to think were appropriate for a child. The faces children themselves make in a mirror are a clue to how far their imaginations can stretch to enjoy a different look! Good books don't necessarily fit a mold, and they certainly don't all look the same.

Sweetness-and-innocence nostalgia, or what adults sometimes think *ought* to suit the state of childhood, can stand in the way of those urgent criteria of fresh art and living literature. When I was just out of graduate school and stuffed with the knowledge of what makes a good children's book, a teacher happened to request that the school library order multiple copies of the same edition of *Wynken, Blynken, and Nod* that I had grown up with. She wanted all her second graders to read it. I was delighted, but my supervisor looked at the book with horror. "We can't order that," she said. "Look at the pictures! There are much better editions available."

I had loved the book simply because it was read to me as a child. Some children will love the telephone directory if you read it to them with feeling. Brushing aside the haze of nostalgia filming my eyes, I saw in this edition of *Wynken, Blynken, and Nod* something I really wouldn't want to foist off on children: it was "cute," not to mention flat, emotionless, and dull. The faces looked like those on a row of kewpie dolls. On second glance, I did not feel anything except a longing for my own past. A child is *living* childhood, not remembering it, so that rosy glow of looking backward doesn't connect with his or her experience of reality.

Children feel strongly, and their books should live up to their emotional potential. What's more, their visual reaction precedes their verbal understanding. They *see* and know before they *speak* and know. A picture book, then, has a visual impact as important as its verbal impact. Since children will absorb the images they see, they shouldn't be cheated with a constant stream of boring, empty pictures. What they stare at *does* make an impression. Most people have had the experience of picking up a book or picture they had in childhood and feeling a certain power in it because of its association with childhood impressions during a time when everything seems bigger and more wondrous than it does in later life. The resulting imprint can be either a piece of strong Sendak art or a weak, imitation-Disney cartoon. The richer the early diet of art, the more deep-rooted will be the child's appreciation of art later on. A lot of pleasure can grow from picture books, much of it depending on the parents' choice.

There is a long and honorable tradition of artists who have made art for children live up to the same standard as art for adults. George Cruikshank, Walter Crane, Randolph Caldecott, Howard Pyle, Edmund Dulac, Arthur Rackham, and Maxfield Parrish were not artists for children but simply artists whose audience sometimes happened to be children. Their craft and vision were the best possible for any person who happened to look at their work, and that is still the ideal for a picture-book illustration.

Take, for example, the work of Paul Zelinsky, who has illustrated a range of original stories and fairy tales. Although his illustrations for *Rapunzel* won the Caldecott Award, my favorite of his fairy tale picture books is *Rumpelstiltskin,* which was a Caldecott Honor book. Oil paintings rich in Italian Renaissance style, setting, and costume unfold this version of the Grimms' strange tale of greed compounded and, finally, confounded. Zelinsky has caught the human complexity represented in fairy tales and layered it visually into absorbing art. Graphically articulated with lavish attention to detail, these illustrations have a romantic but distant tone, one that is completely different from his art for Anne Isaacs's *Swamp Angel,* which are oil paintings on wood that are dominated by forest browns warmed with russet. The tall-tale characters in *Swamp Angel* find larger-than-life expression in Zelinsky's outsized figures, sweeping lines, and action-packed compositions. Illustration, in cases like these, makes absorbing art for any age as well as an enduring picture book to share with children. Good art is no less effective for becoming story art. Illustrating for children simply adds another dimension to the artist's work.

Of course, good art between book covers isn't necessarily a good picture book, just as the art in a good picture book isn't necessarily of museum quality. Condescending pastel cuteness can be vapid, but elegant adult-oriented art can also be lifeless. Child appeal, that special way of looking at things from the ground up, is what gives picture-book art an extra special twist and each good picture book its individual merit. As an otherworldly fairy tale, Zelinsky's *Rumpelstiltskin* offers classic beauty; in *I Lost My Bear,* an equally wonderful book of a very different kind, Jules Feiffer uses ebullient, casual lines and comic strip–style exposition to convey a funny and authentically childlike view of the drama occasioned by misplacing a toy.

In *Flossie and the Fox,* which is an updated classic battle between the good girl and the bad guy, the child's-eye view is very strong. What saves the story from being a tired replay of the trickster and victim is the conspiracy of words and pictures that lets young readers recognize, while the fox does not, that Flossie has the upper hand all along. This orally tuned southern story follows Flossie through the woods with her basket of eggs, which are coveted by a fox whom Flossie refuses to recognize as a predator. "I don't believe you a fox, that's what," she tells the aggressive and increasingly aggrieved animal. While the African-American protagonist speaks dialect, the fox speaks the King's English—and loses the battle of wits with the girl because she fearlessly pretends not to believe what he is until she reaches safety. In the end Mr. Fox manages to outrun the hounds, but Flossie delivers her eggs with a cocky grin. The illustrations in brown, gold, green, and russet are literal but flexible, with a vivid natural world that projects the action in lively tempo. Just scary enough, this is a rural South miniadventure with folkloric dimensions.

According to psychiatrists such as Bruno Bettelheim, it's reassuring for children to know that villains can be recognized and overcome. But, like the tales of old, whatever moral exists is less important than the very dashing story. In general, the less a moral shows through, the better. Children know a sermon from a story and, like most people, prefer the story. Of course, story and message are not necessarily incompatible, and the occasional moral never hurt anybody. In Barbara Cooney's delicately illustrated *Miss Rumphius,* Alice's grandfather tells her to do at least one thing to make the world more beautiful. After a lifetime of working and traveling, she remembers his words, sows seeds of the lupine flower along the road by the sea, and passes on the advice to her niece. Treating the beautification theme on a smaller scale, Lynne Rae Perkins's *Home Lovely* depicts the gardening efforts of a young girl settling into life in an isolated mobile home; and Sarah Stewart's book *The Gardener* introduces us to a girl who sets a city rooftop abloom. Possessing their own special beauty, these books make a point even as they draw young listeners into the story.

The message that works without degenerating into a piece of propaganda is rare, though, and most of us would prefer hearing something totally entertaining, especially about ourselves. Books like Russell Hoban's classic *Bedtime for Frances* offer the truth about human behavior but in disguise—in this case, the disguise of a badger family's life. Frances is having a hard time getting to sleep. She has been through the ritual glass of milk, piggyback ride to bed, goodnight kisses from Mother and Father, may-I-have-the-door-open request, long meandering song, finding a tiger in the room, finding a giant in the room, getting a piece of cake to quiet her hunger pangs, discovering a dangerous crack in the ceiling, attending to the forgotten toothbrush. Suddenly, the curtains blow out in a peculiar way. The teddy bear is not much help.

> "Maybe there is *something* waiting, very soft and quiet. Maybe it moves the curtains just to see if I am watching." She went into Mother and Father's room to tell them. They were asleep.
>
> Frances stood by Father's side of the bed very quietly, right near his head.
>
> She was so quiet that she was the quietest thing in the room. She was so quiet that Father woke up all of a sudden, with his eyes wide open.

When that sleeping father raises one eyelid and says, "Umph!" together with a lot of other things that finally get Frances into bed, there's no question about who he really sounds like: every good-hearted, very tired father who has ever mumbled his children through nighttime fears.

While the Frances books are convincingly familiar, some fantasies rely on exaggeration. Plunking something absurd right into the middle of an ordinary situation to see what happens is a favorite picture-book trick. Susan Meddaugh's *Martha Speaks* offers the completely believable and hilariously funny chronicle of the family dog given speech. From its droll faux-scientific explanation to the truthfulness of the family's eventual exhaustion with the yammering Martha ("She talked and talked . . . until her family could not stand it and said, 'Martha, *please!*' "), this is the impossible made humorously mundane.

Margaret Mahy's *Boy Who Was Followed Home* exemplifies the uninhibited thinking in which children delight and from which adults could benefit.

> One day a small, quite ordinary boy, called Robert, was coming home from school. He looked over his shoulder and there was a hippopotamus following him.

> Robert was surprised and pleased—pleased because he had always liked hippopotami, and surprised because nothing like this had ever happened to him before.
>
> When he got home the hippopotamus followed him up the steps and tried to come in at the door. Robert thought his mother would not like this, so he shooed it away.
>
> It went and lay down in the goldfish pool on the lawn.

Things go from bad to worse, till the inevitably suitable but unexpected climax. Meanwhile, Steven Kellogg's illustrations have compounded the details of the dilemma. Lavender hippopotami crowd the elegant lawn, jostling each other and the beleaguered members of the household. One of them peers into a classroom filled with children in every memorable posture of mischief, boredom, and earnest endeavor. When a disreputable-looking witch is telephoned to solve the problem, she appears with an entourage of pastel-colored vermin and vipers. And the concluding surprise behind Robert, after forty-three hippopotami have finally been induced to slink away with reproachful looks, is a triumphant parade of glorious, golden-brown giraffes following him home the next day.

In this book's ending the pictures tell it all. In other cases, an entire book may feature art with no text. Wordless picture books are fun for children to pore over independently or make up their own words for. Raymond Briggs's book *The Snowman* is the dream of a boy whose snowman has come alive, romped through his house with him, and swept him up for a ride through the night sky before his bittersweet awakening to the melting sun. The illustrations are done in comic-strip fashion but with subtle colors and loving care. In *Clown,* Quentin Blake depicts, without text, the drama of a castoff toy clown who is bounced around until he finally finds a loving home. More sophisticated is *Anno's Journey,* offering detailed panoramas for children to pore over as a traveler passes through Europe.

Sometimes the most beautiful picture books convey a very personal realism. In *Grandfather's Journey* by Allen Say, a Japanese-American narrator reflects on the experience of his immigrant grandfather, never quite at peace in either place once he has lived in both. Paintings with the resonance of an antique photo album underscore the story's authenticity. As in *Miss Rumphius,* connection and continuity with family bring new understanding.

In some ways children's books have taken the place of extended families in our mobile society. Without grandparents, aunts, uncles, and cousins living nearby to pass along stories, children find relatives—and later, friends—in books. Literary adoption extends a sense of community across immense distances. After I gathered the family stories my mother told me into a picture book called *Seven Brave Women,* I heard from children all over who wanted my ancestors! I assured them that they had their own, equally strong family trees. They just needed to find the closest limb (parent, grandparent, and other relatives or foster folks) and start climbing.

The importance of relationships between young children and the aged is deep. Tomie dePaola's *Nana Upstairs, Nana Downstairs* and Charlotte Zolotow's *My Grandson Lew* are tender treatments of a child recalling close bonds with grandparents who have died. The cycle of life and death and the immortality of ordinary people loving each other are caught with a shorthand wisdom and warmth astonishing for such brief portrayals.

Books like this can give listeners a chance to think or talk about the death of an older person they know, either in preparation for the fact or after it has happened. The book does not have to parallel the child's exact situation. One warm story about a boy's attachment to his aging dog, *I'll Always Love You* by Hans Wilhelm, started a cathartic conversation about a death in our family. Perhaps open discussion can free new generations from the kind of irrational terrors that haunted a friend of mine who could not board an airplane because she was told as a child that her dying grandfather, whom she never saw again, had "gone for a ride in the sky." Many difficult subjects, from divorce to disabilities, have been presented for the better understanding of young children; many have also been the focal points of good stories.

I'll deal with nonfiction on its own in chapter 9, but don't overlook it when you're picture-book browsing. Any kind of factual information can be conveyed humanly, if not humorously, in picture-book form. DePaola's *Charlie Needs a Cloak,* for instance, teaches the rudiments of the wool-to-cloth process in a series of graphic jokes that poke fun at both shepherd and sheep. The only creature that makes good is an inconsequential mouse who keeps nipping useful tidbits into his hole, a comment on life if ever there was one. Ruth Heller should get an award for presenting oviparous species in *Chickens Aren't the Only Ones.* She manages to design an informative but unforced rhyming text in bright, posterlike illustrations that will capture the youngest scientist.

In the sprinkling of fantastic and realistic picture books mentioned so far, most of the art has been traditionally literal, but there have been intriguing innovations of technique and medium in contemporary children's book illustration. Leo Lionni's *Swimmy* and Ezra Jack Keats's *Snowy Day* were hailed, in the early sixties, for their freshly expressionistic use of collage, and both artists explored that medium throughout their careers. John Steptoe's early art in *Stevie* and *My Special Best Words* outlines his characters with the intensity of a neon sign in the rain. Leo and Diane Dillon, two-time Caldecott winners, have a large body of illustrative work that includes African folktales with stylized designs and strikingly varied techniques. The filmmaker Gerald McDermott's abstract interpretation of folklore in his book *Arrow to the Sun* has often found children more receptive than their elders. Molly Bang ventures with a medium sensitive to each story, whether it's paper cut-out pictures for *The Paper Crane* or patterned collage paintings for *The Grey Lady and the Strawberry Snatcher.* Brian Karas's illustrations for Diane Stanley's *Saving Sweetness* offer quiet invention in their subtle combination of photocollage landscape and spiky, dot-eyed hand-drawn characters.

In chapter 8 I'll discuss folklore for older readers, but its place here is indisputable. Folklore and the new stories patterned after it are a staple of the genre, showcasing narrative art that introduces children to Medieval, Renaissance, and Primitive styles as well as to other cultures of the world. From Iceland's *Flumbra,* retold by Gudrún Helgadóttir and ruggedly illustrated by Brian Pilkington, to Japan's *Boy of the Three Year Nap,* retold by Dianne Snyder with elegant paintings by Allen Say, children can absorb other patterns of tradition.

There's broad tonal range as well, with the same folktale getting wildly varied treatments. James Marshall's *Red Riding Hood* lightens Perrault's story considerably. "It is I, your delicious—er—darling granddaughter," says the wolf, and later, "I'm so wicked . . . *So* wicked." On the last page, as proof that Red Riding Hood keeps her promise never to speak to another stranger, she spurns the overtures of a large green crocodile. Marshall's version may be counterproductive to the moral, however; this is one wolf *not* to be missed. Another is Ed Young's haunting, white-eyed wolf set against the blood-red cover of *Lon Po Po: A Red Riding Hood Story from China.*

So many fairy tales and folktales have been illustrated as picture books that a certain backlash has set in—or, rather, a parody. Takeoffs on "The Wolf and the Three Little Pigs" are as abundant and amusing as the "straight" versions. If you want to have some fun with your picture-book audience, try coupling James Marshall's slyly cartooned rendition of *The Three Little Pigs* with Jon Scieszka's unreliable narrative of *The True Story of the Three Little Pigs by A. Wolf,* surrealistically illustrated by Lane Smith, and Eugene Trivizas's *Three Little Wolves and the Big Bad Pig,* irreverently illustrated by Helen Oxenbury. You'll see that the traditional moral of being industrious gets quite a twist as these tongue-in-cheek satires suggest alternative villains and ever more alternative solutions. For fans of the Pig family, by the way, Mary Rayner has a collection called *Mrs. Pig Gets Cross,* in which Mrs. Wolf gets foiled with great flair.

Children can also experience myriad real worlds by riding the rails of a contemporary story: To a rundown, rural home like the one Helen Griffith describes and James Stevenson pictures in *Grandaddy's Place* and *Georgia Music.* To Vera Williams's version of a city apartment where a little girl saves her pennies toward *A Chair for My Mother* after their furniture is burned up. To a highly textured tailor's shop in *The Purple Coat* by Amy Hest and Amy Schwartz. To an isolated farm off the Maine coast in Barbara Cooney's *Island Boy.* To *The Village of Round and Square Houses* that Ann Grifalconi discovered in West Africa. To the South African shoe stores Niki Daly shows in *Not So Fast Songololo.* To a cave under the ice at low tide with a north Canadian Inuit child in Jan Andrews's *Very Last First Time.* To the funny frontier of Roy Gerrard's *Wagons West!* To the sad frontier of Paul Goble's *Death of the Iron Horse.* To times past when children taught themselves to read from the Bible, as does the diminutive heroine in Carol Purdy's *Least of All.* To a crossing of the English Channel with Alice and Martin Provensen's *Glorious Flight.* Or to a guided global tour, as in Marjorie Priceman's culinary fantasia *How to Make an Apple Pie and See the World,* wherein the closure of the market necessitates a whirlwind trip to Italy for semolina wheat, to France for eggs, to Sri Lanka for cinnamon ("Find a kurundu tree and peel off some bark. If a leopard is napping beneath the tree, be very quiet"), to Jamaica for sugar, and so on, before returning home to whip up a tasty pie.

Good illustrators tailor an artistic vision to fit a story or text, to set it off and suit it and tell even more than the words do. They create an art that children and adults can share in their own homes. Many people don't take the time to go to a museum anymore, but books comprise a museum that comes to you. Most people have watched their kids proudly bring home drawings and paintings that become fewer and fewer and finally stop altogether. Sometimes the only images that flash by us, day after day, are on the television screen and billboards. There are children who don't know that any other kinds of pictures exist. It's gratifying to be able to show them something richer.

Picture-book art and literature are hard to talk about separately because they belong together by definition in a complementary and even symbiotic relationship; one enriches the other. And small children should no more be swindled in literature than in art. They will use the words they hear, and they shouldn't be cheated of hearing and viewing the best. The short story is one of the most difficult forms of literature, with a discipline all its own. How much harder to make it complex enough to be good yet simple enough to be understood by a young child! The picture-book text must be pithier, developed more actively, more briefly, but just as believably as an adult short story. Folktales are ideal short stories for children because by their very nature they are trimmed of any excess detail, right down to the bones of archetypal character and stark pattern of action.

Most modern stories, by contrast, develop through details of dialogue and description that must be selected with excruciating care and an eye for the truest, most vivid, pared-down, relevant language. The details should relate to a child's experience, although that is often broader than many adults assume. In *Tell Me a Mitzi,* author Lore Segal and artist Harriet Pincus joke about everything from parents to presidents. New York City in all its grubby glory is revealed through the eyes of Mitzi and her brother, Jacob. Theirs is an average family, the kind that succumbs to the common cold. You don't find too many fairy godmothers dealing with diaper changes, thermometers, and chicken soup.

In Mavis Jukes's *Like Jake and Me,* every action and image furthers the portrayal of a young boy who's insecure about his new stepfather's affections and his mother's pregnancy. Still at the loose-tooth stage, Alex desperately wants to prove to himself and Jake that he's competent enough to be helpful. But it's not till Jake admits needing help himself—to get rid of a spider crawling inside his collar—that Alex and Jake realize how close they can be. By the end of a brief but fine-tuned book, this family has resolved a crisis and evolved a new mutual respect for each other.

The ideal picture-book short story can be funny or serious or sad, but, like the illustrations, it should be moving one way or the other. It can be familiar or fantastic, but the characters must be as palpably individualized as people you know in real life, the plot developed as naturally as day following night. (Says one little girl to her father in a *Saturday Review* cartoon, "Read it again, only this time with more emphasis on character development and less on plot mechanics.") Only hack writers will depend on artificial contrivances, or artificial language, to force a story along. Hackneyed writing is just as tiresome as hack art. Witness: "Billy Boll Weevil was an insect. He lived on a cotton farm. The farmer did not like Billy Boll Weevil. 'Go!' he said. The farmer's wife did not like Billy Boll Weevil. 'Go!' she said. The farmer's son did not like Billy Boll Weevil. 'Go!' he said. The farmer's daughter did not like Billy Boll Weevil." Guess what she said? After a tediously repetitious search for help, Billy Boll Weevil advises the farmer to plant peanuts and thereby becomes a local hero instead of a pest.

Children themselves think and articulate more imaginatively than that. A six-year-old I know suggested to her mother, who was grumbling about the cost of shoes, that somebody invent a pair that grew with your feet. The truth is that most kids have very inventive ideas. It takes a clever artist and an original writer to live up to such naturally energetic thoughts and actions.

Art without action is often lost on children. Most mood pieces amount to coffee-table juvenilia, beautiful but not quite balanced between aesthetic beauty and practical appeal. Sometimes they do work well as a kind of retreat—like Uri Shulevitz's *Dawn*—but in general young children are not given to meditative books. They can tolerate a long text, such as Marianna Mayer's adaptation of *Beauty and the Beast,* if it has the kind of movement and emotions that Mercer Mayer has rippled through his accompanying illustrations. The Mayers' book will rivet five- to seven-year-olds and also give them, and any attendant adults, art worth exploring.

Only some of the great picture books available are included here. It is a matter of choice, a matter of stimulating the imagination with the richest books. The picture book you read—and so give—to a child can move your own eye and mind and heart.

Further Adventures with Picture Books

Aardema, Verna. *Borreguita and the Coyote: A Tale from Ayutla, Mexico,* illustrated by Petra Mathers (4–7). Knopf, 1991.

Flat, surrealistic landscapes dramatized by the intense hues of a southwestern springtime form backdrops for this Mexican tale in which a little lamb, Borreguita, fools hungry Coyote three times.

Allard, Harry. *Miss Nelson Is Missing,* illustrated by James Marshall (5–8). Houghton, 1977.

Sweet Miss Nelson, whose students in Room 207 break all her rules, disappears and is replaced by the wicked Miss Viola Swamp! Sly watercolor illustrations clue the reader into the mysterious swap.

Andrews, Jan. *The Very Last First Time,* illustrated by Ian Wallace (5–7). McElderry, 1986.

In her Inuit village in northern Canada, Eva Padlyat walks under the frozen sea at low tide to collect mussels. Deep-toned paintings project an eerie sense of her underworld adventure.

Anno, Mitsumasa. *Anno's Alphabet* (6–8). Crowell, 1975.

This alphabet book for children old enough to appreciate the art of illusion features graceful letters that seem cunningly sculpted from wood.

Aylesworth, Jim. *The Gingerbread Man,* illustrated by Barbara McClintock (4–7). Scholastic, 1998.

A favorite old tale gets fresh treatment with action-packed pictures and a read-aloud text that will have kids chanting, "No! No! I won't come back! I'd rather run than be your snack!"

Bemelmans, Ludwig. *Madeline* (4–7). Viking, 1940.

The setting is a Paris convent school many years ago, but the rhyming story about a feisty little girl who gets what she wants despite a mischievous streak appeals to each new generation of listeners.

Blake, Quentin. *Clown* (5–8). Henry Holt, 1996.
In this wordless but touching picture book, illustrated with sure lines and soft colors, a toy clown consigned to the garbage bin eventually brings beauty and warmth to the family of the girl who takes him in.

Burton, Virginia. *Mike Mulligan and His Steam Shovel* (5–8). Houghton, 1939.
Mike Mulligan's steam shovel wins a contest, digs her way to an honorable retirement, and converts a villainous boss in the process, all depicted in bold color cartoons that have perennial appeal.

Cooney, Barbara. *Miss Rumphius* (5–8). Viking, 1982.
Elegant paintings portray the life of a woman who works, travels, and, in her old age, makes her New England coast more beautiful by sowing flowers.

de Brunhoff, Jean. *The Story of Babar* (5–7). Random, 1933.
Babar's development from orphaned baby to king of the elephants is as satisfying as any hero's mythical journey.

Demi. *One Grain of Rice: A Mathematical Folktale* (5–8). Scholastic, 1997.
Intense crimsons and rich golds emphasize the power of royalty, while Demi's tiny, precise figures set against vertically geometric backgrounds seem especially suited to this Indian story about a clever village woman who tricks a greedy raja into providing food for his hungry people.

Diakité, Baba Wagué. *The Hunterman and the Crocodile: A West African Folktale* (4–7). Scholastic, 1997.
Rhythmic art and narrative distinguish this tale about Donso the Hunterman and his near-disastrous encounter with Bamba the Crocodile.

Ehlert, Lois. *Eating the Alphabet: Fruits and Vegetables from A to Z* (4–6). Harcourt, 1989.
"Apple to Zucchini, come take a look" at this brilliantly illustrated, delicious picture book in which children can practice letters, identify foods, and experience colors.

Feiffer, Jules. *I Lost My Bear* (4–8). Morrow, 1998.
Lively cartoon illustrations exaggerate the humor in a young girl's search for her beloved but misplaced toy.

Freeman, Don. *Corduroy* (4–6). Viking, 1968.
A toy bear who fears that missing a button on his overalls will prevent anyone from wanting him finds a home with a warmhearted little girl.

French, Fiona. *Snow White in New York* (5–8). Oxford, 1986.
Elegance is French's hallmark, and it's evident in this spoof of the old fairy tale, with svelte figures and geometric shapes gracing the Art Deco illustrations.

Goble, Paul. *Buffalo Woman* (5–8). Bradbury, 1984.
Art stylized with Plains Indian motifs unfolds a Native American folktale about a

man who follows his wife into the animal world. Equally intriguing is *The Girl Who Loved Wild Horses,* in which a young woman follows the herd she loves and becomes one with them.

Griffith, Helen. *Grandaddy's Place,* illustrated by James Stevenson (5–7). Greenwillow, 1987.
Gentle watercolor cartoons accompany a story of Janetta's first visit to her grandfather's farm, which proves such a happy occasion that the two spend a summer together in *Georgia Music,* another poignant book by the same author and artist.

Grimm, Jacob, and Wilhelm Grimm. *Snow White and the Seven Dwarfs,* translated by Randall Jarrell, illustrated by Nancy Ekholm Burkert (5–8). Farrar, 1972.
Exquisite artwork enriches this classic tale of "the fairest of them all."

Hearne, Betsy. *Seven Brave Women,* illustrated by Bethanne Andersen (6–9). Greenwillow, 1997.
Handsomely textured paintings illustrate the narrative of a young girl who describes generations of brave women in her family, each making history in her own way and each demonstrating that "there are a million ways to be brave."

Henkes, Kevin. *Lilly's Purple Plastic Purse* (5–8). Greenwillow, 1996.
Lilly, the older sister in *Julius, the Baby of the World* (1990), is in love with her teacher, until he enrages her by taking away her brand-new, precious, but distracting purple plastic purse. Energetic illustrations feature an endearing world of mouse persons.

Heo, Yumi. *The Green Frogs: A Korean Folktale* (4–7). Houghton, 1996.
Two disobedient frogs learn a hard lesson when they finally follow their mother's last wish, which is why they're still crying to this day. Appropriate to a water-based story, the art looks like amoeba soup floating across the pages while the bug-eyed, stick-limbed characters cavort defiantly around their bespectacled mother.

Hest, Amy. *The Purple Coat,* illustrated by Amy Schwartz (4–6). Macmillan, 1986.
In what is clearly a yearly ritual, mother takes Gabrielle to Grampa's tailor shop for a new coat, but they disagree about the color. The patterns and texture of the art are an ingenious extension of a story about fabric.

Hoban, Russell. *Bread and Jam for Frances,* illustrated by Lillian Hoban (5–8). Harper, 1964.
Only bread and jam will make this determined young badger happy, but she finally gets more than her fill, as the humorous pictures convey.

Hoffman, Mary. *Amazing Grace,* illustrated by Caroline Binch (4–8). Dial, 1991.
Skillfully composed, richly toned paintings portray an expressive black girl in various postures of imaginative play as she projects herself into the heroic center of every story and wins a lead role in the school play.

Hogrogian, Nonny. *One Fine Day* (4–7). Macmillan, 1971.
An Armenian cumulative tale follows a fox that gets his tail cut off for drinking a woman's pail of milk and must then go to each of a series of animals to ask a reciprocal favor until he can make enough swaps to pay the woman to sew his tail

back on. The rhythmic repetition and soft-hued art make this a winning read-aloud story.

Hooks, William. *The Three Little Pigs and the Fox,* illustrated by S. D. Schindler (4–7). Macmillan, 1989.

With a perfect storytelling balance of invention and convention, Hooks relates an Appalachian variant of "The Three Little Pigs," illustrated with fresh, funny watercolors that are well drafted and cleverly expressive.

Hyman, Trina Schart. *Little Red Riding Hood* (5–7). Holiday, 1982.

Rustic scenes beautifully drawn and colored will appeal to listeners of this dramatic fairy tale.

Isaacs, Anne. *Swamp Angel,* illustrated by Paul O. Zelinsky (5–8). Dutton, 1994.

Angelica is a larger-than-life homespun heroine who builds her first log cabin at the age of two, lifts wagons out of the swamp, and tosses a giant bear straight up into the sky, where he crashes into a pile of stars. No tall tale ever had better illustrations than these large-scale, action-packed oil paintings on wood.

Isadora, Rachel. *Ben's Trumpet* (5–7). Greenwillow, 1979.

Striking black-and-white art deco motifs echo the 1930s setting and catch the exquisite rhythms of jazz as an African-American child begins to fulfill his dream of becoming a trumpet player.

Johnston, Tony. *The Ghost of Nicholas Greebe,* illustrated by S. D. Schindler (6–9). Dial, 1996.

When a dog pilfers one of the late Nicholas Greebe's bones, Nicholas takes up haunting and the bone brings bad luck to all who encounter it until the happy reunion of bone and owner.

Jukes, Mavis. *Like Jake and Me,* illustrated by Lloyd Bloom (6–8). Knopf, 1984.

When they search for a scary wolf spider, a boy and his stepfather find they have more in common than they thought; movingly detailed writing with strong, impressionistic art.

Karas, G. Brian. *Home on the Bayou: A Cowboy's Story* (5–8). Simon, 1997.

So what's involved in moving from the desert out West to a swamp down South? Dirty water? A grandpa who wears rubber boots? A broken lasso? A bunch of new kids who laugh at you and a school bully who calls you cowpie? A mother you're so mad at for moving that you'd rather eat cactus spines than talk to her? Karas's fun-poking pictures show it all, segueing from sandy tans to frog-and-gator-green smudged with Spanish-moss gray.

Kellogg, Steven. *Chicken Little* (4–5). Morrow, 1985.

Wash drawings bursting with vitality spoof a favorite cumulative folktale. Fans of this one will enjoy *Pecos Bill, The Island of the Skogg,* and other Kellogg picture books characterized by delicate color and exuberant line work.

Kuskin, Karla. *The Dallas Titans Get Ready for Bed,* illustrated by Marc Simont (5–8). Harper, 1986.

Even more fun than *The Philharmonic Gets Dressed,* this takes the Dallas Titans football team off the field, into the locker room for showers, and finally home to bed—a poetic romp with robust pictures and lots of information about the game and the gear.

Lester, Julius. *Sam and the Tigers: A New Telling of Little Black Sambo,* illustrated by Jerry Pinkney (6–8). Dial, 1996.

A controversial old story gets hilarious (and politically correct) treatment here by two award-winning African Americans who have collaborated on a witty text and roguish illustrations. You'll never see a more intense cast of tigers, especially from the rear view.

Lied, Kate. *Potato: A Tale of the Great Depression,* illustrated by Lisa Campbell Ernst (4–7). National Geographic Society, 1997.

Against a background of burlap-brown paper grows an organic story of a family devastated by the Depression and saved by a trip from Iowa to Idaho, where the narrator's grandparents scour picked-over potato fields at night to trade for "groceries, clothes, and even a pig." If the figures look a little rumpled, they also look engagingly happy, which just goes to prove that a potato goes a long way toward satisfying all kinds of hunger, even for stories and pictures.

Livingston, Myra Cohn. *Up in the Air,* illustrated by Leonard Everett Fisher (5–8). Holiday, 1989.

With its lilting rhymed narrative and expressionistic paintings, this sonorous celebration of airplane travel will enhance any child's excitement over flying.

Lobel, Arnold. *On Market Street,* illustrated by Anita Lobel (5–8). Greenwillow, 1981.

In illustration of Arnold Lobel's clever text, each of Anita Lobel's elaborate characters is made of objects representing a letter in the alphabet, from the apple peddler to the zipper man.

Lowell, Susan. *The Bootmaker and the Elves,* illustrated by Tom Curry (5–9). Orchard, 1997.

"The Shoemaker and the Elves" gets a bouncy revision in this Wild West setting where "a cowboy bootmaker who was so poor that even his shadow had holes in it" gets some magical help.

Mahy, Margaret. *The Boy Who Was Followed Home,* illustrated by Steven Kellogg (5–7). Dial, 1986.

Surprised but rather pleased to be followed home from school by a growing number of hippopotami, Robert is the subject of a fantasy with amiably detailed illustrations that hold an even bigger surprise for young listeners.

Marshall, James. *George and Martha* (5–8). Houghton, 1972.

Two funny, affectionate hippopotami—beady-eyed but large-bodied—teach each other what caring and sharing are all about. Don't miss Marshall's funny versions of *The Three Little Pigs* (1989), *Red Riding Hood* (1987), and other folktales.

Martin, Jacqueline Briggs. *Grandmother Bryant's Pocket,* illustrated by Petra Mathers (6–8). Houghton, 1996.

A cozy book with appealing diminutive figures in intense hues, this historical tale features eight-year-old Sarah, who overcomes the fear engendered by a barn fire in which her dog Patches perished.

Mayer, Marianna. *Beauty and the Beast,* illustrated by Mercer Mayer (5–8). Simon, 1987.
This classic French fairy tale gets lively treatment in Mayer's vivid art, which moves with a cinematic quality across the pages.

McCloskey, Robert. *Make Way for Ducklings* (4–8). Viking, 1941.
Young listeners still hold their breaths till the mother mallard finds a safe place for her ducklings in the Boston Public Garden. The humor that characterizes the author-artist's drawings for this picture book also distinguishes his *Homer Price* and other popular works.

McCully, Emily. *Mirette on the High Wire* (5–8). Putnam, 1992.
Young Mirette becomes a high-wire walker in Paris under the tutelage of a famous performer, Bellini, whom she saves when his nerve fails during a big comeback. Richly hued pictures give striking perspective on the daring heroine's high-wire work. An equally inspiring female character appears in *Beautiful Warrior: The Legend of the Nun's Kung Fu.*

McKissack, Patricia C. *Flossie and the Fox,* illustrated by Rachel Isadora (5–7). Dial, 1986.
By pretending she doesn't believe he's a fox, Flossie outwits her predator and gets her basket of eggs safely through the woods in this southern African-American tale glowingly illustrated with woodsy hues.

Meddaugh, Susan. *Martha Speaks* (5–8). Houghton, 1992.
Family dog Martha learns how to talk after lapping up some alphabet soup ("The letters in the soup went up to Martha's brain instead of down to her stomach"). Unfortunately, Martha never shuts up; fortunately, she saves the family from a burglary by calling the police! Young listeners will love the cartoon speech balloons that float around the happy line-and-wash pictures of Martha holding forth.

Perkins, Lynne Rae. *Home Lovely* (5–8). Greenwillow, 1995.
With the help of Bob the mailman, Tiffany enriches her new trailer home with a thriving vegetable garden.

Pinkney, Brian. *The Adventures of Sparrowboy* (5–8). Simon, 1997.
CHIRP, CHIRRR, RRRRRP, ZAP, WHOOSH! After reading the Falconman comic strip every day, Henry finds himself flying high as Sparrowboy. His rescues are modest, but the illustrations make the most of them with dramatic colors, suddenly shifting perspectives, and fast action.

Priceman, Marjorie. *How to Make an Apple Pie and See the World* (5–8). Knopf, 1994.
A simple pie recipe turns into a glorious world tour when the local market is closed and the listener is sent all over the globe to collect ingredients.

Rackham, Arthur. *Mother Goose, the Old Nursery Rhymes* (3–6). Marathon, 1978.
Pen-and-ink sketches, silhouettes, and full-page color art illustrate these nursery rhymes as well as the traditional tales in *The Arthur Rackham Fairy Book.*

Rey, H. A. *Curious George* (4–7). Houghton, 1941.

Children will forever identify with the little monkey who wreaks havoc but never loses the affection of his protector, the man in the yellow hat.

Ringgold, Faith. *Tar Beach* (5–8). Crown, 1991.

Vigorous acrylic paintings based on one of the artist's story quilts project the fantasy of eight-year-old Cassie, who dreams of flying above New York's George Washington Bridge from her nighttime rooftop.

San Souci, Robert D. *Sukey and the Mermaid,* illustrated by Brian Pinkney (5–8). Four Winds, 1992.

In an organic blend of fantasy and South Carolina island folklore, an African-American girl escapes from her oppressive stepfather with the help of a dark-skinned mermaid, beautifully depicted amid wild seascapes.

Say, Allen. *Grandfather's Journey* (5–8). Houghton, 1993.

Stately paintings evocative of an old photo album portray the bittersweet dilemma of a Japanese immigrant to the United States who, although happy in his new country, longs to return to the old.

Scieszka, Jon. *The True Story of the Three Little Pigs by A. Wolf,* illustrated by Lane Smith (6–9). Viking, 1989.

Supported by sophisticated, surrealistic art, this satire on the traditional tale ends with the wolf, who simply started out to borrow a cup of sugar from the mean-spirited neighborhood pigs, in prison for homicide (porkicide?) but proclaiming his innocence. If you and your charges enjoy postmodern picture books, don't miss *The Stinky Cheese Man and Other Fairly Stupid Tales* and *Math Curse* by the same author-artist team.

Segal, Lore. *Tell Me a Mitzi,* illustrated by Harriet Pincus (4–8). Farrar, 1970.

A sturdy sister and brother star in three hilarious tales of child life in New York City, a setting urbanely reflected in rounded, richly humorous pictures.

Sendak, Maurice. *Where the Wild Things Are* (4–6). Harper, 1963.

A series of beautifully choreographed paintings follows Max from naughty escapades through a dream trip to the land of wild things and back home, where someone loves him best of all.

Seuss, Dr. *Horton Hatches the Egg* (4–7). Random, 1940.

Few can resist the fun of Dr. Seuss's wacky rhymes, especially when they frame a story about the ultimate rewards of loyalty. Horton is an elephant who gets stuck sitting on a bird's egg, but the hatchling turns out to have a remarkable resemblance to—and love for—Horton!

Sheppard, Jeff. *The Right Number of Elephants,* illustrated by Felicia Bond (3–6). Harper, 1990.

Wildly exaggerated scenes depict a countdown from the number of elephants required to pull a train out of a tunnel (ten) to the number required to be a very special friend (one).

Stanley, Diane. *Saving Sweetness,* illustrated by G. Brian Karas (5–8). Putnam, 1996.
A runaway orphan captures the heart of the sheriff who's been sent to capture her, and they end up a happy family in these innovative collages with a Wild West theme.

Steig, William. *The Amazing Bone* (5–8). Farrar, 1976.
A succulent pig and her loyal bone foil the intentions of a wily fox, all caught with graphic flair by the brilliant *New Yorker* cartoonist who created *Sylvester and the Magic Pebble, Doctor De Soto, Brave Irene,* and other award-winning favorites.

Steptoe, John. *Stevie* (6–8). Harper, 1969.
Neon-hued paintings extend the idiomatic first-person narrative of a boy reminiscing about the crybaby he used to resent his mama baby-sitting but who later became "kinda like a little brother."

Stevens, Janet. *Coyote Steals the Blanket: A Ute Tale* (5–8). Holiday, 1993.
With a bold mix of crayon and watercolor, the artist achieves a motion-picture effect in her depictions of Coyote, who steals a beautiful blanket from a huge rock, almost gets flattened as a result ("RUMBLE, RUMBLE RUMBLE"), and is saved by modest, moral little Hummingbird.

Stevenson, James. *Could Be Worse!* (6–8). Greenwillow, 1977.
Watercolor cartoons trace Grandpa's preposterous adventures on air, land, and sea in a tongue-in-cheek tall tale that escalates with the chorus, "Could be worse!"

Stewart, Sarah. *The Gardener,* illustrated by David Small (6–9). Farrar, 1997.
A new kind of secret garden blooms on a city rooftop in this Depression-era story about a girl who faces upheaval and hard work head on, with red hair blazing in every gracefully illustrated scene.

Titherington, Jeanne. *A Place for Ben* (3–6). Greenwillow, 1987.
In these softly shaded, precise colored pencil drawings, Ben finally finds and furnishes a private place to play, only to discover he's glad for the company of his little brother.

Tripp, Wallace. *A Great Big Ugly Man Came Up and Tied His Horse to Me* (5–8). Little, 1973.
The jolliest of pictures depict the silliest of situations in this collection of nonsense verse.

Trivizas, Eugene. *The Three Little Wolves and the Big Bad Pig,* illustrated by Helen Oxenbury (4–8). McElderry, 1993.
Big-time role reversal has a seriously mean pig hounding three beleaguered young wolves, who eventually convert their foe into a flower child—all comically depicted in watercolors that explode or dance off the page, depending on the nonstop action.

Van Allsburg, Chris. *Jumanji* (6–9). Houghton, 1981.
With velvety shading, brilliant light-dark contrasts, and unusual perspectives, Van Allsburg's drawings highlight a story about two children who start playing a jun-

gle-adventure board game they can't seem to stop. For a visually suspenseful alphabet book, try Van Allsburg's *Z Was Zapped,* in which each letter meets an untimely demise by the book's end.

Viorst, Judith. *Alexander and the Terrible, Horrible, No Good, Very Bad Day,* illustrated by Ray Cruz (5–8). Atheneum, 1972.
Here's a title children will chorus as they look at Ray Cruz's pen-and-ink drawings of a boy's day gone haywire.

Ward, Lynd. *The Biggest Bear* (5–8). Houghton, 1952.
Soft-brown, spacious illustrations accompany the story of a boy whose woods-orphan grows out of bounds.

Wells, Rosemary. *Benjamin and Tulip* (4–7). Doubleday, 1973.
With a few skillful pen-and-ink lines, this classic bully-victim situation takes on unforgettable character as a raccoon gets her comeuppance for pestering her neighbor.

Williams, Vera B. *A Chair for My Mother* (4–6). Greenwillow, 1982.
Having saved their pennies since a fire devastated their apartment, a little girl, her mother, and her grandmother manage to buy a big, comfortable chair. The illustrations are as rosy as the upholstery.

Young, Ed. *Lon Po Po: A Red Riding Hood Story from China* (5–8). Philomel, 1989.
This wolf's glowing eyes are enough to frighten anyone except the girl who saves her sisters by tricking him. Intense artwork transports listeners into a story world less polite and more daring than that in the European versions.

Zelinsky, Paul. *Rumpelstiltskin* (5–8). Dutton, 1986.
Golden paintings in Italian Renaissance style unfold the Grimms' tale of greed compounded and, finally, confounded. The artist's other exquisitely illustrated fairy tales include *Hansel and Gretel* (1984) and *Rapunzel* (1998).

James Marshall

4

Jumping from Picture Books to Older Literature

Reading is a doorway for some children, but for lots of others it's a stone wall. Books may have seemed easy when encountered on a parent's lap, but now they're a whole different project requiring new and sometimes daunting skills. Before setting off into the land of literature with your young reading partner, you need to remember the enormity of this transition and that the new reader brings his or her own tastes, obstacles, and inclinations to it.

I know reading problems firsthand because I had to solve one. My first daughter was not a whiz kid who taught herself to read at the tender age of three. She was one of those individuals, often labeled stubborn, who do things in their own sweet time. In the second grade she tested at a first-grade reading level. She thought reading was hard and she was afraid to fail at it so she decided to postpone the whole project. Fear is the first step down the road to failure. Her worried teacher was beginning to suggest special tests for eyes, brain, perception, coordination, and digestion. The child seemed bright enough, but maybe something was physically wrong.

Panic loomed. At first it seemed outrageous that *my child* wouldn't like to read. I had all these books I could hardly wait to share with her. On second thought, it made sense that a librarian-writer's child would have a complicated reaction to books. I just had to figure out what to do about it. A lot of parents do. There are many reasons children don't read, but there are also many ways to cope with their reluctance and/or other difficulties. The best cure is motivation, a book that hooks them. Children who can't read the first page of a geography textbook have been known to whiz through *National Geographic.* Young dinosaur enthusiasts who find ordinary words quite indigestible seem to gulp down names such as *Carcharodontosaurus* and *Yangchuanosaurus shangyouensis.* Failures in the basal reading series may tackle model airplane instructions without a pause or problem.

To motivate a child you need to find a special "motivating book." You can track down that book and then leave it on the kitchen table, hoping the child will pick it up and be drawn in. Or you can read it out loud to the child and clinch the deal. As the above-mentioned nonreader said once, "If you read the first chapter, then I get interested." The British writer and critic John Rowe Townsend maintains that "a book is not a labor-saving device" and that "a reading child can be identified before conception." In other words, a lot depends on the adult's attitude as well as the book's magic. The right combination of the two makes the best teaching tool possible.

Any interested adult will do. No special training is necessary, but patience helps. In my case, training was sometimes handy, but dealing with children and books on a personal level was a learning experience completely different from the professional experience. Instinct told me to lay off the tests until time and a couple of good books had had their chance. After all, everyone travels at his or her own pace. But I did start leaving irresistible books lying around the house—easy, funny books like James Marshall's *Three Up a Tree* and reassuring, sensitive books like Beverly Cleary's *Ramona the Pest* (more about this later), which hooked my nonreader.

The resulting laughter, tears, and companionship that my first daughter has found in books spelled "success" at reading: by the fourth grade she was testing at tenth-grade level. But the real reward is her habit of reading, thinking, feeling, articulating, writing, entertaining herself for hours at a time, experiencing other people's minds and lives through the looking glass of their writing.

This is not an isolated phenomenon, and it is not confined to worried writers' children. There have been reports ranging from unexpected responses of handicapped children—the most detailed is Dorothy Butler's *Cushla and Her Books* (now out of print, but look for it in your library)—to whole schools "going book," as in Pennsylvania districts that have a SQUIRT program. During Super Quiet Undisturbed Individual Reading Time, everybody reads—children, teachers, clerical staff, principal, custodian. The phone in the secretary's office is off the hook. With adults practicing what they preach, any activity seems contagious. Kids will if you will.

As far as textbooks and teaching machines go, it makes more sense to achieve literacy *through* literature than to achieve literacy *before* giving children literature. Nobody learns to swim on dry land, and most basal reading series, perhaps updated from Dick and Jane but still written to a prescribed formula, are a desert of nonliterature. Here is the entire text of a typical book given to children learning how to read, with illustrations resembling those in a 1950s mail-order catalog. If this deadens your senses, just think how it must kill the interest of a restless new reader.

> "When will it be my birthday?" asked Mary.
>
> "Soon," said her father.
>
> "Will my birthday come soon?" asked Mary.
>
> "Soon," said her mother.
>
> "I wish my birthday would hurry," said Mary.
>
> "Will my birthday come soon?" asked Mary.
>
> "It won't be long," said Grandfather.
>
> "I wish my birthday would hurry," said Mary.
>
> "There are just ten more days," said Grandmother.
>
> "Will my birthday come soon?" asked Mary.
>
> "Soon," said her teacher.
>
> "I wish my birthday would hurry," said Mary.
>
> "Just a few more days," said Father.
>
> "I can't wait for my birthday!" said Mary.
>
> "Just four more days," said her brother.
>
> "Hurry up, birthday!" said Mary.
>
> "My birthday is tomorrow," Mary said happily.
>
> "Happy birthday, everybody!" shouted Mary. "My birthday hurried up. Now I wish it would slow down."

Read out loud, this sounds like someone chopping onions for an hour and a half. One six-year-old dubbed it the "worst book alive," but it's not really alive, and, unfortunately, it's not really that unusual. It's quite often the kind of thing foisted on six-year-olds who trail groaning into the reading circle.

A dull book simply dulls both child and adult, whereas a live-wire book keeps them reading. Reading is more than mechanics, it's magic. Emotional appeal is probably the biggest factor to nonreaders: Do they enjoy the way this book makes them feel? Individually, emotional relevance can translate into anything from dogs to baseball cards, dollhouses to jump-rope chants. Combined with compelling writing and art, the vital interest factor is an absolute winner.

Sylvia Ashton-Warner, an educator in New Zealand, couldn't find that kind of book when she was teaching Maori children to read, so she let them whisper an important word to her. She wrote each one on a scrap of paper, which the next day was returned to her hand in tattered, moist shreds but scrawled on a mind forever: "ghost," "mother," "afraid," "fight." Words like "the" or "and" stopped those children cold, but they never faltered over the hard words they had asked for. In her riveting book *Teacher,* Ashton-Warner describes how they eventually wrote their own textbooks with their own important words.

Many of the words the children chose had serious overtones. But there is a period, often when reading is just getting started and isn't solid yet, when the best approach seems to be light and low-key. It's hard enough to concentrate and get the sentences to run together correctly, much less figure out what's happening and what it all means. At that point, the funny and familiar seem to work best. The step backward, from hearing complex stories read out loud to figuring them out with enough speed and ease not to lose track of the meaning, can be discouraging.

Normally, the big crossover from listening to reading comes sometime during a period between first and third grades. It can be earlier or later, but at some point the child has to jump from hearing and looking at picture books as a source of literature to reading "chapter books" for independent enjoyment and school use (though, as stated in the previous chapter, this doesn't have to mean throwing picture books away). If children don't move into reading ease, it eventually affects their education, work life, financial possibilities, and adult environment. Learning to read well determines a child's entire future, so those years from six to eight are crucial.

Of course, reading preparation begins at birth, and reading practice is an ongoing process. *The Braid of Literature* by Shelby Anne Wolf and Shirley Brice Heath describes a nine-year study that showed how deeply two little girls integrated the books they heard throughout their development. But the period of transition to independent reading ease is especially difficult without strong motivation, which points to the most important elements of fiction for children this age—namely, suspense and humor. Children will read to find out what happens next and to laugh. This gets back to just which books should be left for reluctant readers. And that brings us to important names like Arnold Lobel, James Marshall, and Beverly Cleary, who have made more budding young readers smile and read on than almost any writer except Judy Blume, who for the most part comes a little later in the reading game.

Although two of our greatest pioneering creators of beginning-to-read books have died, their work lives on. Arnold Lobel's Frog and Toad series represents some of the best in a whole genre with limited vocabulary, a good story percolating through it, and enough pictures to ease a page full of print. Beginning-to-read books can be read aloud as picture books by an adult, but they also can be picked up and read independently by the listeners who later want another crack at the story on their own. Having heard and liked the story provides them with a push in the right direction. At best, children have been known to learn how to read this way without even realizing it, which shortcuts a good deal of painful effort on everyone's part. At the very least, the easy words and appealing format of beginning-to-read books make a great practice field. Even the arrangement by chapters gives kids the sense that they're ready for "real books."

Lobel, who died in 1987, happened to have a gift for this elemental level of writing and drawing; he stayed simple and sweet without getting corny. His stories and art almost always have humorous insight but hold their own at an action level as well. His innate sympathy for small creatures extended throughout a humble world of frogs, toads, grasshoppers, mice, and owls, all with their own vanities, all drawn with earthy tones, telling detail, and a gently mocking earnestness that win you over to regular visits.

James Marshall, who died in 1992, was more than mocking. He was just plain funny, a characteristic that he seemed to extend without strain to easy-readers as well as picture books. His George and Martha series can serve as either, being some of the shortest stories in American literature. The third story in the first collection is five lines long, with pictures of one hippopotamus spying on another through the bathroom window, only to find himself crowned by the bathtub: "George was fond of peeking in windows. One day George peeked in on Martha. He never did *that* again. 'We are friends,' said Martha. 'But there is such a thing as privacy!'" Marshall shone brightest where few other author-illustrators are naturally at ease, demonstraing his brilliance in the sets of beginning readers that include *Three up a Tree* and *Fox and His Friends.* These books keep children laughing and learning how to read. Marshall even made fun of chopped-onion prose when one of his characters, Lolly in *Three by the Sea,* quotes from her school reader: "The rat saw the cat and the dog. 'I see them,' says the rat. 'I see the cat and the dog.' The dog and the cat saw the rat. 'We see the rat,' they said. And that was that." And for too many children, it is—unless they get hold of a lively book like Marshall's.

Other authors and artists have added their own flair to the easy-reading genre. Another loyal and entertaining pair of characters are the cows Minnie and Moo, in Denys Cazet's *Minnie and Moo Go to the Moon* and *Minnie and Moo Go Dancing.* Jean Van Leeuwen's Oliver and Amanda Pig stories have something of the same affectionate but unsentimental storytelling style as Lobel's, but they focus on family rather than friends. Crosby Bonsall's brief mysteries are fun, and Syd Hoff's cartoon animals are broadly popular. Regional flavor lifts some of the beginning-to-read books high above the ordinary. *Wiley and the Hairy Man* by Molly Bang is a spooky southern swamp tale with imaginative, moss-soft drawings. Alvin Schwartz's *In a Dark, Dark Room and Other Scary Stories* is great for beginning readers because it combines the repetition of folktale patterns with the appeal of spooky suspense. Betsy Byars's book *The Golly Sisters Go West* and its sequels include tall tales in which two adventuresome women with minimal experience brave the frontier. The dialogue and antics are convincingly like those of rivalrous young siblings anywhere on the block, but the Old West setting adds flair. The accompanying watercolors proffer a generous dollop of humor, especially in the riotous postures of the two main characters and their horse's expressions.

Realism also holds its own in beginning-to-read books. Witness Betsy Byars's *My Brother, Ant* about the trying but affectionate preschool sibling of a heroic young narrator. Barbara Ann Porte excels at quickly establishing a genuine character and situation in her books about a motherless boy named Harry. The novelist Cynthia Rylant shows a particular talent for the beginning-to-read genre in her Henry and Mudge series. Henry is a boy who wants a dog—nothing unusual. But the puppy he gets, Mudge, *is* unusual. By the time Mudge stopped growing (in the first book), "he weighed one hundred eighty pounds, he stood three feet tall, and he drooled. 'I'm glad you're not short,'" says Henry appreciatively. A more good-hearted duo you couldn't find, even when they get into trouble with each other and everyone else. All of these books could stand on their own as young literature, but their additional feature of reading ease makes them an invaluable starter for rising readers.

You may have noticed that many beginner books run to series. The characters and settings become habitual, which is especially appropriate for uncertain readers with low confidence. There are moments when habit is comforting. Once you've mastered the names Harry, Henry, or Mudge, you can play with them, so it's a shot in the arm when more stories about them appear, as long as the spontaneity, structure, and style are consistently strong.

Just one reading size larger than beginners is the kind of story Beverly Cleary writes in *Henry Huggins* and the Ramona books. Cleary captures the everyday world of families with a fine eye for detail and a memory like an elephant for exactly what it feels like to be young in school or home situations. Children recognize themselves instantly and adults are bounced back into their own pasts with the speed of a time machine: what it's like not to have a sheep costume ready for the Christmas program; what it's like to stomp around in the rain on a pair of homemade tin-can stilts; how hard it is when a father loses his job and a child watches helplessly as parental tension mounts and the beloved cat Picky-Picky refuses to touch the cheapest brand of pet food but gnaws the Halloween pumpkin instead.

Although Cleary's books are funny, they have for children a "there but for the grace of God go I" poignancy. When Ramona anticipates cracking her hard-boiled egg on her head like the other kids in the lunchroom cafeteria, she has no way of knowing her mother has given her an uncooked egg by mistake. The shock of raw egg dripping down her neck sends her running, and every reader will know how keenly she feels the humiliation. Each chapter of Cleary's books is a complete episode, a satisfying beginning-middle-end in itself, easy to read and identify with. In staying true to her picture of perpetually normal family living, Cleary also pokes fun at adults. At one point, beleaguered Mr. Huggins, watching a spoiled young visitor litter his living room during a party, whispers into the air, "How much Kleenex in a box, anyway?" To which a thrifty guest replies matter-of-factly, "Two hundred and fifty sheets," precisely summarizing her own personality in one blow.

The trick with these books is for you to read the first chapter aloud and involve your children, and then turn them loose. They can finish comfortably and go back to the same series for more. Cleary has built up that circle of security that adults look for in their escape reading, with a slightly more innocent ear for dialogue. Of course, she's not the only writer who does this, but she's been doing it well for forty years. There are plenty of variations to throw on the table for spice. Betty MacDonald's series of books about *Mrs. Piggle-Wiggle* has something of the same perennial appeal. *The Enormous Egg* by Oliver Butterworth and *Mr. Popper's Penguins* by Richard and Florence Atwater are golden oldies with a similar light, episodic quality.

The transition between learn*ing* reader and learn*ed* reader is a challenging stage to write for. It doesn't attract the number of artists who want to create beautiful picture books for younger listeners or the number of writers who want to develop more complicated novels for older readers. Consequently, it's hard to find really good books for precarious readers ages seven to nine. Quality and popularity do crop up hand in hand, however, even for that age group and should be cherished all the more for the fires they can light under a hesitant reader. Easy access begins with an irresistible title: *The Monster in* *the Third Dresser Drawer* was followed by *The Kid Next Door and Other Headaches: Stories about Adam Joshua,* both by Janice Lee Smith, an author who knows the ways of childlife ("What do you do if you're afraid to be brave?"). Books such as Russell Erickson's Warton and Morton series about two toads' sometimes terrifying adventures or *Marvin Redpost: Why Pick on Me?* (you're right, it has to do with his nose) offer children energetic stories as well as reading exercise.

Entertaining novels and nonfiction for readers in the primary grades have gotten a new boost with increased incorporation of children's literature into elementary school reading programs. Publishers have recognized the "chapter book" gap and consciously cultivated materials that fill the need as imaginatively as possible, often in a format deliberately bridging the gap between the oversized picture books and the smaller, print-intensive look of novels. Harper and Row's series I Can Read Books was inaugurated with a title many adults may remember from their own childhoods, Else Holmelund Minarik's still-effective *Little Bear,* with illustrations by Maurice Sendak. Other notables in the series include Peggy Parish's *Dinosaur Time,* an automatic favorite because of the subject, and Barbara Brenner's *Wagon Wheels,* a gripping piece of historical fiction about three African-American pioneer boys who make their way alone from a dugout in Nicodemus, Kansas, to a new homestead their father has built 150 miles away. Random House has a Step into Reading series with books on popular topics such as *The Titanic: Lost . . . and Found* by Judy Donnelly and a Stepping Stone series to which some excellent writers have contributed. Henry Holt publishes the Redfeather Books, which range in subject matter from cheerful school stories to gentle reality-based fantasy to intriguing early nonfiction; Karen Hesse's accessible dog story *Sable* is a worthy representative. *Julian's Glorious Summer,* along with Ann Cameron's other books about an African-American seven-year-old and his family, are smoothly crafted and full of zest, as is *Aliens for Breakfast,* in which Jonathan Etra and Stephanie Spinner detail what happens when young Richard Bickerstaff sits down to a bowl of cereal spiked with a freeze-dried alien.

Whereas decoding is serious business that involves struggling from one word to the next, reading is a game with the prize of another good book. Kids who love science fiction and have gulped down *Aliens for Breakfast* and the subsequent *Aliens for Lunch* can take on *Stinker from Space* by Pamela Service, which is a little harder but just as exciting. Many of the "transition" books focus on the familiar world of school, as their titles tell: *Millie Cooper, 3B* by Charlotte Herman; *The Flunking of Joshua T. Bates* by Susan Shreve; *Class Clown* by Johanna Hurwitz. The classroom is a world unto itself. Shifting friendships, moral choices, problems of self-esteem and self-control are magnified into a secondary cosmos. Classroom antics sometimes seem like the stuff of a shallow sitcom, but the best authors can catch the deeper dynamic without getting heavy-handed. They can project kids' exuberance and anxieties in light, crisply detailed fiction.

As the reading level rises, so does the range of choices, as will be obvious in the next chapter. Graduates of the younger school stories can indulge in *Kevin Corbett Eats Flies* by Patricia Hermes, *There's a Boy in the Girls' Bathroom* by Louis Sachar, *Buddies* by Barbara Park, or *Nerd No More* by Kristine Franklin. Some books seem born for reluctant readers. One of my favorites is Thomas Rockwell's *How to Eat Fried Worms,* which makes ten- to twelve-year-olds laugh out loud (gross humor is pretty reliable for this age group). It's the story of two boys' bet that one will eat fifteen worms within fifteen days or forfeit fifty dollars. Billy is determined to do it, his rival to prevent him. The punch line, inevitably, is that after choking down the required number of worms in various desperate recipes, Billy starts to like them and keeps eating them after the bet is won. Keith Robertson's *Henry Reed, Inc.* and its successors were surefire hits before "reluctant reader" became a catchword. Now there are books especially designed for reluctant older readers. Marilyn Sachs's *Thunderbird* is about a girl who doesn't like to read but loves cars—and, it turns out, loves a boy who's a Brain with a capital "B."

For many readers, paperbacks are less intimidating than hardcover books. Most of the best children's books are now available in paperback editions and are often within the price range of a weekly allowance, giving youngsters a chance to make their own choices—which is a terrific stimulus to reading. And don't expect your child always to choose what you consider top quality. Formula fiction and syndicated series have always been wildly popular. Nancy Drew, that best-selling female James Bond of the younger set, has been updated and reenergized in new paperback titles. Today she's rivaled by paperback series ranging from the Animorphs series to the Sweet Valley High, Twins, and Kids books; the Saddle Club to Silver Skates; R. L. Stine's Goosebumps to Ann Martin's Baby-Sitters Club books. And there are always new series coming over the horizon, some of which will undoubtedly be the next big grade-school thing.

Nancy Drew isn't a soaring achievement, nor are her compatriots on the series shelf, nor are the comic-book super heroes, and so forth. But everybody needs a break. Although it should be clear by now that quality counts, few of us read at peak capacity all the time. Quality has its limitations, just like everything else. In that period of crucial consolidation into reading ease, anything interesting counts. For a little relaxation and regression later on and right over the adult threshold, children and teenagers have a right to their own versions of escape reading, which they'll find and enjoy, one hopes, without too much hindrance.

However, their "junk books" don't require your support or participation. Balancing fluff, pulp, and other juicy tidbits with some adventures in high-class taste does. It wouldn't hurt, for instance, to know some books a step up from formula mysteries, with the same allure and better writing. At a young level, there's Crosby Bonsall's *Case of the Cat's Meow* and his other easy-to-read books, while transition readers will enjoy David Adler's Cam Jansen series. Betty Ren Wright has written some effective early ghost stories that offer an alternative to Goosebumps books.

Older readers whose reading problems stem more from reluctance than decoding deficiencies relish the suspense of Caroline Cooney's *Face on the Milk Carton,* Amy Ehrlich's *Where It Stops, Nobody Knows,* Mary Downing Hahn's *Following the Mystery Man,* Joan Lowery Nixon's *Other Side of Dark,* Betty Ren Wright's *Dollhouse Murders,* Lois Duncan's *Locked in Time,* Avi's *Wolf Rider,* and many more. These are writers who will draw your children in and take them far beyond formula. A reading specialist once wrote to me about speaking at a conference: "Examples of books with just enough action, well-developed characters, plenty of punch, yet not overwhelming vocabulary are especially welcome." The good news is that they exist.

My own reluctant reader, by the way, paid me back in kind. On the recommendation of a fellow reviewer, I gave her one of those transitional book-hooks. It's no great literary feat, the reviewer had said, but it would keep a nine-year-old occupied. It did. My nonreader consumed it in one gulp and said the next day, quietly but with great determination, "Mom, *you'd better read this book.*" I took the hint and was startled to recognize a character remarkably, I might say *uncomfortably,* like myself—a loving but work-minded mother of a loving but doll-playing daughter who needed to be liberated from her mother's liberation.

We discussed the book and its conflicts and agreed on some adjustments in my schedule that made my daughter's life a lot more comfortable. You just never know when you're going to have to follow your own advice and where it's going to take you. My daughter and I spent more time together, and collecting doll furniture got to be a kind of hobby for both of us. The dollhouse reminded me of the art of miniature paintings, of literary miniatures—children's books that, like the child herself, were small but no less beautiful.

Many years later my other daughter, aged sixteen, brought me a well-thumbed paperback called *Reviving Ophelia* and said "Mom, *you'd better read this book.*" By this time I was a veteran, and I knew I was about to find out something important. Through this book my daughter told me, in ways that she could not express and I might not have understood, what her adolescent world was like. The book changed her life because she saw patterns of behavior from the perspective of someone studying them instead of someone suffering them. It changed our relationship because of the world we suddenly shared through the book. This rite of passage was a natural outcome of lifelong book bonding. Start early if you can—or start whenever and wherever the child is.

Jumping from Picture Books to Older Literature

EASIES

Bang, Molly. *Wiley and the Hairy Man* (6–8). Macmillan, 1976.
A spooky southern swamp tale picks up suspense with shadowy, moss-hung pictures, proving that easy-to-read books don't have to stint on atmosphere.

Benchley, Nathaniel. *Snorri and the Strangers,* illustrated by Don Bolognese (6–8). Harper, 1976.
Centuries before Columbus's arrival, a group of Norwegian settlers meet Native American inhabitants in a book that proves early reading can be just as interesting as early history.

Bernier-Brand, Carmen T. *Juan Bobo: Four Folktales from Puerto Rico,* illustrated by Ernesto Ramos Nieves (6–8). HarperCollins, 1994.
Juan Bobo was entertaining young Puerto Rican listeners long before appearing in print, and now he's beckoning to new readers with four deliciously silly tales (he tries to carry water in baskets and then dresses his pig for church), all accompanied by cleverly comical art with neon flashes highlighting lush island colors.

Bolognese, Don. *Little Hawk's New Name* (6–8). Scholastic, 1995.
Energetic line and watercolor pictures illustrate this story of a Plains Indian boy who helps his grandfather at a buffalo hunt, wins a horse race, and earns honor among his people.

Bonsall, Crosby. *Mine's the Best* (5–7). Harper, 1984.
The vocabulary of two children arguing is naturally limited, which makes this cartooned story ideal for beginning readers.

Brenner, Barbara. *Wagon Wheels,* illustrated by Don Bolognese (6–8). Harper, 1978.
Three motherless African-American boys and their father leave the post–Civil War South to settle in Kansas, after which the brothers make a 150-mile trek alone to the permanent homestead their father has established farther west. The illustrations are expressive wash drawings in brown and gold.

Byars, Betsy. *The Golly Sisters Go West* (6–8). Harper, 1986.
Slapstick comedy in an easy-to-read format follows the fortunes of two pioneer women who fuss at each other like kids, but their horse is the real star of the show, and of the funny pictures as well. The sisters return in *Hooray for the Golly Sisters*

and *The Golly Sisters Ride Again,* both fun for new readers. In a contemporary but equally humorous vein, try *My Brother, Ant* and its sequel.

Cazet, Denys. *Minnie and Moo Go to the Moon; Minnie and Moo Go Dancing* (6–8). DK Ink, 1998.
An intrepid pair of cows find that their promising ideas always seem to lead them into giggle-worthy trouble.

Cohen, Miriam. *First Grade Takes a Test,* illustrated by Lillian Hoban (6–8). Greenwillow, 1980.
First grade isn't too soon to worry about standardized tests. As these kids work their way through self-doubts that shake up the classroom, the brightly colored art reassures readers that everything will turn out all right.

Eastman, P. D. *Are You My Mother?* (6–8). Beginner, 1966.
An easy, light-hearted story about a baby bird who searches for his mother, this is an old book but still a favorite.

Giff, Patricia Reilly. *Good Luck, Ronald Morgan!* illustrated by Susanna Natti (6–8). Viking, 1996.
Dog training is a challenge with the hole-digging, book-chewing, cat-chasing pup that Ronald got in *Happy Birthday, Ronald Morgan!*

Griffith, Helen. *Alex and the Cat,* illustrated by Sonja Lamut (6–8). Greenwillow, 1997.
Humorous interplay between bumptious dog Alex and the wry family cat vividly delineates each of the two characters for new readers, who will also enjoy the soft-hued illustrations set off in plenty of white space.

Hoban, Lillian. *Arthur's Honey Bear* (6–8). Harper, 1974.
An endearing monkey child thinks he's ready to sell his stuffed bear along with other toys he has outgrown—until his little sister claims it.

Hoff, Syd. *Mrs. Brice's Mice* (6–8). Harper, 1988.
Beginning readers have always found it easy to identify with Hoff's animal characters—here, an individualistic mouse proves to be a hero when he goes his own way; the words are easy and the color cartoons as appealing as in other favorites of Hoff's, such as *The Horse in Harry's Room* or *Captain Cat.*

Hopkins, Lee Bennett. *Blast Off! Poems about Space,* illustrated by Melissa Sweet (6–8). HarperCollins, 1995.
Cosmic wonder is reflected in these simple poems about the moon, sun, stars, planets, and meteorites—all glowing in the accompanying watercolor art.

Kline, Suzy. *Song Lee in Room 2B,* illustrated by Frank Remkiewicz (6–8). Viking, 1993.
In the same series as *Horrible Harry and the Green Slime* (1989), this book focuses on a young Korean-American girl who overcomes her shyness in the course of some classroom adventures.

Lobel, Arnold. *Frog and Toad Are Friends* (5–8). Harper, 1970.
Five captivating stories about a frog, a toad, and the miniadventures of their lov-

ing friendship comprise the first in a warmhearted, witty series, all illustrated with gently humorous drawings in green and brown.

Marshall, Edward. *Fox All Week,* illustrated by James Marshall (6–8). Dial, 1984.
Fox gets into almost as many scrapes as kids who are learning to read, and they identify with him as they gulp down this series.

Marshall, James. *Three up a Tree* (6–8). Dial, 1986.
One of the best easy-to-read series features a group of kids who tell each other tall tales, heightened by the writer-artist's tongue-in-cheek drawings.

Minarik, Else Holmelund. *A Kiss for Little Bear,* illustrated by Maurice Sendak (5–8). Harper, 1968.
The kiss that Grandmother sends to Little Bear is carried on its way by a hen, a frog, and a cat—and that one little kiss leads to love, as Maurice Sendak shows in his enticingly old-fashioned pictures.

Parish, Peggy. *Amelia Bedelia,* illustrated by Fritz Siebel (6–8). Harper, 1963.
Amelia takes her employers' instructions literally and is saved from the results of "dressed chicken" and "dusted furniture" only by the merits of her lemon meringue pie. In addition to her popular Amelia Bedelia series, Parish has written easy-reading nonfiction, including *Dinosaur Time.*

Petersen, P. J. *I Hate Company,* illustrated by Betsy James (7–9). Dutton, 1994.
In this funny, unpatronizing look at youthful upheaval, Dan's life is turned upside down when his mother's friend and her three-year-old son move in for an indefinite stay.

Pinkwater, Daniel. *Ned Feldman, Space Pirate* (7–10). Macmillan, 1994.
Fast-paced and zany, this book relates Ned's adventures with Captain Lumpy Lugo from the planet Jivebone, some giant space chickens, and a yeti.

Porte, Barbara A. *Harry's Pony,* illustrated by Yossi Abolafia (6–8). Greenwillow, 1997.
As in other books in the Harry series, the protagonist handles a genuine problem—here, the pony he's won in a contest but can't keep in his neighborhood—with good-hearted aplomb reflected in light line-and-wash illustrations.

Ross, Pat. *M and M and the Bad News Babies,* illustrated by Marilyn Hafner (6–8). Knopf, 1983.
Two friends, Mandy and Mimi, earn money to stock their fish tank by babysitting a lively pair of twins in this realistic, briskly funny easy reader.

Rylant, Cynthia. *Henry and Mudge,* illustrated by Suçie Stevenson (6–8). Bradbury, 1987.
The friendship of Henry and and his dog Mudge is chronicled in a funny, gracefully written series of more than a score of other titles, including *Henry and Mudge and the Sneaky Crackers: The Sixteenth Book of Their Adventures.*

Schwartz, Alvin. *In a Dark, Dark Room and Other Scary Stories,* illustrated by Dirk Zimmer (6–8). Harper, 1984.
Folktales, especially ghost stories, make great practice reading because of the quick-

paced suspense, and these have been effectively simplified and rigorously illustrated to keep kids on the edge of their seats.

Seuss, Dr. *The Cat in the Hat* (6–8). Beginner, 1966.
This early easy-to-read book is still one of the best as it plays with rhyming words and a chaotic character children love.

Sharmat, Marjorie. *Nate the Great and the Pillowcase,* illustrated by Marc Simont (6–8). Delacorte, 1993.
How can you miss with two dogs named Fang and Sludge, an ace boy-detective with a steady supply of new mysteries to solve, and deadpan humor punctuated with flexible and affectionate art?

Van Leeuwen, Jean. *Amanda Pig and Her Big Brother Oliver,* illustrated by Ann Schweninger (6–8). Dial, 1982.
Although Amanda and Oliver appear as pigs in the soft-toned drawings, their squabbles and amusements would fit right into any loving family's daily life.

Yolen, Jane. *Commander Toad in Space,* illustrated by Bruce Degen (6–8). Putnam, 1980.
A science fiction adventure for the youngest reader follows the fortunes of a stellar amphibian who became popular enough to launch a series.

EASY UPS

Atwater, Florence and Richard. *Mr. Popper's Penguins* (9–11). Little, 1938.
The Popper family is unexpectedly joined by a flock of penguins, who make it necessary to alter certain aspects of the house and who considerably liven up the Popper children's lives.

Blume, Judy. *Tales of a Fourth Grade Nothing,* illustrated by Roy Doty (7–10). Dutton, 1956.
Peter's got problems, not the least of which is a two-year-old brother who's driving him crazy!

Bulla, Clyde. *The Sword in the Tree,* illustrated by Paul Galdone (8–10). Harper, 1956.
This exciting Arthurian story is only one of many brief, easy-to-read historical fictions written by Clyde Bulla, who had a gift for economical language, strong action, and sturdy characterizations.

Butterworth, Oliver. *The Enormous Egg,* illustrated by Louis Darling (8–11). Little, 1956.
When his hen lays a gigantic egg, Nate finds himself the proud owner of . . . a dinosaur!

Cameron, Ann. *The Stories Julian Tells,* illustrated by Doris Leder (7–9). Random, 1987.
Julian is so scared of riding a bike that he lies about preferring to work for his dad all summer—and gets rewarded with a new bike! Julian's younger brother gets top billing in *The Stories Huey Tells* (1995). Both boys and both books have lots of natural appeal.

Cleary, Beverly. *Ramona and Her Father,* illustrated by Alan Tiegreen (8–12). Morrow, 1977.

When Mr. Quimby loses his job, Ramona tries to help. The results, like all of Ramona's performances in the bestselling series, are as funny as they are familiar.

Cooper, Ilene. *The New, Improved Gretchen Hubbard* (9–12). Morrow, 1992.

In one of many authentic situations developed in the Kids of Kennedy Middle School series, which includes *Queen of the Sixth Grade, Choosing Sides,* and *Mean Streak,* Gretchen slims down and discovers that being cute has its own problems.

Danziger, Paula. *Amber Brown Is Not a Crayon,* illustrated by Tony Ross (7–9). Putnam, 1994.

The brisk, empathetic writing here ensures that readers relate to third-grader Amber Brown, whose best friend Justin moves away.

Dickinson, Peter. *Chuck and Danielle,* illustrated by Kees de Kiefte (8–10). Delacorte, 1996.

Seven episodes about a nervous whippet named Chuck lead to triumph for the trembling dog and his faithful mistress, not to mention a reward from McDonald's!

Donnelly, Judy. *The Titanic: Lost . . . and Found,* illustrated by Keith Kohler (7–9). Random, 1987.

A straightforward but involving account of the *Titanic*'s launching, capsizing, and discovery.

Erickson, Russell. *A Toad for Tuesday,* illustrated by Lawrence Di Fiori (7–9). Lothrop, 1974.

Warton's capture by an owl who plans to eat him on his birthday makes a suspenseful episode in the serial adventures of toad brothers Warton and Morton.

Etra, Jonathan, and Stephanie Spinner. *Aliens for Breakfast,* illustrated by Stephen Bjorkman (8–10). Random, 1988.

Richard's bowl of Alien Crisp cereal sports a cosmic visitor who saves Earth from invading Dranes.

Franklin, Kristine. *Nerd No More* (8–10). Candlewick, 1996.

Cursed by his mother's television appearances as "Mrs. Science," Wiggie is determined to change his nerdy image.

Gilson, Jamie. *It Goes Eeeeeeeeeeeee!* illustrated by Diane de Groat (7–9). Clarion, 1994.

Richard (from *Itchy Richard*) and his friends in Mrs. Zookey's second-grade class are preparing for Endangered Animal Month, which sends classmates Patrick and Dawn Marie off to track bats for their report.

Greene, Stephanie. *Owen Foote, Soccer Star,* illustrated by Martha Weston (7–9). Clarion, 1998.

In this sequel to *Owen Foote, Second Grade Strongman* (1996) eight-year-old Owen manages to stand up for himself and his best friend despite a problematic coach and teammate.

Hartman, Victoria. *The Silliest Joke Book Ever,* illustrated by R. W. Alley (6–9). Lothrop, 1993.

"How does an up-to-date shepherd tell time? With a digital flock." This is one of more than a hundred jokes, packaged with jovial watercolor drawings, that offer wordplay to stretch a child's vocabulary in a nondidactic way and with a currency very much in touch with a high-tech world.

Herman, Charlotte. *Millie Cooper, Take a Chance,* illustrated by Helen Cogancherry (8–10). Dutton, 1985.

In a warm school-and-family story set in the forties, Millie schemes to get her first bicycle, reads her favorite poem aloud to the class, and worries about getting enough valentines.

Hermes, Patricia. *Kevin Corbett Eats Flies,* illustrated by Carol Newsome (9–11). Harcourt, 1986.

Kevin galvanizes the attention of his fifth-grade peers by swallowing a goldfish, a shortcut to popularity proven by his past record of eating flies.

Hesse, Karen. *Sable,* illustrated by Marcia Sewall (7–9). Henry Holt, 1994.

Easy to read and as basic in appeal as an animal story can be, this is young Tate's account of how she got a dog her mother didn't want and how she got to do the woodworking her father didn't want her to try.

Hill, Kirkpatrick. *Toughboy and Sister* (9–12). McElderry, 1990.

A suspenseful survival story about two children, ages eleven and eight, left alone in a remote Alaskan fishing cabin far from their Athabascan Indian village. The sequel, *Winter Camp,* offers further adventures.

Hopkinson, Deborah. *Birdie's Lighthouse,* illustrated by Kimberly Bulcken Root (6–9). Schwartz/Atheneum, 1997.

In 1855, ten-year-old Bertha ("Birdie") helps her father tend the lighthouse and ultimately faces a terrifying storm, depicted in watercolor-and-ink illustrations that heighten the drama.

Hurwitz, Johanna. *Class Clown,* illustrated by Sheila Hamanaka (8–10). Morrow, 1987.

Lucas Cott is one of those not-always-endearing characters who seem to appear in every class: the wise-cracker, the cut-up, the kid who reacts too fast for his own control system to censor. Readers will appreciate the way Lucas channels his energy into running a successful class circus.

Hutchins, Hazel J. *The Three and Many Wishes of Jason Reid,* illustrated by Julie Tennent (8–10). Viking, 1988.

Eleven-year-old outfielder Jason Reid gets more than he wished for from a garbage-can elf who grants him a baseball glove that will catch anything, immunity from surprise or questioning about the glove, and . . . three more wishes.

King-Smith, Dick. *The School Mouse,* illustrated by Cynthia Fisher (8–10). Hyperion, 1995.

This prolific author's winning style and vigorous characterizations make him a favorite, whether in this story of a mouse inspired to scholarship, in his series about animal-crazy Sophie, or in *Babe, the Gallant Pig,* featured in the popular film *Babe.*

Lindgren, Astrid. *Pippi Longstocking,* illustrated by Louis Glanzman (8–10). Viking, 1950.

To grownups, Pippi may seem like a brat, but to kids she's a laudable trickster who gets away with doing absolutely anything she wants to.

MacDonald, Betty. *Mrs. Piggle-Wiggle,* illustrated by Hilary Knight (7–9). Lippincott, 1957.

Mrs. Piggle-Wiggle may look a little peculiar, but she knows some amazing ways to make children behave.

Mahy, Margaret. *Tingleberries, Tuckertubs and Telephones,* illustrated by Robert Staermose (8–10). Viking, 1996.

In this madcap adventure, Saracen's dear old granny is a retired ace detective who can't wait to get on the trail again when an old nemesis, the pirate Grudge-Gallows, escapes from prison.

Park, Barbara. *Buddies* (10–12). Knopf, 1985.

Two weeks at a girls' camp presents Dinah with a problem of what to do with an unpopular cabinmate who clings to her like a leech.

Pollack, Pamela. *The Random House Book of Humor for Children,* illustrated by Paul O. Zelinsky (8–10). Random, 1988.

This anthology of thirty-four funny excerpts, from Mark Twain to Judy Blume, will lead children straight to the original books for a rich banquet of reading.

Quattlebaum, Mary. *Jackson Jones and the Puddle of Thorns,* illustrated by Melodye Rosales (8–11). Delacorte, 1994.

In this witty, easygoing story, Jackson Jones wants a basketball for his birthday, but much to his dismay—and the delight of the local bully—he instead receives a plot in the local community garden.

Robertson, Keith. *Henry Reed, Inc.,* illustrated by Robert McCloskey (9–12). Viking, 1958.

Henry Reed and Midge Glass are two inventive children who start a business of their own, with hilarious results, in pure and applied research.

Rockwell, Thomas. *How to Eat Fried Worms,* illustrated by Emily McCully (8–10). Watts, 1973.

Ten-year-old Billy hopes that worms can be delicious, because he's just made a bet that he'll eat fifteen of them!

Sachar, Louis. *Marvin Redpost: Why Pick on Me?* illustrated by Barbara Sullivan (7–9). Random, 1993.

Both honest and funny, this entry in the Marvin Redpost series—which includes *Marvin Redpost: Kidnapped at Birth?* and *Marvin Redpost: Alone in His Teacher's*

House—will have "transition" readers laughing out loud as our third-grade hero suffers a popularity plummet when the class bully labels him a nose-picker.

Sachs, Marilyn. *Thunderbird* (10–12). Dutton, 1985.
Tina seldom reads a book, and her chief interest in life is repairing the old Thunderbird she's bought. Then she falls for the class brain who's devoted to environmental causes and everything changes.

Service, Pamela. *Stinker from Space* (9–11). Scribner's, 1988.
A first-class, funny science fantasy that will hook middle-grade readers right from the first scene, when Tsynq Yr evades a Zarnk enemy cruiser, crashes to Earth, and has to inject his mind into the body of a skunk for lack of a better host.

Shreve, Susan. *The Flunking of Joshua T. Bates,* illustrated by Diane de Groat (7–9). Knopf, 1984.
Joshua is miserable about the unfairness of having to repeat third grade, but a new teacher who looks forbidding coaches him through his crisis. This and tempting titles such as *Joshua T. Bates in Trouble Again* will draw readers into the Joshua T. Bates series.

Smith, Janice Lee. *The Monster in the Third Dresser Drawer,* illustrated by Dick Grackenback (7–9). Harper, 1981.
Adam Joshua is a young individualist who suddenly has to deal with moving, the arrival of a baby sister, a strict babysitter, and loose teeth, all of which he manages with aplomb.

Sobol, Donald. Encyclopedia Brown series (8–12). Morrow and Lodestar.
The mysteries solved by the whiz kid who stars in the Encyclopedia Brown series have proved irresistible even to reluctant readers.

Spinelli, Jerry. *Tooter Pepperday,* illustrated by Donna Nelson (7–9). Random, 1995.
Feisty heroine Tooter rails against her new home on a farm—there's no pizza delivery or nearby McDonald's—but she does find some things that fascinate her there, including an egg that must be turned in its incubator every day in order to hatch.

Walsh, Jill Paton. *Matthew and the Sea Singer,* illustrated by Alan Marks (7–9). Farrar, 1993.
An unwanted orphan, Matthew has a golden singing voice that leads to his kidnapping by seal-folk and, later, a daring rescue by his friend Birdy in a story that's deeper than its reading level implies and illustrated by watercolors with a lightly mythic resonance.

Wojciechowski, Susan. *Beany (Not Beanhead) and the Magic Crystal,* illustrated by Susanna Natti (7–9). Candlewick, 1997.
The likable Beany returns in this breezy sequel to *Don't Call Me Beanhead!* and offers more of her spunky, funny, fair-minded observations in dealing with a "magic" crystal with the power to grant just one wish.

Wright, Betty Ren. *The Ghost of Popcorn Hill,* illustrated by Karen Ritz (8–10). Holiday, 1993.

An eerie situation develops when two brothers discover their rustic old cabin is haunted by a previous inhabitant—and by the ghost of an Old English Sheepdog! Large print and homey pencil illustrations invite readers to enjoy this and other mysteries by the same author.

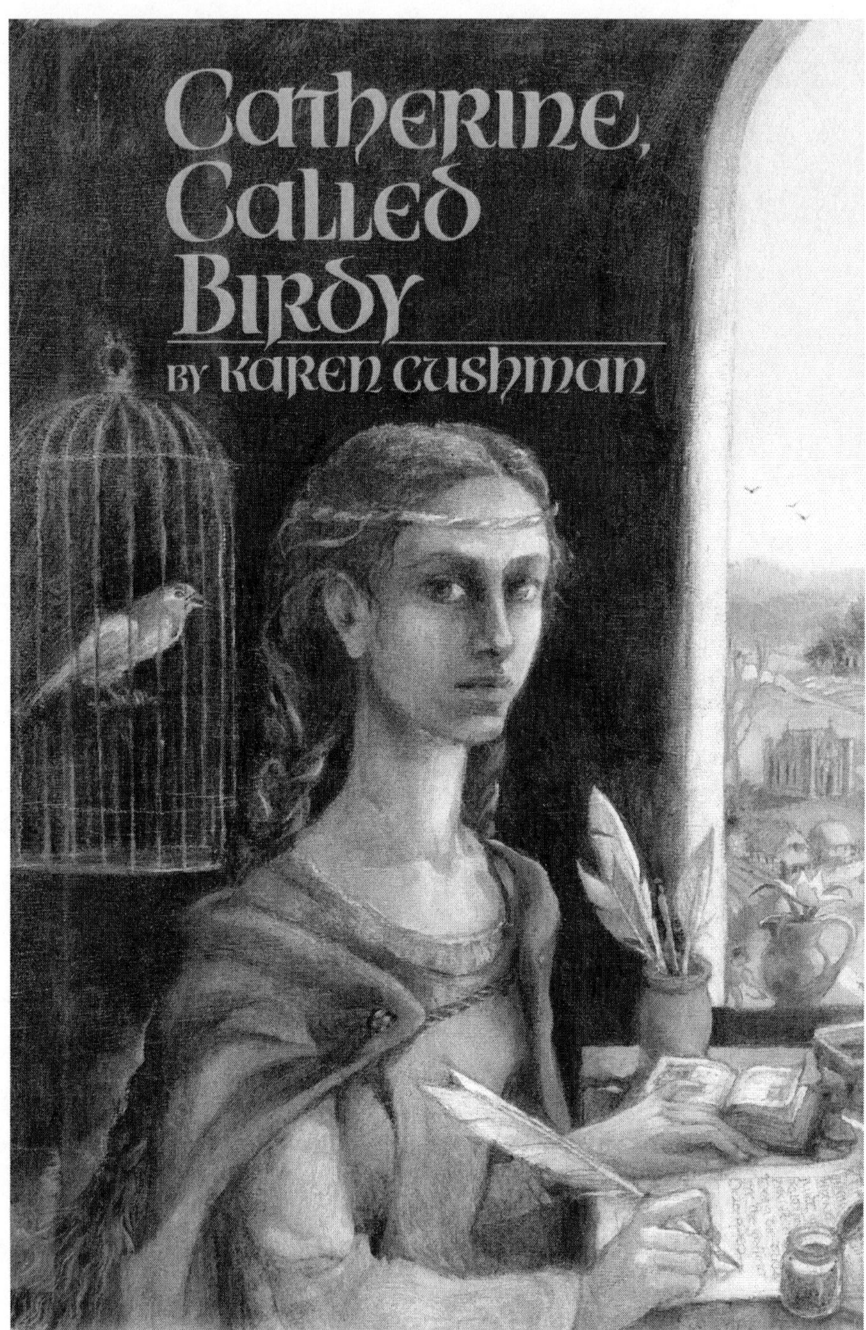

Trina Schart Hyman

5

Fiction for Older Children

Once, in the throes of writing a book, I lettered two reminders to myself. One three-by-five card neatly read "Patience" and the other "Magic." They were the two ingredients I thought I needed for working on a novel, and for months they were taped to the wall above my desk.

One day I sat down at the typewriter and saw that my ten-year-old had added a sign right in the middle of the other two. It was a much bigger piece of paper with a neat circle on it colored red, and underneath it were the words "Big Tomato." Suddenly the light dawned and I realized that "Big Tomato" was a much better symbol for writing than "Patience" or "Magic." First of all, it was not abstract but concrete, which is a mark of good fiction. Second, it was not colorless but vivid, like good writing. Third, it was an everyday detail, not a grandiose scheme (which only succeeds when it's built on everyday details). Finally, a tomato is, in its own way, something of a miracle. The same could be said of a good novel.

The novel is not necessarily realistic, but it is *real,* like a big tomato. And as with big tomatoes, at least tomatoes in certain seasons of the year, there are so many novels for young readers that they can become rather overwhelming. But if you look more closely, what initially may seem to be a shelf of indistinguishable books starts to sort itself out. For one thing, the child you're browsing for probably has some established likes and dislikes. If he or she makes retching noises when channel-surfing past "Dr. Quinn, Medicine Woman," it might be best to avoid frontier fiction (though it's worth checking to see if your child flips the channel back when no one is looking). If he or she can't stop talking about last summer's camping trip, an outdoor adventure or survival story may be right up your child's alley. That doesn't mean you have to lock a child into reading the same kind of book all the time—after all, one of the great pleasures of reading is broadening your horizons, discovering that you're really enjoying a book you didn't expect to. But there's also something special about a book that comes from somebody who has paid enough attention to you to know that this title might be particularly suited to your individual taste. Kids deserve both those literary experiences—the unexpected splurge and the tailored fit.

Type of literature isn't the whole story, of course. Fiction ranges in complexity from the cheerful antics of personified animals, such as those in *The School Mouse* by Dick King-Smith, to young adult dramas like Nancy Werlin's *Killer's Cousin,* in which a teenager comes to terms with his role in his girlfriend's death while beginning to realize his young cousin has a terrible secret of her own. Fantasy can be domestic, gentle, and reality-based, as in Sylvia Waugh's book *The Mennyms* and its sequels about a family of life-sized rag dolls who survive quietly in human society, or it can be grand and dramatic, like Philip Pullman's *Golden Compass.* Tales of the supernatural can work on the picture-book level of Tony Johnston's sly *Ghost of Nicholas Greebe* or create an irresistibly sinister atmosphere, as in Robert Westall's *Stones of Muncaster Cathedral.* An adult friend of mine was hooked into a lifelong habit of mystery reading by an early acquaintance with the Freddy the Detective series by Walter Brooks.

If you're in the bookstore or library with a young reader in tow, you may be able to avail yourself of a consultation, but if you're not, this is where the "don't panic and grab *Black Beauty*" dictum comes in. You don't want to stand in the aisles reading the whole book (which wouldn't guarantee success with another reader anyway); rather, you want to have a taste of the titles you're considering. Even if you're armed with the information that the birthday girl likes fantasy, look beyond the unicorn on the cover to see if the opening grabs you, if the dialogue sounds believable, if the characters seem compelling—it could be the book used up all its atmosphere on the cover, or that it's actually historical fiction set in medieval France, or that it's exactly the book she'll love. Sampling the book first isn't a guarantee, but it's an easy way to hedge your bets.

Not knowing the exact age range for which a book is appropriate shouldn't worry a participating adult too much. It's just a matter of finding a book with plenty of room for a growing mind. The recommended lists in this book suggest an age range for each title, but those ranges are merely rough guidelines (some of the books in the previous chapter and following chapter, for instance, have ranges that overlap with the titles in this one). Individual children vary so much in abilities and interests that their involvement can take them to unexpected levels, and a book may reach much higher- or lower-age audiences than intended. The age of the audience doesn't affect the potential for quality. Central to children's literature is the idea that *the same high quality can prevail in books from preschool through puberty.*

It's true that there are dominant concerns special to each age group, and the writer who can articulate these has a rare talent. Even more amazing is the writer who can span many age levels in one book through the sheer power of craft. That's what makes E. B. White so well loved: in *Charlotte's Web,* for example, a pig's acceptance of a spider's death makes a story of friendship that evokes responses on many levels.

There are some ages when children do have special reading needs, in particular when they are just consolidating their skills. But once past that barrier, their reading depends on their interests, which may depend on adult interests. There's always one sure route around age categories—namely, reading aloud. It's emotionally satisfying, and it leads the way to books a child will love reading alone.

Fantasy is perhaps the genre most likely to produce books appreciated by child and adult reader alike, whether read together or separately. But even fantasy must be real, and consistent. Magic must be a world that works. People often think of children's fantasy, for instance, as involving sweet little fairies tiptoeing through the tulips. Those tulip fairies are a long way from the high art that some fantasy has become. J. R. R. Tolkien in *The Lord of the Rings,* Ursula Le Guin in *A Wizard of Earthsea,* Lloyd Alexander in the Prydain Chronicles, Susan Cooper in *The Dark Is Rising,* and Madeleine L'Engle in *A Wrinkle in Time* have all disproved that myth with their monumental series. Youngsters who prefer the fantastic in a cozier form still have plenty to choose from, however. William Mayne's stories of Hob, the friendly house spirit who guards a family from small nuisances and larger evil, never get frilly about their half-real, half-fanciful world. Hob is purposeful and rough-edged, defeating the enemy in his own homely way in *Hob and the Goblins.* Mayne makes Hobbishness an everyday affair—and therein lies its magic.

The more fantastic a piece of fiction is, the harder the writer must work to make it believable. Great children's books come when writers capture the dreams of childhood with their skills grown wise. Every child dreams of heroic ventures. Lloyd Alexander has captured those dreams with the wiles of wit, invention, timing, and characters who become each reader's close friends or archenemies. Meet Cabarus, the villain of *Westmark:* "As chief minister, he was entitled to sumptuous chambers in the new Juliana. He declined them. He kept his same quarters, setting an example of frugality and modesty; righteousness being always more believable when combined with dreariness."

Lloyd Alexander's villains are often the more powerful for being lost heroes, distorted by fatal flaws we all share. And his heroes are convincingly human—guileless, vulnerable, faulty, sometimes silly. The hero of *Westmark* is introduced with characteristic irony. "As for Theo, he loved virtue, despised injustice, and was always slightly hungry." Alexander's plots are remarkable for complexity and pace—two elements not always compatible in literature. Even his descriptions lend either suspense or comic relief. His fantasy is realistic, his realism fantastic.

In dealing with younger children's fiction, whether fantasy or realism, you're once again up against the requirement of brief development. Long pages of indulgent description or unadulterated intricacies of characterization without benefit of action will just draw a yawn. Plot is simply more compatible with a child's concentration span than elaborate style, but that's no excuse for not developing the best possible style and characters, along with a gripping plot. The details have to be chosen with selective self-discipline, but those very limitations, like a sonnet form, are a challenge for a good writer. Brevity, after all, is the soul of wit, and some of the best descriptions are brief caricatures. In novels, as in picture-book writing and art, it is freshness that counts. Children—or people in general—are deluged with the ordinary, the well meant but mummified, the TV-dinner titles. What's really exciting is fiction that *has* to be read because it *had* to be written, not because it *ought* to have been written. The idea of it was just too compelling or funny or sad not to overflow. And when it overflowed, it was channeled by skillful writing.

Sometimes it comes as a big surprise that it takes more than a knowledge of children to write a children's book. Not even imagination is enough. Good intention is a wonderful thing, but good intention without the spark of inspiration isn't much at all, and inspiration without craft is nothing. The skills of fiction are the same for adults' and children's books. A plot can be suspenseful or inevitable, but there needs to be some element of surprise in its unfolding. Predictable plots are pretty dull. Ditto for predictable characters. No two people are alike; yet in mediocre children's books a stereotyped character—a hero or villain with no distinguishing characteristics or surprises—is often allowed to pass as a mouthpiece for a writer's message.

Children's literature is particularly susceptible to delivering messages through characters and situations. A message is not the same as a theme, which is an idea that emerges from real, unique characters as they evolve their story. It's the characters who must shape the plot, theme, tone, style, and setting—or the book will be hollow rather than convincing. Caricatures can heighten comedy and archetypes can deepen folklore, but stereotypes will flatten fiction.

One of my touchstone characters in modern realistic children's fiction is Harriet the Spy. She's the one who broke through the tradition of children being good all the time. She fluctuates as we all do from high to low to high again, from lovable to obnoxious and back again. When she first appeared, adults thought her spying was controversial, but children immediately recognized her as one of their own kind yet different from anyone else. One of her idiosyncrasies is tomato sandwiches; another is practicing what it would feel like to be an onion. She's unique all right. There will never be another Harriet who loves tomato sandwiches and rolls around on the floor like an onion. It's these specific twists that contribute to good characterization for adult books or children's books.

Individualized characters generate their own problems and find their own solutions. The problems may vary from defying a comfortable school clique to surviving a concentration camp. The solutions may range from accepting the decrees of society to defying them. If the characters are original, the plot has a chance to be original too. But plot also involves further techniques of storytelling, such as a tight movement from beginning to middle to end. Plot—finding out what happens—is the great spellbinder.

There's a wonderful passage in John Irving's adult novel *The World According to Garp.* It describes a publisher's infallible system for predicting that a book will be popular. Nobody knows that he gives the manuscript in question to a woman who cleans his office and who hates to read. If she finishes it, he knows it will be a winner.

> "If you hated it, why'd you read it, Jillsy?" John Wolf asked her.
> "Same reason I read anythin' for," Jillsy said. "To find out what *happens.*"
> John Wolf stared at her. ". . . So you read it to find out?" John Wolf said.
> "There ain't no other reason to read a book, is there?" Jillsy Sloper said. . . . "It feels so true," she crooned, making the word *true* cry like a loon over a lake at night. . . . "A book's true when you can say 'Yeah! That's just how damn people *behave* all the time.' *Then* you know it's true," Jillsy said.

Like Jillsy Sloper, children and many other people (if truth be told) will sit still only so long for descriptions of psychological complexity. They want to know what happens next, and they want it to ring true. Endings in folklore may seem patterned, but there's suspense in a higher and higher accumulation of events that up the ante to a climactic, satisfying conclusion. The events and endings of realistic fiction are more unexpected, the way our own lives are.

The heroine of Bette Greene's *Summer of My German Soldier* is a southern Jew who during World War II helps a German prisoner of war—one of the few people in her life who has treated her kindly—to escape, an act that the rest of her society regards as criminal. Because the writer takes such care in building a real character through unique details, natural dialogue, and carefully chosen scenes, the reader experiences Patty Bergen's personal agony of being rejected by parents and peers from whom she desperately wants acceptance and approval. Because of being so involved in her as a real person, the reader cares deeply that she is experiencing painful alienation at the book's conclusion, winding up in a reform school as punishment for showing moral compassion. It's not a happy ending—indeed, children's literature in the last few decades has begun to reflect the fact that not all stories end happily ever after—but it's the inevitable one for this story.

Since the characters and plot have held true, the theme emerges powerfully, forcing us to ask, What is justice, personal and social? What place does love really have in a society riddled with prejudice? Who are society's real villains and who are its heroes—behind all the labels? How does one know what is right and how does one find the courage or will or desperation to do it? If Patty Bergen had been popular and "well adjusted," would she have valued a lowly black servant as her best friend the way she did, or was that a function of her need? You just don't find this kind of plot or character or theme in mass-market series books.

Children don't *always* have to read for depth, of course, any more than adults do. Humor, entertainment, easy pleasure, simple information, and a host of other attractions can be valid reasons to read a particular book at a particular time. But there are books that offer the young reader, in an accessible and age-appropriate fashion, a chance to grow and to explore important and complicated questions that human beings struggle with all their lives. These are the books that children whose reading is limited to the pleasurable ease of formula fiction are missing out on.

The same depth *can* be found in fantasy, science fiction, mystery, comedy, or historical fiction. It can be found in realistic stories of families, friends, and their survival against the odds of war or peace, natural or manmade environments. The world should not be boiled down to a thin broth of simplistic concepts for children. It is daring for writers to touch the sparks of reality and fantasy in a child's mind, which ranges from narrow experience to wide-open possibilites. The presentation or the technique can be simple, but the vision behind it must be rich. It has to be as complex as the world is and as people are. That takes a lot of mastery, a lot of technical footwork. It takes a lot of work to let the complexity of things, or even hints of the complexity of things, show through a simple presentation.

A plot that develops from well-realized characters will have a logical force giving the book a natural urgency that children and adults respond to and remember. A plot that is imposed on characters, in which events have no reason for their occurrence beyond the author's functional need for them, makes a contrived book, and artificial contrivance is the greatest plague in children's literature. It mars fiction, nonfiction, poetry, and picture books alike. It accounts for fake dialogue, awkward transitions, and patronizing information. Books should grow naturally, not be forced.

Fiction doesn't work with the abbreviated conventions of folklore. In fiction as in life, people have many sides to their characters. Even in a fantasy of good versus evil, such as *The Lord of the Rings,* Tolkien's lowest character, Gollum, is more poignant for his flashes of goodness, which make us sympathetic enough to grieve for his departure from the side of the good. The writer who has insight into the human condition and who has patience to probe it in fiction can move any reader beyond the printed page into the human realm. A writer who can do so in connection with the experiences of childhood may be able to pull off a good book for children.

No good children's book tries to provide all the answers. One of the hardest things for adults to acknowledge to children is that we *don't* have all the answers. A problem-solution equation doesn't amount to literature. A mentally handicapped child, for instance, may appear as a stereotype, a case study, or the object of a lesson on "adjustment." In well-developed fiction, however, that child becomes a complex personality. Virginia Euwer Wolff's *Probably Still Nick Swansen* and Sylvia Cassedy's *M.E. and Morton* both bring mentally handicapped characters into sharp focus without becoming "problem novels."

The intention to teach a lesson or deliver a sermon often overwhelms children's novels. Intention should be generated by story, not story by intention. Katherine Paterson, who is deeply religious, shows how convictions and craft can coexist to the detriment of neither. She has an ability to build, with absorbing intensity, distinctive worlds of character and situation. She also has an emotional hotline into the deepest concerns of childhood, peopling, plotting, setting, and styling stories into the kinds of simple, natural shapes that carry the most complex meanings: the death of a friend in *A Bridge to Ter-*

abithia, the release of defenses against having never been loved in *The Great Gilly Hopkins,* the fierce quest for identity in *Jacob Have I Loved,* the acceptance of a great gift of talent in *Come Sing, Jimmy Jo,* the delving into some crucial questions of identity in *Jip: His Story.*

These stories are all characterized by a moral toughness that leaves no room for the sweet or the didactic or even the easy way out. In *A Bridge to Terabithia,* Jess will forever feel pain and guilt over his friend Leslie's drowning, but there is redemption in bequeathing to his sister the imaginative legacy of his dead friend. The heroine of *Jacob Have I Loved* never comes to terms with her twin sister through a stormy childhood and adolescence; only her adult observations finally bring a separate peace. The hero of *Come Sing, Jimmy Jo* has to see beyond the weakness and betrayal in both his parents' actions, past the pathetic hysteria of his country music fans, to where his own strength lies, in the mountains, in mountain music, and in the old mountain woman and her son who have raised him in their own image. *The Great Gilly Hopkins* leaves the protagonist losing her first real mother figure but changing in the realization of what she has lost. To the only person who has ever persisted past her obnoxious ways into her neglected heart, Gilly Hopkins says,

> "Dammit, Trotter. Don't try to make a stinking Christian out of me."
>
> "I wouldn't try to make nothing out of you." There was a quiet at the other end of the line. "Me and William Ernest and Mr. Randolph kinda like you the way you are."
>
> "Go to hell, Trotter," Gilly said softly.
>
> A sigh. "Well, I don't know about that. I had planned on settling permanently somewheres else."
>
> "Trotter"—She couldn't push the word hard enough to keep the squeak out—"I love you."
>
> "I know, baby. I love you, too."

These are astutely moral novels that never become moralistic.

Paula Fox is another writer whose caring reveals itself in craft. Although her crafting is distinguished by a singular internal clarity, it also has a depth of imagery that takes readers deep into the core of the characters. In fact, I once heard her say that her approach to characterizations resembled peeling an onion, getting closer and closer to the center. An action exists to reveal the actors in all their complexity, yet not a word appears that doesn't need to be there. To balance the requirements of nuance and clarity is no mean feat. Each of her books is distinguished by unforgettable portraits of a young protagonist facing some strategic choice of maturation and an adult who has made those choices, for better or worse. The plots, of course, are completely different. In *One-Eyed Cat,* a boy purges his guilt over blinding an animal with the first proud shot of his rifle. *Lily and the Lost Boy* reenacts a Greek tragedy of sacrifice and redemption.

The children in these books do not emerge unscarred from their encounters, but they and their readers are stronger for the echoes of understanding that reflect off the incident. Part of the reason for this is that Fox creates a kind of echo chamber with her prose. It is hard, clear, compact, and smooth, with thoughts further refined as they bounce from point to point. One leading reviewer, Zena Sutherland, has called her the greatest stylist of children's literature. Above all, there's the patience of credible development in her work. Nothing is told that can be shown, with the result that each reader discovers a truth of his or her own rather than of the writer's prescription. That's a rare achievement in any book, but especially in the context of traditional didacticism that too often marks juvenile fiction.

Even in a book as politically charged as *The Slave Dancer,* which won the Newbery Medal in 1972, Fox allows the situation to speak for itself. This roused great controversy when the book was published, for the narrative is a young fifer's report of a voyage aboard a slave ship, and some critics would have preferred a diatribe. Yet the tragic ironies of injustice are as clear to children as they are to adults. I quote from a twelve-year-old's essay on *The Slave Dancer:*

> The way Paula Fox writes this book is to pick out small, insignificant people and show their misery, because those are the people who make up the majority of slaves. She took a small white boy, and without any blood and gore, showed him some of the most horrible things in the world.
>
> She also showed a lot of human nature. Purvis, for example, was the best man on the whole ship, but he put on a pretense of being a rough sailor. Ben Stout, on the other hand, acts kind and gentle, but is really a nasty cruel person. There are bad men, and there are bad men."

Trust in the power of craft and the perception of the reader characterizes the best writers in any genre. That Fox brings this respect to nine-year-olds as well as ninety-year-olds is rare indeed. A good children's book provides privacy for free thought, for reflection on the human condition and its moral implications. That's not to say that her work is without its moments of gripping tension. A reviewer said of Fox's 1967 book, *How Many Miles to Babylon,* that "the suspense devices are worthy of Hitchcock." Most important, however, Fox projects the imaginative life of children not as fey or droll but as intense and all powerful.

While Paterson and Fox write seriously about serious subjects, other writers shed humorous light on dark days. Betsy Byars is well known for her ability to render sad situations from a good-humored protagonist's perspective. *The Burning Questions of Bingo Brown* is a very funny book about first love between two classmates whose teacher is desperately smitten with an aerobics instructor.

There are many points to admire here. One is the high-spirited reflection of classroom conversations and dynamics, which Bingo observes during his perpetual journeys to the pencil sharpener. A second is the smooth blend of plot and subplot, as the reader realizes that it's the child who's normal and the adult who has lost control. However, neither is stereotyped. Bingo grows wiser with the usual spurts and setbacks of preadolescent realization. Mr. Markham is a sensitive, witty, intelligent teacher who is unstable and makes the terrible mistake of attempting suicide but who has the affection of his class and recovers his balance. The honest, capable handling of Bingo's guilt by his mother, who at first appears to be something of an airhead, is another coup. There is a range of humor, from hilarious ("He, who had been in love three times in one day and had already had four mixed-sex conversations!") to ironic ("Bingo knew his name would not be picked. He had never been chosen for anything in his life"). Maintained in both style and incident, these passages are too numerous to mention, although some, like the description of Bingo's perfect grandmother, are memorable. This is a story that children are going to get a lot out of and love, while adult readers will appreciate both craft and content.

Byars also has a seriocomic series about a family named Blossom. In the first book, *The Not-Just-Anybody Family,* Junior falls from the roof in an attempt to fly and is hauled off to the hospital with two broken legs. His sister and brother, after running into the woods to avoid an encounter with the police, are faced with the prospect of rescuing their grandfather, who they correctly assume is in jail (for disturbing the peace after reckless teenagers run their car over some cans he has collected for refund). Their mother is away on the rodeo circuit. Their dog is on the run, looking for Pap. The ins and outs of this plot are so well woven, and often spliced with cliff-hangers, that readers will (a) read fast to see what happens, (b) laugh at the slapstick action, (c) fall in love with this quirky family, and (d) savor the happy ending. Along the way, they'll also learn a bit about human behavior.

Another superstar of humorous series is Lois Lowry's Anastasia. Whether Anastasia is adjusting to a new baby brother, getting a job, or courting her gym teacher's approval by learning how to climb a rope, she's the subject of sparkling wit on the part of her creator, and she's won a raft of followers.

Readers do recognize signature styles, and those who like one book inevitably will come back for more.

Slightly older readers will relish Phyllis Reynolds Naylor's books about motherless Alice (starting with *The Agony of Alice*), which are funny and understanding about the perils of daily life. Alice, initially a sixth grader but growing up through various episodes of self-discovery as the books continue, is midway between her shy friend ("Elizabeth wrapped her arms tightly around her body, as though she wasn't about to let *hers* do any changing, ready or not") and her adventurous friend ("Pamela always had the latest information about everything. Listening to Pamela was like having a map of a city without any roads on it. You knew where you were supposed to go, but you didn't know how to get there"). With endearing persistence, Alice works a place out for herself with the help of her loving if occasionally bemused father and brother.

The spirited irreverence of Roald Dahl (who died in 1990) brings readers back for almost anything he wrote, often starting with *Charlie and the Chocolate Factory.* His capacity for imagining the ridiculous and detailing it believably is exemplified by *The BFG,* about a giant whose vegetarian diet puts him at odds with some cannibalistic comrades. Dahl's hallmark is entertainment in defiance of didacticism. From his child's-eye view, manners and morality are immaterial to the more basic justice of turning an absurd adult world on its ear. If he teaches any lesson, it is by poking fun at superficial conventions, but wordplay and satirical characters are what really energize his stories.

Even stories that appear to depend on quick wit, like Dahl's, require consistent development. One editor calls writing fiction the slow art of revelation. Writers want so badly to *tell* a reader—especially a child—what's what, but that won't work. Writing fiction means making the reader not just listen politely but *live through* the action along with characters who have been slowly revealed, just the way people get to know other people, one glimpse at a time, with the future of the person or event unknown and the message left up to the reader's own discovery. Does a good adult book need a moral? The rich portrayal of human beings and what happens to them has provided enough reason for many adults to enjoy reading a novel. Children deserve the same kind of enjoyment in their fiction.

Juvenile fiction extends as far as imagination and skill can take it. Today children's fiction is going farther and farther, now that writers have grasped it as real literature worth their best energy and interest. An adult friend of mine read and loved *Summer of My German Soldier* without knowing that it was a novel published for children. This doesn't mean that the good novel for children should be identical to the good novel for adults; but it does mean that the good novel for children should be *just as good* as the good novel for adults—with the extra requirement of being relevant to the child's particular experiences. That's not easy to do, of course, which is why it's not always done. Children's books are no more perfect than adults'. But it's something to shoot for, to remember in looking for a good novel. The same process that moves adults in Joseph Heller's *Catch-22* moves children in James and Christopher Collier's *My Brother Sam Is Dead.* Both books make the tragic ironies of war real through a carefully built, slowly revealed story. There should be no shortcuts in writing for children.

From the examples of good juvenile fiction so far, it must be clear that no subject is off-limits in this field anymore. Fiction ranges from treating terrible problems to inventing idyllic fantasy worlds. Characters may have AIDS, or they may simply have trouble picking out the right birthday present for a parent. They may be lost, deserted, "tessered" to a different time on a distant planet, or determined to learn how to cook. They may be giant chickens, mentally or physically disadvantaged children, genius detectives, or opera-singing crickets. It's an open season in children's books. This is partly what makes them so interesting to some adults and partly what makes them so disturbing to others. The controversies will crop up in a later chapter, because they're an issue separate from quality.

Quality itself has many faces. One trailblazer in children's fiction is Virginia Hamilton, whose award-winning books extend the imaginative world by joining the traditional and the innovative: the grafting of folklore and realism in themes and language, for instance, or the interplay of past and present in a realistic ghost story. Her work is important in opening up the way for future writers and their experimental ideas. Just as important is the way she explores the black experience with humane insight rather than political self-consciousness.

In *The House of Dies Drear,* a mysterious figure emerges from the days of slavery into the lives of a midwestern family. *The Magical Adventures of Pretty Pearl* blends mythology and history with a god-child's wandering from Mount Kenya, where she lived with her brother John de Conquer, down through the world and woods of the American South, into hiding with black and Cherokee refugees, and then into the company of the giant hero John Henry himself. The protagonist of *M. C. Higgins the Great* struggles to unite a legacy of hill-country music and community with commercial invasions that loom in a slag heap over his future. *Sweet Whispers, Brother Rush* materializes a family ghost to help a child understand her neglectful mother and dying brother. *The*

Planet of Junior Brown deals with the sorrows of children who have been cut off from their roots, the bare emotional survival of those who must substitute peer for generational support.

Hamilton's Jahdu tales use words in strong, rhythmic patterns of folkloric storytelling that are renewed to fit and follow the small roving rascal who dares to come from a mythical past even as far as the streets of Harlem. Jahdu's favorite word as he runs in and out of trouble is "Woogily," an exclamation that will stand by any child in times of trouble. Virginia Hamilton's recharging tradition with currents of creative energy and untried techniques carries literature from the past through the hands of the living present into a lasting future.

The best-selling author Judy Blume is a very different kind of experimental writer, one who ventures into areas that some adults consider controversial but that children recognize as common concerns. Her style is simple and smooth—mostly dialogue or a kind of first-person conversation with the reader that's as easy and accessible as watching television. Blume's great talent is remembering her childhood secrets and reaching the juvenile majority who have the same secrets. She captures the desperately important trivia of growing up: Who likes me and who doesn't? Am I too fat? Why do Mom and Dad fight? *Are You There, God? It's Me, Margaret* is certainly one of the truest pictures of an ordinary suburban preadolescent worrying her way toward a place in the universe—a universe defined by family, friends, and getting her period. What could be more natural?

The only limitation to an exclusive diet of Blume's books is the sameness of experience. Her books circle a certain kind of average-modern-suburban problem. As a vivid writer, Blume deals realistically and truthfully with these concerns, but her readers look into a roomful of themselves—which is sometimes exactly what a young reader wants. There are also gifted writers, however, who use their startling acuity about daily kid life to place it in a broader context of maturation or to provide subtler insight as well as faithful reflection. Rachel Vail has a precise ear and total sympathy for adolescence, catching the fevered desperation behind junior high thought processes, both the delicate nuances of social relationships and the confusion about those nuances. In *Wonder,* Jessica gets her nickname from her first-day-of-school dress, which she thought had a sophisticated polka-dot look until an in-crowd princess cracks that it "looks like a Wonder Bread explosion" and blights Jessica's life. There's no sense that it's all a tempest in a teapot, either: "Are you sleeping with my father?" Whit demands of his drama teacher in *Do-Over,* and we know her stalling means "Yes." Vail doesn't preach; she just lets life unfold between the book's covers, where kids who feel like they can't control it in the everyday world can take their time and let it sink in.

Sometimes the world in a novel is far from everyday. In Gary Paulsen's *Hatchet*, an airplane crash strands a boy in the Canadian wilderness with only his hatchet to aid him in survival. The late Scott O'Dell was a master of bringing the distant to life: in *Island of the Blue Dolphins* he created an unusual, riveting saga of a Northwest Native American girl who remains on an island to find her brother when her people flee a hostile tribe. Before he died, O'Dell endowed an award each year for the kind of accessible but accurate historical fiction he advanced in his own writing career. Some of the winners are set in less-distant worlds: Mary Downing Hahn's *Stepping on the Cracks* tells of the American homefront during World War II, where neighborhood kids tend and hide a local youth who's a deserter from the army.

Books can close the distance between earlier times and contemporary ones. New titles aren't the only good titles; a child may well love a good book that his or her parents or even grandparents loved in their childhoods. While many of the best older books are out of print (though perhaps still available in your local library), some are being brought back in new editions and in paperback. The decades of change mean that many of the earlier books are dated now, but some still work well. They are innocent of the altered times yet fundamentally knowing in a way that children sense and respond to. Eleanor Estes's book *The Moffats* and Marguerite Henry's *Misty of Chincoteague* radiate a strong sense of warmth and security, a kind of commonplace happiness of growing up that some children may never have but still look for, no matter what their ages.

Good writing and popular appeal can be found in every imaginable children's book setting, from a midwestern foster home to an underground Paris subway, from a British garden to a Greek mountainside to the exploration of outer and inner space. Readers can pick whatever is most relevant and appealing. There's a whole gardenful of big tomatoes out there.

Fiction for Older Children

Aiken, Joan. *The Wolves of Willoughby Chase* (10–12). Doubleday, 1963.
A Dickensian tale of two children who prevail, after dramatic adventures, over a wicked governess.

Alexander, Lloyd. *The Book of Three* (10–12). Henry Holt, 1964.
The first in an imaginative, action-packed hero cycle about Taran, an assistant pig-keeper whose destiny it is to be a Welsh king. Alexander's graceful style and skill at building a suspenseful plot sustain all his novels, including the involved Westmark trilogy.

Armstrong, Jennifer. *Black-Eyed Susan,* illustrated by Emily Martindale (8–10). Crown, 1995.

The love Susie and her father have for their sod house on the prairie contrasts with Susie's mother's desolation over what she sees as a wild and lonesome existence.

Babbitt, Natalie. *Tuck Everlasting* (9–12). Farrar, 1975.

Winnie stumbles on a mysterious family and their remarkable secret—the Tucks have found the source of everlasting life. But is it a blessing or a curse?

Bawden, Nina. *Carrie's War* (10–14). Harper, 1973.

Two children evacuated from London during the Blitz settle in a small Welsh town where a nearby farm and the household that takes them in become a world as challenging and complex as the one they left behind.

Blume, Judy. *Are You There, God? It's Me, Margaret* (9–11). Bradbury, 1970.

Twelve-year-old Margaret has lots of questions about growing up and learns to answer them herself in one of the first juvenile novels to deal with menstruation and with a child's confusion about religion resulting from her parents' Jewish-Christian marriage.

Bond, Michael. *A Bear Called Paddington,* illustrated by Peggy Fortnum (8–10). Houghton, 1960.

The endearing bear has a special gift for getting into all kinds of trouble.

Boston, L. M. *A Stranger at Green Knowe,* illustrated by Peter Boston (9–12). Harcourt, 1961.

My favorite in an outstanding time-shift fantasy series, this is the story of two strangers at the twelfth-century English manor house of Green Knowe, where a lonely young Asian boy discovers a gorilla who has escaped from the zoo and finds brief refuge with him. To start at the beginning of the series, read *The Children of Green Knowe* about a boy who, while staying with his great-grandmother, meets child-ghosts of earlier members of the family who died during the great plague of the 1600s.

Brooks, Walter R. *Freddy the Detective,* illustrated by Leslie Morrill and Kurt Wiese (9–11). Knopf, 1932.

A clever pig sets out to solve some mysterious problems on the Bean farm where he lives.

Byars, Betsy. *The Burning Questions of Bingo Brown* (10–12). Viking, 1988.

With her particular talent for rendering sad situations from a good-humored protagonist's perspective, Byars has written a very funny book about the first love between two classmates whose teacher is desperately lovesick over an aerobics instructor. Fans who have already tracked down all the books in the Bingo series should also check out Byars's Blossom family saga or one of her more serious novels such as *Cracker Jackson.*

Cole, Brock. *The Goats* (11–13). Farrar, 1987.

Two social misfits, marooned on an island by the cruel trick of fellow campers, undertake a journey that rekindles their self-confidence and forges a bond between them.

Collier, James Lincoln, and Christopher Collier. *My Brother Sam Is Dead* (11–13). Four Winds, 1974.

Impetuous and idealistic, sixteen-year-old Sam defies his Tory father to join the Continentals in their war against the British in 1775.

Coman, Carolyn. *What Jamie Saw* (9–12). Front Street, 1995.

With unfaltering control and economy, the author puts us at the heart of a crisis in which Jamie and his mother flee from his abusive stepfather.

Conford, Ellen. *The Luck of Pokey Bloom,* illustrated by Bernice Lowenstein (9–12). Little, 1975.

A blithe family story in which Pokey keeps trying to win contests and, at the same time, to understand her impossible brother. Since *Pokey*'s success, Conford's light school stories have become a popular staple.

Cooper, Susan. *The Dark Is Rising,* illustrated by Alan Cober (10–13). McElderry, 1973.

The seventh son of a seventh son, eleven-year-old Will is irretrievably drawn into the eternal struggle between good and evil in this powerful fantasy set during the twelve days of Christmas.

Creech, Sharon. *Walk Two Moons* (10–13). HarperCollins, 1994.

On a road trip to Idaho with her loving grandparents, Sal comes to terms with her mother's desertion and death in this tender, surprising novel reminiscent of Barbara Kingsolver's homespun odysseys for adult readers.

Curtis, Christopher Paul. *The Watsons Go to Birmingham—1963* (10–13). Delacorte, 1995.

A series of funny episodes delineates an African-American family traveling from their Michigan home to visit relatives in Birmingham, Alabama, where the tone suddenly turns dark when four children are killed in a church bombing.

Cushman, Karen. *Catherine, Called Birdy* (11–14). Clarion, 1995.

A high-born medieval heroine with a rebelliously modern voice engages readers in various episodes of her daily life as related in a diary she has promised to keep.

Dahl, Roald. *The BFG,* illustrated by Quentin Blake (9–11). Farrar, 1982.

In a book popping with playful nonsense words, the ugly but appealing Big Friendly Giant defies his fellow flesh-eaters and befriends little Sophie, who helps him satisfy his hunger without consuming "human beans."

Danziger, Paula. *The Cat Ate My Gymsuit* (11–14). Delacorte, 1974.

"I hate my father. I hate school. I hate being fat," says Marcy, whose life becomes more tolerable with the help of an English teacher but gets turned upside down again when the teacher is dismissed. This was the first novel by a writer who has become highly popular with junior high readers.

Dorris, Michael. *Morning Girl* (9–11). Hyperion, 1992.

Morning Girl and her brother, Star Boy, alternately narrate chapters describing their everyday lives just before the arrival of Columbus to their island. The irony of their spiritual wealth compared to the explorer's view of them as poor and fit only for servitude has a shocking effect on readers already involved with the characters.

Ehrlich, Amy. *Where It Stops, Nobody Knows* (11–14). Dial, 1988.
Suspense builds as the narrator, Nina, begins to question her mother's constant moving around and stumbles on the truth of her real parentage.

Enright, Elizabeth. *Gone-Away Lake* (8–10). Harcourt, 1957.
Near a swamp that was once a lovely lake, two cousins find a tumbledown cottage that their families decide to restore in the sequel *Return to Gone-Away Lake,* Enright has another series, beginning with *The Saturdays,* about four lively siblings who pool their weekly allowances to give each in turn a chance to spend the whole amount.

Fine, Anne. *The Tulip Touch* (10–12). Little, 1997.
Tulip's increasingly destructive behavior reflects an abusive home life, but Natalie must finally betray her to escape the dangers inherent in their friendship.

Fitzgerald, John D. *The Great Brain* (9–14). Dial, 1967.
Ten-year-old Tom Fitzgerald, the shrewdest con artist west of the Mississippi, gets in and out of trouble through a series of schemes.

Fitzhugh, Louise. *Harriet the Spy* (8–12). Harper, 1964.
Lonely Harriet learns more than she expects to by keeping a secret notebook about family and friends.

Fleischman, Sid. *The Whipping Boy,* illustrated by Peter Sís (9–11). Greenwillow, 1986.
A round tale of adventure and humor, this book follows—at top speed—the fortunes of Prince Horace (better known as Prince Brat) and his whipping boy, Jemmy, who has received all the hard knocks for the prince's mischief . . . until the two leave the palace.

Fox, Paula. *One-Eyed Cat* (10–14). Bradbury, 1984.
A masterpiece of character portrayal focuses on a boy's resolution of guilt about a cat he believes he has maimed with a shot from his first gun. Fox, who has received many honors in addition to the 1974 Newbery Medal for *Slave Dancer,* is one of the great stylists of children's literature.

Freeman, Suzanne. *The Cuckoo's Child* (10–12). Greenwillow, 1996.
Lonely for her parents, who have disappeared at sea, Mia tries to settle with her aunt in small-town Tennessee after growing up in Beirut. The year is 1962, and the character dynamics resonate with the difficulty of unexpected adjustments.

George, Jean Craighead. *Julie of the Wolves,* illustrated by John Schoenherr (10–12). Harper, 1972.
In search of her father, an Inuit girl of the far north treks across the frozen tundra in the company of a pack of wolves.

Giff, Patricia Reilly. *Lily's Crossing* (9–12). Delacorte, 1997.
Against the seismic upheavals of World War II, Giff plays out the private tremors of two children who live in a safe place, Rockaway Beach, N.Y., but are nevertheless threatened with the loss of those they love.

Greene, Bette. *Summer of My German Soldier* (12 and up). Dial, 1973.
A German prisoner of war hides in a small Arkansas town during World War II—and nobody knows except a young Jewish girl.

Greene, Constance. *A Girl Called Al,* illustrated by Byron Barton (9–11). Viking, 1969.
Plump, individualistic, and caustic, Al (short for Alexandra, a name she hates) moves with her divorced mother into an apartment down the hall from the seventh-grade narrator, who describes the often humorous episodes of their developing friendship.

Hahn, Mary Downing. *Stepping on the Cracks* (9–12). Clarion, 1991.
When eleven-year-old Margaret finds a pacifist hiding out during World War II and helps him with food and medicine, she incurs the wrath of her parents, who are grieving over the death of her older brother on the front lines.

Hamilton, Virginia. *M. C. Higgins, the Great* (11–13). Macmillan, 1974.
Swaying atop his pole in the Appalachian mountains, M. C. Higgins surveys a domain of beauty threatened by strip miners and outsiders who don't respect his family's way of life.

Holman, Felice. *Slake's Limbo* (10–13). Scribner's, 1974.
Unable to bear life on the streets of New York City, a neglected boy makes a home in the subway until he can develop inner strength and find people to trust.

Konigsburg, E. L. *From the Mixed-Up Files of Mrs. Basil E. Frankweiler* (8–12). Atheneum, 1967.
Claudia knows she has to run away, but grubby hideouts are not her style. The Metropolitan Museum of Art has all the elegance she wants—and much, much more.

Le Guin, Ursula. *A Wizard of Earthsea,* illustrated by Ruth Robbins (10–12). Parnassus, 1968.
In a world of high fantasy, young Ged must learn that enchantment can be used for evil as well as good, depending on the heart of the magician.

L'Engle, Madeleine. *A Wrinkle in Time* (10 and up). Farrar, 1962.
There is only one way for Meg to rescue her missing father—by passing through another time dimension and depending on the power of love.

Levoy, Myron. *Alan and Naomi* (10–13). Harper, 1977.
With subtlety and emotional realism, Levoy relates the story of an American boy who tries to help a young Jewish refugee who was the victim of Nazi terrorism in France.

Lewis, C. S. *The Lion, the Witch, and the Wardrobe* (10–12). Macmillan, 1951.
A spellbinding parable about four children who pass through an old English wardrobe into the magical land of Narnia, where they help Aslan, the lion ruler, free his subjects from the evil White Witch.

Lively, Penelope. *The Ghost of Thomas Kempe,* illustrated by Anthony Maitland (10–12). Dutton, 1973.

Young James Harrison bears the brunt of the havoc caused by a seventeenth-century sorcerer who reappears in modern England.

Lowry, Lois. *Anastasia Krupnik* (9–11). Houghton, 1979.
Ten-year-old Anastasia lists the things she loves and hates, but she changes her mind about several items, especially the baby brother she dreads until he's actually born.

MacLachlan, Patricia. *Sarah, Plain and Tall* (9–11). Harper, 1985.
A warm, satisfying, and lyrically written story of a woman who answers an ad to become a frontier widower's wife and mother to his two orphaned children.

Mayne, William. *Hob and the Goblins* (9–12). DK Ink, 1994.
Household spirit Hob must defend his adopted family from goblins in search of their treasure.

McKay, Hilary. *The Exiles* (10–14). McElderry, 1992.
Four obstreperous sisters spend an outrageously funny summer in the English Lake Country with formidable Big Grandma, who forbids them to read and sends them instead to explore the great outdoors, with the occasional disastrous result.

Merrill, Jean. *The Pushcart War,* illustrated by Ronni Solbert (10–12). Addison-Wesley, 1964.
A seriocomic tale of a war between truck drivers and pushcart vendors on the streets of New York City.

Myers, Walter Dean. *Scorpions* (11–13). Harper, 1989.
Harlem presents Jamal and Tito with a one-way ticket to trouble in the form of pressure to join a gang called the Scorpions, once led by Jamal's big brother before his imprisonment for murder.

Naylor, Phyllis Reynolds. *Shiloh* (9–11). Atheneum, 1991.
Sympathy for a mistreated beagle that he rescues from a brutal neighbor leads soft-hearted Marty to lie and steal, raising some intriguing ethical questions via a suspenseful plot and complex characterizations. Readers interested in a side-splitting series should also check out Naylor's Alice books, beginning with *The Agony of Alice* and continuing with a spate of episodes through *Achingly Alice.*

Norton, Mary. *The Borrowers,* illustrated by Beth and Joe Krush (9–11). Harcourt, 1953.
Young readers have always enjoyed the detailed doings of these tiny people who live in hidden corners of a house, with narrow escapes from huge human occupants and their pets.

O'Dell, Scott. *Island of the Blue Dolphins* (10–12). Houghton, 1960.
Nature becomes both friend and enemy to a young Indian girl as she struggles to survive on a deserted island.

Paterson, Katherine. *A Bridge to Terabithia,* illustrated by Donna Diamond (10–12). Crowell, 1977.
The moving story of a backwoods boy who befriends a newcomer, creates an imaginary world with her, and then must cope with bitter loss when she drowns.

Paulsen, Gary. *Hatchet* (11–14). Bradbury, 1987.
A plane crash in the Alaskan wilderness leaves Brian stranded, with only his hatchet to aid him in survival.

Pearce, Philippa. *Tom's Midnight Garden* (10–12). Lippincott, 1958.
This winner of the British Carnegie Medal is a smoothly crafted time-travel fantasy about a boy whose midnight visits to a garden take him to the past for friendship with a girl who's now an old woman living in his house.

Peck, Richard. *The Ghost Belonged to Me* (12 and up). Viking, 1975.
This comic but hair-raising ghost story sports a cast of individualistic characters in a turn-of-the-century midwestern town, and it comes with a slew of sequels.

Pullman, Philip. *The Golden Compass* (11–15). Knopf, 1996.
The first in a complex, gripping fantasy trilogy in which a young girl follows a big destiny with cosmic implications, continued in *The Subtle Knife* (1997).

Rodgers, Mary. *Freaky Friday* (10 and up). Harper, 1973.
Thirteen-year-old Annabel gains some sympathy for her mother's point of view after she wakes up one morning to find that they have switched places.

Selden, George. *The Cricket in Times Square,* illustrated by Garth Williams (9–11). Farrar, 1960.
Chester Cricket discovers the joys of Times Square and friendship with an unforgettable cat and mouse pair. He also wins the hearts of commuters with his operatic voice!

Speare, Elizabeth. *The Sign of the Beaver* (10–12). Houghton, 1983.
An eighteenth-century boy survives winter in an isolated New England cabin with the help of an Indian who befriends him.

Stolz, Mary. *The Noonday Friends,* illustrated by Louis S. Glanzman (9–11). Harper, 1965.
Stolz exercises her amazing perceptions and sure style in realizing the dynamics of a relationship between two girls who have only lunchtime to be together, since one must babysit for her little brother at home after school.

Turner, Megan Whalen. *The Thief* (10–13). Greenwillow, 1996.
Imprisoned after boasting of his master thievery, young Gen finds himself freed on condition of retrieving a legendary stone that will empower his king—and endanger himself. Hidden motives and identities will surprise the reader of this ingeniously plotted fantasy.

Vail, Rachel. *Wonder* (10–13). Jackson/Orchard, 1991.
Seventh grade becomes a nightmare for Jessica when shifting social hierarchies suddenly make her the butt of the popular girls' teasing.

VanOosting, James. *The Last Payback* (10–12). HarperCollins, 1997.
When eleven-year-old Dimple's twin brother is killed in a gun accident at his friend's house, Dimple plans revenge and—in a breathtaking climax—almost gets it.

Voigt, Cynthia. *Dicey's Song* (11–13). Atheneum, 1982.
A Newbery Medal winner and one of a series of well-characterized novels about the Tillerman family, this book chronicles Dicey's adjustment to life with her stubborn grandmother, who took in Dicey and her three siblings after their mother abandoned them.

Waugh, Sylvia. *The Mennyms* (10–13). Greenwillow, 1994.
In an old British house live a family of human-sized rag dolls magically imbued with life and trying to get through daily travails without incurring the suspicion of their neighbors.

White, E. B. *Charlotte's Web,* illustrated by Garth Williams (7–9). Harper, 1952.
A classic tale of loyalty and loss, this story portrays Wilbur the Pig and his friendship with a remarkably talented spider who saves him from the fate of most barnyard animals.

White, Ruth. *Belle Prater's Boy* (10–12). Farrar, 1996.
A skillfully styled novel set in 1950s Appalachia features two cousins—one beautiful and the other ungainly—facing the dark secrets of their family past with affection for each other and, ultimately, respect for themselves.

Williams, Vera B. *Scooter* (8–10). Greenwillow, 1993.
Every day Elana launches her scooter through the housing project with irresistible energy, reporting on and participating in the activities of the community until she's filled up her summer with new friends.

Yumoto, Kazumi. *The Friends,* translated by Cathy Hirano (10–13). Farrar, 1996.
In a touching story that reaches across cultures, three sixth-grade Japanese boys, determined to confront death in the form of a corpse, spy on an old man who they believe will soon die but who instead offers them a lively (and much-needed) friendship.

Postscript to the Paperback Edition

J. K. Rowling's fantasy series of Harry Potter books, starting with *Harry Potter and the Sorcerer's Stone* (9 and up; Scholastic Press, 1998), has taken the publishing world by storm. Although these stories about orphaned Harry and the magical powers he develops at the Hogwarts School of Witchcraft and Wizardry are fairly long and complex, they're also fast-paced, funny, and inventive—a magnetic combination for both reluctant and habitual readers. Of the many fantasy novels that have enriched children's literature, these have been especially successful in bonding generations, with children and adults finding a common delight akin to sharing fairy tales. Harry would certainly have blazed a trail into our discussion of fiction had he materialized before the manuscript for this third edition of *Choosing Books for Children* was completed.

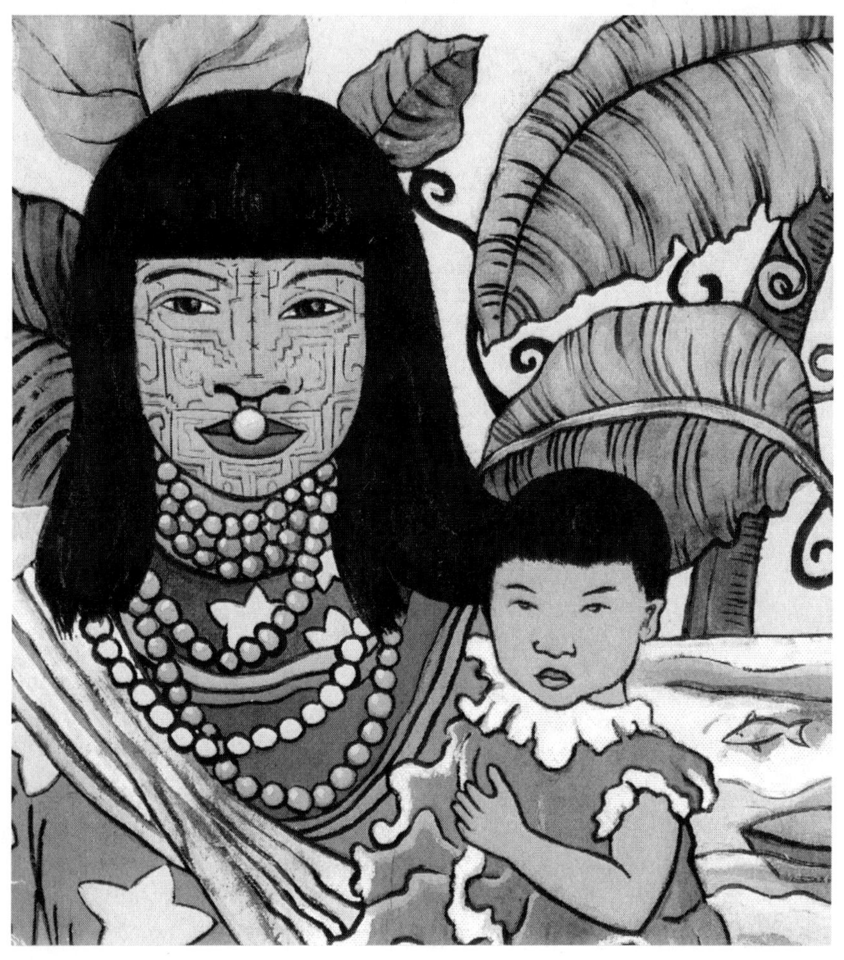

Elly Simmons

6

Books for Young Adults

Defining the difference between a young adult and an adult depends on which one you're talking to. Young adults generally are thirteen to nineteen years old, but whatever their age, their behavior patterns are likely to vacillate from moment to moment depending on which hormone is running rampant. If it's hard to define a young adult, it's twice as hard to agree on what young adult literature is. Nevertheless, it's published and it sells, so it must exist. In addition to reading children's and adults' books—both often on the sly, but for different reasons—adolescents read books especially tailored to their experiences. Popular and serious fiction, useful nonfiction, and poetry collections have contributed to a pioneering genre that banks on teens' spending their allowance and/or first earnings on a book or on their connecting with a librarian who champions a young adult collection.

What teens buy with their money and what libraries buy for their collections may be two different things, including a variable mixture of classics and comics, award-winners and best-sellers. What's consistent, though, are the basic themes that attract adolescents during this eclectic stage of reading. It doesn't take a developmental psychologist to remind you what most teens are going through: physical and sexual changes, along with struggles for peer approval, self-identity, self-confidence, social responsibility, and independence from the family. This is a constellation of concerns that determines much of their response to literature. Like everyone else, they're reading for emotional satisfaction as well as information and aesthetic adventure.

A fourteen-year-old may cry over the diary of Anne Frank one day and regress into Archie comics the next. Adolescence is a seesaw. One of the hardest things about parenting an adolescent is watching the thump that follows a sky-high glide. Readingwise, there are more choices available today than ever before to accommodate those transitions. Robert Lipsyte, a young adult novelist of the first order, summarized the situation this way in the *New York Times Book Review* (May 18, 1986): "For the last 20 years, a devoted band of editors, teachers, and librarians has been clearing a pathway through the steamy thicket of adolescence and paving it with an amazing variety of books, from urban slice-of-life to dragon tales, historical family dramas to scenarios of terrorism." He went on to decry the mediocrity that threatened this literature because of commercialism and censorship. Unfortunately, his statements hold true today.

Historically, commercialism and censorship are no newer than their effects on young adult literature. Horatio Alger was producing his hugely popular series of titles at the same time that Louisa May Alcott wrote the landmark *Little Women.* The enormously successful dime novels of the nineteenth century didn't prevent Mark Twain from developing an avid following among teenage readers. We know Twain was read because *Tom Sawyer* and *Huckleberry Finn* were both banned from the Brooklyn Public Library as "bad examples for ingenuous youth"! By all means remove both books, wrote Twain sarcastically. "The mind that becomes soiled in youth can never again be washed clean; I know this by my own experience and to this day I cherish an unappeasable bitterness against the unfaithful guardians of my young life, who not only permitted but compelled me to read an unexpurgated Bible through before I was 15 years old. None can do that and ever draw a clean breath again this side of the grave."

Novels for young adults have always bred controversy (as I'll discuss further in chapter 10) and commercialism. After all, economic independence is an incipient goal for most adolescents. In establishing their own tastes, they can also begin to finance them. Most professionals working with books and young adults try to strike a balance between the popular and the literary. What's popular on a mass-market level is clear, but a lot of adults still don't know how many great trade books—of fiction, nonfiction, and poetry—have been published for young adults in the past several decades.

You may hear more about adult classics—*The Catcher in the Rye, Lord of the Flies, A Separate Peace*—that young adults have adopted for their own (or been coerced into reading as a classroom requirement). You may not realize that Robert Cormier and S. E. Hinton, whose books are now being enjoyed by the children of their original readers, were only the best-known crest of a wave of terrific writers for young adults, a wave that includes M. E. Kerr, Cynthia Voigt, Gary Paulsen, Lois Duncan, Richard Peck, Walter Dean Myers, Margaret Mahy, Chris Crutcher, Sue Ellen Bridgers, Bruce Brooks, Paula Fox, John Donovan, Norma Klein, Avi, Nancy Garden, Jacqueline Woodson, Francesca Lia Block, and a host of others who have rocked young adult literature back on its heels and, in many cases, revitalized and even re-formed it.

This is not to say that preteens and teenagers shouldn't read adult books. They should and do. By the age of fifteen, according to Dr. Richard F. Abrahamson at the University of Houston, most adolescents are reading more adult than young adult books. The American Library Association's Young Adult Library Services Association includes adult books in its annual list of Best Books for Young Adults, and it also sponsors the annual Alex Awards, which go to ten adult books that especially appeal to young adults. Yet parents who keep up with adult books to share with teens—for example, Bobbie Ann Mason's *In Country,* Michael Dorris's *Yellow Raft in Blue Water,* or Tobias Wolff's *This Boy's Life: A Memoir*—may not have a clue that there is literature written specifically for adolescents. Moreover, high school teachers often stick to a strict "classics" curriculum that doesn't include either contemporary young adult or adult books.

Keeping up with popular culture is not the problem. We certainly know which rock groups are big because they're LOUD, and if your family is anything like mine it's hard not to know which movies, television programs, and video or computer games are popular. Many a parent has also had the latest Stephen King novel swiped from the bedside table only to find it weeks later among the dust bunnies under the resident sixteen-year-old's bed. But here's something different to try with your teenager: the exploration of literature written especially for them. You'll find yourself amazed by the quality and challenged by the content. Margaret Mahy's novel *Memory,* for instance, is a poignant account of the relationship between a nineteen-year-old, "swollen with apparitions" on the fifth anniversary of his sister's death, and an old woman with Alzheimer's disease who offers him shelter. She half believes him to be a long-lost love—then again, she also puts cheese in the soap dish and soap in the sugar bowl. The memories of both characters are clearer than their reality, but in their developing affection comes peace of mind for each. The wit and detail with which these two individualists are portrayed puts adult and young adult fiction on equal footing.

Maybe you wouldn't expect to turn to young adult literature for a novel that conveys the experience of living in a Peruvian jungle. Yet Joan Abelove's *Go and Come Back* does exactly that—and from the viewpoint of an indigenous teenager named Alicia. Here's her first reaction to the two New York anthropologists who are visiting her jungle village for a year's work on their dissertations: "They both wore no beads, no nose rings, no lip plugs, no anklets. They didn't pierce their noses or their lower lips. They didn't bind their ankles or flatten their foreheads. They did nothing to make themselves beautiful." In addition to being undecorated and devoid of the body fat required for true beauty, the two white women have plenty of strange ideas, and many of the Isabos enjoy watching them make mistakes and ask stupid questions. But there are tensions, as well, especially revolving around the stinginess of the "old white ladies." The villagers "save" by sharing everything they have and depending on others to do the same, whereas the strangers "save" by withholding what the villagers want and need, from beads to rice. Moreover, Alicia and her people accept primal facts of sex and death with a forbearance ("whatever it would be" is a favorite expression) that unsettles the anthropologists.

Alicia's mother simply dismisses the foreigners: "Do not think of them as people." Yet Alicia slowly becomes involved in a kind of friendship with one of them, Joanna, and determines to teach her manners (lying, for instance, to save face with kinsmen), cleanliness (bathing twice a day in the river), generosity (figuring out what people want before they ask), and a better understanding of life generally. "They knew so little and they asked so much," Alicia says. The narrator's voice, which could have become a gimmick of viewpoint reversal, relies instead on wit and consistency for ultimate effect. The aspects of humor and tragedy in the situation are skillfully counterpointed: on the one hand, we are laughing at the dual perception of dental floss as tooth cleaner and fishing line; on the other, we are feeling for Alicia and Joanna as they struggle with conflicting expressions of sadness over the death of a baby Alicia has adopted. Although Alicia's lifeways naturally make more sense than the Anglos', since this is her story, the authorial tone never mistakes cultural adulation for respect.

Too often U.S. teenage fiction has portrayed other cultures from the outside. While Abelove is not a member of the fictional Isabo, she lived for two years in the setting of her novel. She may not be an insider, but she knows enough to know what she doesn't know. And, paradoxically, she has shed light on insiders by representing their attention to what she does know—namely, being an outsider to them. For an audience of young adults, concerned as they are with outsiders and insiders, it's a particularly brilliant concept.

Another first novel that truly bridges the interests of young adults and adults is Kyoko Mori's *Shizuko's Daughter.* This book is written in a spare, intricately balanced style that interweaves several viewpoints without losing sharp focus. The book opens with the calm, carefully deliberated suicide of eleven-year-old Yuki's beautiful but unhappy mother, Shizuko, who turns on the gas while her daughter is taking a music lesson at the piano teacher's house. Most of the remaining scenes, each dated sometime in the next seven years, detail Yuki's grief, survival, and understanding of her mother's death. But *Shizuko's Daughter* journeys far beyond the "problem novel" genre. Instead, it is a fully realized portrayal of a Japanese family to the depth of three generations and at least six individuals, including the cold father and stepmother Yuki defies, as well as the warm grandparents whose richly traditional patterns of living bring aching recollections of Yuki's mother. The tension of the characters themselves serves as driving action. The strong will and sense of artistry that isolate Yuki finally save her as well.

Readers will be moved beyond cultural boundaries by the author's ability to render nuances of childhood with an immediacy devoid of nostalgia. Most impressive, technically, is Mori's narrative voice, which subtly translates aesthetic observations into readers' experiences: the color and texture of flowers, of clothing, of pottery, of human love's pain and release. Such authenticity illuminates the fictional realities and motivations without intrusion or distraction, so that readers will feel themselves enlightened by an encounter with the rare achievement: a powerfully understated story.

Going to a distant time as well as a distant place is James Berry's *Ajeemah and His Son,* about eighteen-year-old Atu and his father who are ambushed in Africa by slave traders while journeying to present a bride price, two pieces of gold hidden in Ajeemah's sandals, for Atu's betrothed, Sisi. The story of their agonizing voyage across the sea and their bondage on Jamaican sugar plantations ends in tragedy for one, survival for the other. In eighty-three pages of hypnotic prose, Berry telescopes a story covering thirty-three years, from Ajeemah's capture to the marriage of his daughter two years after the abolition of slavery in the British West Indies. The narrative achieves a kind of poetic momentum, punctuated by intense scenes and rhythmic dialogue that focus the characters as singular individuals pinioned by history. Most unforgettable is the impact of slavery on children: the family that Ajeemah is forced to leave behind in Africa, the eldest son turned brutal by slavery, the Jamaican daughter who brings to the future only a vague, sad discomfort with the traditions that have sustained her father. The tale ends on a note of hope, but it is hope mixed with bitter irony, not the false hope of happily ever after.

That young adult literature, despite some corrosive effects of commercialism, still gives adolescents a chance to learn and care about situations worlds away is a hopeful sign. If publishers can take the risk of developing writers like these, we can ask ourselves for the courage and energy to introduce their brave books to brave young readers. In doing so, we offer young adults the chance to break out of a desperate sense of isolation that seems to trap so many of them, each of whom feels that he or she is the only one going through various traumas of growing up in a dangerous world.

A lot of these books deal with serious subjects, but that doesn't mean there's no sense of humor in young adult literature. Imagine a game where you know enough to make the next move exciting but not enough to know what it's going to be. That's *Holes,* as primal as its title. You and any reasonable (or unreasonable) youth of your acquaintance will get sucked into this one—but it's not a black hole by any means. Spiraling between past and present, Louis Sachar, whose light middle-grade fiction (*There's a Boy in the Girls' Bathroom; Marvin Redpost: Alone in His Teacher's House*) has won him popular acclaim, surpasses conventional plot for a more innovative mix of realism and legend, with elements of mystery that keep the surrealistic events suspenseful.

Stanley Yelnats arrives at Camp Green Lake, a Texas juvenile correctional facility. The name is ironic because there hasn't been a drop of water in this desert setting for a hundred years and the blazing sun has long since killed off everything that was ever green. Stanley is innocent of anything except being in the wrong place at the wrong time, a fate that has plagued his family since his Latvian great-great-grandfather broke a promise to a helpful gypsy. Some of this Stanley knows, and some he doesn't. Readers sometimes find out before he does, or sometimes at the same time, a trick of pacing and alternating scenarios that Sachar has mastered to intense effect. Every revelation of the past ups the ante of the present.

The ominous warden, who wears nail polish that's color-enhanced with rattlesnake venom, also has a past, as do the inmates, especially one nicknamed Zero—someone even the (deceptively) kindhearted counselor calls worthless. Most of all, the "lake" has a past, and as the boys are ordered to dig holes—each boy, one hole five feet cubed, every day—we discover how all these pasts intersect for a dangerous climax and a hole that holds more than dirt. Sounds grim, doesn't it? Except that it's not. Sachar inserts humor that gives the suspense steep edges—the tone is as full of surprises as the plot. Although nothing is quite what it seems in this wildly inventive novel, the patterns of language and narrative assure us that everything will eventually make sense. And it does, in ways that I won't reveal lest readers be denied the satisfaction of finding out for themselves. Between the jigsaw-puzzle plot and the signifying wordplay, this is a smart book whose mystery kids will want to solve on their own. And they won't mind the compact chapters—poetic in a strictly action-packed way.

One last note: a lot of nearly perfect books (Natalie Babbitt's *Tuck Everlasting* comes to mind) are written by women and are strongest in their appeal to girls, though boys certainly enjoy them in a classroom or group situation. But *Holes* is written by a man and projects magnetic attraction for boys as well as girls. Tough, true-hearted, and ultimately tender, this nearly perfect book—the 1998 Newbery Medal winner—is a member of that endangered species, the family read-aloud. You can even have a contest: Which listener will notice first that Yelnats is Stanley spelled backwards? Did you?

Clearly, drama doesn't have to preclude humor, which can range from goofy slapstick to absurdist irony to sly satire. Ron Koertge's books are about serious things, but they're very funny nonetheless. *Confess-o-rama,* for example, is about a teenager named Tony who has to adjust to a new town after his third stepfather follows his father and his first two stepfathers into death. ("Four dads," muses a new acquaintance. "That's about one stormy moor and a couple of witches away from Shakespeare.") It's a witty, affectionately dark comedy. Another example is *The Rules of the Road,* Joan Bauer's literary counterpart to the road movie, in which a tough and funny heroine named Jenna is devoted to shoe quality and is half-shanghaied, half-inspired to drive from Illinois to Texas with the shoe company director to ensure perpetuation of the company's standards at a stockholder's meeting. Jenna speaks for many of us when she says:

> It seemed to me that the people who made the rules of the road had figured out everything that would help a person drive safely right down to having a sign that tells you you're passing through a place where deer cross. Somebody should stick up some signs on the highway of life.
>
> CAUTION: JERKS CROSSING.
>
> Blinking yellow lights when you are about to do something stupid.
>
> Stop signs in front of people who could hurt you.
>
> Green lights shining when you're doing the right thing.
>
> It would make the whole experience much easier.

For Jenna, the road offers the control and liberation that real life often lacks.

The fourteen-year-old African-American protagonist of Rita Williams-Garcia's *Like Sisters on the Homefront* doesn't run away; rather, she's sent away. A veteran of city streets and already pregnant for the second time, Gayle is forced by her mother to stay with deeply religious and highly conventional relatives in Georgia. This adolescent never stops being her own tough-talking, earthy self, but she does come to appreciate family in a way that affects her future.

The need for family and the problems kids have with their families dominate many young adult novels. In Angela Johnson's *Toning the Sweep,* another fourteen-year-old African-American girl, Emmie, deepens bonds of kinship with her mother, who is still bitter over the 1964 murder of her own father by Alabama racists, and her grandmother, who is dying of cancer. The videotape Emmie makes teaches her much about the two older women and even about herself; by the time the summer is over, the lifelong tensions among the three have eased. Emmie's gradual understanding and even the dramatic incident of her grandfather's death unfold through subtle action at a pace natural to the protagonist's development. There are no long explanations or sudden epiphanies, and Johnson trusts the reader to discover, as do the characters, how events of the past circle into the present.

Lorri Hewett examines a similar theme in *Lives of Our Own,* wherein two girls, one black and one white, start to realize that the connections of previous generations may make them family. Hewett also takes a nuanced look at outsiderhood and insiderhood, making it clear that race is just one of the many ways people are divided against themselves. That fact is also apparent in Marsha Qualey's *Revolutions of the Heart,* in which the anti-Indian prejudice of a small Wisconsin town causes friction in a girl's family when she develops a friendship with a Cree boy. In Michael Cadnum's *Zero at the Bone,* a teen's family faces the complicated possibilities that result from his older sister's disappearance. The family struggles to come to terms with the tragic possibility of foul play and the bitter possibility of her cruel desertion of her family, trying to rebuild itself in her absence. A brother-sister relationship also plays a central role in M. E. Kerr's *Deliver Us from Evie,* except that when Evie leaves her Missouri farm family it's a coming out as well as a coming of age—and she leaves with the daughter of a powerful local banker.

In many of these young adult novels, the protagonists are struggling to redefine their families, but in others they're inventing them anew. *Family Pose* by Dean Hughes portrays a night-shift hotel crew that becomes a family for an orphaned runaway. David's foster homes have so damaged him that Paul, the middle-aged bellboy who sneaks him into a hotel room and feeds him, has to work hard to win his trust. The desk clerk, the telephone operator, and the cocktail waitress unite to offer him the affection and respect he craves, but each of them is a loner for different—and complex—reasons. Whether anyone will undertake responsibility for him, or whether they'll shuffle him back into an impassive system, remains in question until the last satisfying but never sentimental page. The detailed setting and the subtly unfolding observation of each character, young and old, give readers the uncanny sense of a life crisis relived.

Weetzie Bat, a punk, young adult fairy tale, is the ingeniously lyrical narrative of two friends, Weetzie and Dirk, who weave a nest out of Hollywood illusions and hardcore loyalty. Weetzie's unhappily divorced parents, Charlie Bat and Brandy-Lynn, take refuge in booze and drugs. In high school Weetzie connects with Dirk, who is gay. When Dirk's grandmother Fifi dies, she leaves the two of them her cottage, and it only remains for them to fill the place with a loving family: Dirk finds Duck; Weetzie brings home My Secret Agent Lover Man. Even Slinkster Dog gets a mate, Go Go Girl, and a bunch of puppies. Weetzie has a baby, Cherokee, who belongs to all of them, as does Witch Baby, who is eventually deposited on their doorstep. Although each of the four main characters is shaken by a terrible loss, the group survives through the knowledge that together they are all each one has individually. "Love is a dangerous angel" and can bring pain, but the bond is primitively strong. "I heard that rats shrivel up and die if they aren't, like, able to hang out with other rats," Duck says.

While the characters in *Weetzie Bat* have just passed into adulthood, they evince the innocence and effervescence of a fancied childhood. The book is full of magic, from the genie who grants Weetzie's wishes to the malevolent witch Vixanne, who visits the family three times. There are beauties and beasts and roses, castles and Cinderella transformations. What *Family Pose* develops with traditionally crafted realism, *Weetzie Bat* achieves through vivid imagery. Block's far-ranging free association has been shaped and controlled into a story with tangibly sensual characters. The language is inventive California hip, but the patterns are compactly folkloristic and the theme is transcendent. "I don't know about happily ever after . . . but I know about happily," Weetzie Bat thinks at the end. The end isn't really the end, though, because there's a whole series that follows, including *Witch Baby, Cherokee Bat and the Goat Guys,* and other titles that have been collected into *Dangerous Angels: The Weetzie Bat Books.* With each one Weetzie's family gets bigger and bigger.

Credibly, even indelibly, young adult literature is telling kids that every adult results from a child, outgrown or not, who needs a family. We can take our families where we find them, or, lacking the luck to find them, we can make new ones. It's a poignant message and one that is desperately needed in an era of broken bonds. Beyond the immediate impact of both stories is another implication: the power of human imagination is such that even books can become family.

There are all manner of possible families waiting for young adults to join them. If your teenager is in love with love, you'll both enjoy Margaret Mahy's book *The Changeover,* Barbara Wersba's *Fat: A Love Story,* and, yes, Judy Blume's *Forever* (if you haven't read it, your fourteen-year-old probably has). Lisa Fiedler's *Curtis Piperfield's Biggest Fan* and *Lucky Me* chronicle the helplessly funny romances of C.C. (Cecily Carruthers), who eventually ends up with her lifelong true love. Robin McKinley is so taken with the love story of

"Beauty and the Beast" that she has written two novels—*Beauty: A Retelling of the Story of Beauty and the Beast* and *Rose Daughter*—combining magic with realism in a way that enhances both.

If you've got a sports fan in the house, try *The Contender* by Robert Lipsyte (would-be sports fans might prefer his *One Fat Summer*), *The Moves Make the Man* by Bruce Brooks, *The Runner* by Cynthia Voigt, *Running Loose* by Chris Crutcher, *Painting the Black* by Carl Deuker, or *Tangerine* by Edward Bloor. These are brilliant books that offer as much depth of characterization as they do game action, with a tonal range from high humor to heartbreaker. And don't forget poetry: read aloud some selections from *American Sports Poems* selected by R. R. Knudson and May Swenson.

Books can focus any interest or concern you and your teenager have been discussing. If you've mentioned a newspaper article about a war raging somewhere and your teenager reacts, you can both explore the issues through fiction such as *Fallen Angels,* Walter Dean Myers's portrayal of a young recruit in Vietnam. There are many faces of war besides those on the battlefield. Robert Cormier's *Chocolate War* targets conflict in a Catholic school, and *After the First Death* is his riveting study of terrorism. S. E. Hinton's novel *The Outsiders* exposes the tragedy of gang war.

Many Holocaust survivors are writing their memoirs as age persuades them to pass on knowledge of their experiences during World War II. Schoschana Rabinovici's autobiography *Thanks to My Mother* and Anita Lobel's *No Pretty Pictures: A Child of War* are moving examples. Maxine Rosenberg's *Hiding to Survive* collects a number of these memoirs. Hanneke Ippisch's *Sky: A True Story of Resistance during World War II* relates the author's experiences as a Dutch teenager who risks her life to save Jews. Hazel Rochman and Darlene McCampbell's *Bearing Witness* is an anthology of Holocaust stories for adults and young adults. Myron Levoy's *Alan and Naomi,* about a Jewish refugee from Nazi persecution, is set in the United States, as is M. E. Kerr's *Gentlehands,* about the American grandson of a concentration camp official who has emigrated and tried to conceal his identity. Uri Orlev's *Man from the Other Side,* translated from Hebrew, is a gripping story about a Polish teenager who guides Jews through the sewers to escape or enter the Warsaw Ghetto, where he is caught in the uprising. The sewers through which Marek travels are a naturally apt metaphor for his journey through the underworld of self-knowledge, which involves danger from within as well as without. Neither sensationalized nor sanctified, this young adult Holocaust novel has instead been profoundly considered and patiently crafted.

Adults often don't realize that teenagers are fighting a private war with drugs, high-risk sex, or peer pressure to engage in other destructive—especially self-destructive—behaviors. An adolescent in your life may be worried about a friend who has talked of suicide. That's something to take seriously, and it so happens that there are a couple of good young adult novels on the subject. One is Richard Peck's *Remembering the Good Times.* Another is Zibby Oneal's *Language of Goldfish.* If you want to introduce some perspective into parent-child relationships, which may become deadlocked at any point in the journey to maturity, try reading up on some other families' situations, such as those in Robert Newton Peck's novel *A Day No Pigs Would Die,* about a boy's evolution of respect for his father, or in Paula Fox's *Moonlight Man,* about a girl's changing perception of her alcoholic father.

U.S. culture has internalized its rites of passage, and many of our best young adult novels are first-person narratives of inner development. In Isabelle Holland's *Man without a Face,* a boy reaches out to a father substitute for guidance on his quest for love and self-respect. In Paul Zindel's novel *The Pigman,* two teenagers relate the tragedy of their relationship with a lonely old man. In Virginia Euwer Wolff's *Make Lemonade,* the fourteen-year-old protagonist's rite of passage involves her babysitting job for a seventeen-year-old with two children. In Barbara Shoup's *Stranded in Harmony,* a high school senior feels that his football captain, cheerleader dating, predictable teen years are going to turn into the adulthood everybody expects him to have rather than the one he wants to have. Desperate to break out, he says, "When I catch a pass and start running, all I can think is, If the goal post is as far as I can go with this sucker, what's the point?"

Some rites of passage involve realms of fantasy or alternative reality. Fans of such fiction are often freely plundering the adult shelves, but there are plenty of young adult–specific gems. Patrice Kindl has a gift for creating memorable and unusual realities, as in *Owl in Love,* the story of Owl, a fourteen-year-old girl by day and an owl by night, who falls for her biology teacher and mistakenly assumes he's destined to be her lifelong mate. If your teenager is into thrillers, horror flicks, or Gothic romance, you'll be glad to know that a spate of first-class vampire books has arrived on the scene: M. T. Anderson's *Thirsty* offers a mordantly humorous and ultimately dark saga, Vivian Vande Velde's *Companions of the Night* plays with the ethics of vampire-human relations, Mary Downing Hahn's *Look for Me by Moonlight* draws on some of the classic motifs of vulnerable heroine and disarming vampire, and Annette Curtis Klause's *Silver Kiss* similarly makes use of passionate emotion.

The point of boarding this omnibus of books is to explore new territory and see what's out there. You may feel as if your adolescent has changed so much you don't even know him or her anymore, but there are meeting grounds, whether in science fiction (try William Sleator's books, for example) or social science reading assignments. There aren't many subjects that don't show up in young adult literature, not many questions that don't get raised. Is sex a pleasure or a problem? You'll find every shade of opinion in a good bibliography of young adult fiction and nonfiction on sex and sexuality. As Hazel Rochman said in discussing trends in young adult literature:

> It's not just that . . . the books are more sexually explicit, though some are, and if not explicit, then candid. But the sophistication is deeper than the age or sex life of the protagonist. There's a complexity in language and character and moral choice. These books tell a good story, but they offer more than a quick read or a neat solution to a problem. They are more than what used to be called "bridge books" to *real,* that is adult, literature. They challenge the patronizing view attacked by Roger Sutton (in *School Library Journal,* Sept. 1986) that assumes all YA books must be "casual, unintimidating, fun, easily slipped into the day-to-day life of the average teen."

That's not to say that "casual" books aren't around and that they don't have their reading merits. It's safe, sound, and secure to find the same characters, plot, point of view, theme, and even length in every book when the rest of the world is tumbling down around you, when your body is playing tricks on you, and when there's more than enough challenge in just getting through the school day.

Yet the heroic aspects of adolescence will not be denied. Given half a chance, young people will search for a better self, a better society, and even a better book. It is not accidental that mythological quests—sometimes for identity, sometimes for justice—were usually undertaken by young adults. Something of that heroism survives in the best books for adolescents. Adults who look for idealism in adolescent literature may be shocked by the realism they find, while those who look for realism may be embarassed by idealism. Paula Fox, who writes with uncanny precision and versatility for children, young adults, and adults, once said: "When the light of the imagination shines, there are no longer children and adults, children's literature and adult literature—only humans trying to be human." In the past several decades, young adult books have grown to the height of human literature.

Books for Young Adults (ages 13–17)

Abelove, Joan. *Go and Come Back.* Jackson/DK Ink, 1998.
Alicia, who lives in a village in the Peruvian jungle, finds the two visiting anthropologists strange in both appearance and habits, thus exposing at a very human level the revelations and limitations of cross-cultural understanding.

Anderson, M. T. *Thirsty.* Candlewick, 1997.
A vampire novel with psychological twists that reveal peculiar similarities between the supernatural and the ordinary teenager, from flip humor to deep despair.

Avi. *Nothing but the Truth: A Documentary Novel.* Jackson/Orchard, 1991.
In the course of only a few days, ninth-grader Philip becomes a national celebrity when his homeroom teacher gets him suspended for humming along with the daily tape of "The Star-Spangled Banner." Yet nothing is as it seems in this collection of diary excerpts, school memos, and newspaper reports that reveal Philip's real motives.

Bauer, Joan. *Rules of the Road.* Putnam, 1998.
Jenna, a sales clerk in a shoe store, chauffeurs the company president from Illinois to Texas and en route learns about driving, business, life, and herself.

Becerra de Jenkins, Lyll. *The Honorable Prison.* Lodestar, 1988.
Marta is seventeen when she and her family are put under house arrest because of her father's editorials against the military dictatorship that rules their Latin American country.

Berry, James. *Ajeemah and His Son.* HarperCollins, 1992.
An intense, hypnotic novel in which Ajeemah and his eighteen-year-old son are ambushed in 1807 by slave traders and shipped to a Jamaican sugar plantation, where their suffering ends in survival for one but tragedy for the other.

Block, Francesca. *Weetzie Bat.* Harper, 1989.
This poetic, punk fairy tale launches an inventive series celebrating West Coast adolescent postmodern culture in which free love generates family loyalty.

Bloor, Edward. *Tangerine.* Harcourt, 1997.
Absurdist comedy blended with soccer suspense makes an unusual novel about the individualistic younger brother of a bullying football star.

Blume, Judy. *Tiger Eyes.* Bradbury, 1981.
After her father is killed in a hold-up, fifteen-year-old Davey learns to reach outside her family to find help and love. This is a fine book, but what teenagers really want to read is *Forever* (see chapter 10).

Bridgers, Sue Ellen. *Notes from Another Life.* Knopf, 1981.
Sometimes it seems that brother and sister Kevin and Wren have only each other—and their music—to sustain them in a difficult family situation.

Brooks, Bruce. *The Moves Make the Man.* Harper, 1984.
How can Jerome—bright, articulate, and the only black student in an all-white school—help his troubled friend Bix? The answers lie on and off the basketball court, as Jerome teaches Bix a new way to play the game.

Cadnum, Michael. *Zero at the Bone.* Viking, 1996.
When his seventeen-year-old sister fails to come home one night, Cray and his parents are plunged into a world of waiting, searching, and wondering.

Childress, Alice. *A Hero Ain't Nothing but a Sandwich.* Coward, 1973.
In this landmark example of the "new realism" in young adult literature, family and friends try to help Benjy, a thirteen-year-old heroin addict.

Cormier, Robert. *After the First Death.* Pantheon, 1979.
In a complex but involving thriller, three teens become both victims and agents of several kinds of terrorism.

Crutcher, Chris. *Running Loose.* Greenwillow, 1983.
Telling a time-honored story with an utterly contemporary voice, Louie Banks finds out there's more to football than winning.

Deuker, Carl. *Painting the Black.* Houghton, 1997.
Ryan Ward's senior year is consumed by his relationship with a gifted but egomaniacal newcomer who uses his athletic prowess at baseball to excuse breaking the rules and sexually harassing female students.

Dickinson, Peter. *Eva.* Delacorte, 1989.
This brilliant science fiction story develops the premise of a thirteen-year-old whose body is destroyed in an auto accident and whose brain is implanted in a chimpanzee. Dickinson explores the differences between animals and humans in sensitive scenes that challenge our assumptions without becoming didactic.

Dines, Carol. *Talk to Me: Stories and a Novella.* Delacorte, 1997.
Dines's subtle, honest portrayal of teenagers besieged by parental and peer problems makes these stories exceptional for their empathetic insight and controlled style.

Farmer, Nancy. *The Ear, the Eye, and the Arm.* Jackson/Orchard, 1994.
This taut science fiction–fantasy set in Zimbabwe in 2194 has the imaginative suspense of a detective story. But in this case the detective is a mutant who attempts to rescue three children from the slave-driving villainess who has kidnapped them.

Fiedler, Lisa. *Curtis Piperfield's Biggest Fan.* Clarion, 1995; *Lucky Me.* Clarion, 1998.
Whether she's finding a boyfriend and agreeing to be just friends with her oldest, dearest male friend (*Curtis Piperfield's Biggest Fan*) or reconsidering the "just friends" proposition (*Lucky Me*), C.C. is a bright and funny teen in Fiedler's charming romantic comedies.

Fox, Paula. *The Moonlight Man.* Bradbury, 1986.
During a long-awaited vacation with her seldom-seen father, Catherine discovers the desperation that lies beneath his glamorous exterior.

Frank, Anne. *The Diary of a Young Girl.* Doubleday, 1967.
This classic document gives teen readers a poignant and personal view of the tragedy of the Holocaust.

Garden, Nancy. *Annie on My Mind.* Farrar, 1982.
In a touchingly romantic novel, Liza and Annie share the ordinary pains and pleasures of first love—as well as the wrenching hurt when their lesbian relationship is made public.

Guy, Rosa. *The Disappearance.* Delacorte, 1979.
A family takes adolescent Imamu Jones into custody after he's acquitted of a crime and then suspects him of being involved in the disappearance of their youngest child. Imamu knows he must find the real criminal if he's to be cleared.

Hahn, Mary Downing. *Look for Me by Moonlight.* Clarion, 1995.
Teenagers who think they get thrills from a horror movie will be riveted by this more subtle but nonetheless gothic thriller in which discontented sixteen-year-old Cynda nearly succumbs to a sinister stranger's vampire kiss.

Hamilton, Virginia. *Sweet Whispers, Brother Rush.* Philomel, 1982.
Fourteen-year-old Teresa (Tree) meets a ghost who reveals frightening secrets about Tree's mother and brother.

Hewett, Lorri. *Lives of Our Own.* Dutton, 1998.
Two girls, one black and one white, discover that their lives may be linked through their parents' shared history in a small Georgia town.

Hinton, S. E. *The Outsiders.* Viking, 1967.
One of the first contemporary "problem novels," this is the empathetic and romantic story of a family of brothers caught up in gang warfare in lower-class Tulsa.

Hughes, Dean. *Family Pose.* Harper, 1989.
David is a runaway whose foster homes have so damaged him that Paul, the middle-aged bellboy who sneaks him into a hotel room and feeds him, has to work hard to win his trust.

Ippisch, Hanneke. *Sky: A True Story of Resistance during World War II.* Simon, 1996.
This vivid narration of the author's work as a teenage Dutch resistance worker (for which the Nazis placed her in solitary confinement) is comprised of brief chapters, each centering on an involving incident, along with photographs, newspaper clippings, correspondence, popular poems, cartoons, and other graphic artifacts.

Johnson, Angela. *Toning the Sweep.* Jackson/Orchard, 1993.
Fourteen-year-old Emmie arrives at Grandmama Ola's home in the California desert with her mother and a video recorder. The three women are saying goodbye: Ola to her friends because she is dying of cancer; Emmie to the childhood retreat she has visited every summer; and Mama to a past that includes the 1964 murder of her father by Alabama racists. It's a powerful crossroads for the reader as well.

Kerr, M. E. *Deliver Us from Evie.* HarperCollins, 1994.
Evie's romance with a powerful banker's daughter shocks the small farming community her family calls home. Kerr is the author of many other inimitable contributions to young adult literature, including *Gentlehands,* in which a boy realizes that his aristocratic grandfather has a secret that stretches back to World War II and Nazi Germany.

Kindl, Patrice. *Owl in Love.* Houghton, 1993.
Owl is a seventh-grade girl by day but an owl by night. Her orderly "wereowl" world

is thrown into chaos when she falls in love with her biology teacher and assists a strange runaway boy.

Klause, Annette Curtis. *The Silver Kiss.* Delacorte, 1990.
Here's a less than classic triangle between two vampire brothers of sworn enmity and a girl whose mother is dying of cancer. The result of this unlikely combination is a passionate novel that's sexy, scary, moving, and irresistible to teens.

Koertge, Ron. *Confess-o-rama.* Orchard, 1996.
Tony, newly moved to town after the death of his mother's fourth husband, finds himself drawn against his will into friendship—and maybe romance—with an eccentric and determined young artist.

Lipsyte, Robert. *One Fat Summer.* Harper, 1977.
Overweight Bob Marks is the hero of his own first-person narrative, but he doesn't know it until the end of the book when he finds out that a hero is not necessarily thin and tough—both of which he has become—but someone with a compassionate bent for doing the right thing—which he is becoming. A seriocomic story of growing up male in the fifties by the author of *The Contender.*

Lobel, Anita. *No Pretty Pictures: A Child of War.* Greenwillow, 1998.
What distinguishes this Holocaust memoir from many others that have been published recently is the author's scrupulous honesty to her perceptions as a child. Lobel projects herself not as a hero or even a victim but as a determined, sometimes irascible survivor. The writing is clean, almost stark, and the tone straightforward enough for a broad age range of readers.

Lynch, Chris. *Slot Machine.* HarperCollins, 1995.
Elvin discovers that the summer camp preparing him for freshman year is designed mainly to scout new sports talent and slot boys into their place in the social structure—and he doesn't seem to fit into any of the slots.

Mahy, Margaret. *The Changeover.* McElderry, 1984.
In this gripping fantasy set in contemporary New Zealand, Laura must save her little brother who is dying from a spell cast by an evil wizard. Other notable young adult books by Mahy include *The Catalogue of the Universe* and *Memory,* in which nineteen-year-old Jonny and Sophie, who has Alzheimer's disease, find mutual love and strength in Sophie's old house, "a crazy stumbling contraption of strange things fitted together."

McKinley, Robin. *The Hero and the Crown.* Greenwillow, 1984.
Part of an exciting fantasy sequence about epic female heroes in the mythic land of Damar, this novel relates Aerin the dragonslayer's defeat of an archwizard who has threatened the kingdom. Readers will also want to pursue *The Blue Sword,* published earlier but set later in the fictional chronology of events.

Mori, Kyoko. *Shizuko's Daughter.* Henry Holt, 1993.
In a powerfully understated story, Yuki survives her beloved mother's suicide, despite her father and stepmother's cold disregard, with the support of her traditional grandparents.

Myers, Walter Dean. *Fallen Angels.* Scholastic, 1988.
"I wouldn't have joined if I had seen anything else to do," but Vietnam was Richie Perry's only way out of Harlem. Myers's account of the war through a young black soldier's eyes is honest, graphic, and compelling.

Newton, Suzanne. *I Will Call It Georgie's Blues.* Viking, 1983.
While Neal has found jazz music as a refuge from his father, a dictatorial minister, his little brother, Georgie, seems to be retreating into nothing at all.

O'Brien, Robert. *Z for Zachariah.* Atheneum, 1975.
In one of the first post–nuclear holocaust novels written for young people, Ann Burden thinks she is the only person left alive until she meets John R. Loomis. But is he friend or foe?

Oneal, Zibby. *The Language of Goldfish.* Viking, 1980.
Thirteen-year-old Carrie dreads leaving her childhood—symbolized by an island in the pond where she and her sister talked to the fish in happier days—and barely survives a suicide attempt in this subtly developed novel set in the suburbs where "people . . . did not have crazy children."

Orlev, Uri. *The Man from the Other Side,* translated from the Hebrew by Hillel Halkin. Houghton, 1991.
Neither sensationalized nor sanctified, this Holocaust novel centers on fourteen-year-old Marek who, after discovering that his father is Jewish, becomes involved in the Warsaw Ghetto Uprising as a "sewer guide."

Peck, Richard. *Remembering the Good Times.* Delacorte, 1985.
Kate is talented, Trav is brilliant, and Buck thinks of himself as just an average guy, but he's the one who remembers and tells the story of the bond between the three friends and the tragedy of Trav's suicide. Peck can be a stern, sometimes didactic writer, but his wit and understanding of young people raise *Remembering the Good Times* far above the usual "problem novels."

Peck, Robert Newton. *A Day No Pigs Would Die.* Knopf, 1972.
In an autobiographical rite-of-passage story, thirteen-year-old Rob grows and learns on a Shaker farm in Vermont in the 1920s.

Pullman, Philip. *Ruby in the Smoke.* Knopf, 1987.
This nonstop Victorian thriller matches wits between a feisty young heroine and a monstrous villainess who both struggle for possession of a fabled gem. First in a trilogy about brave Sally Lockhart, the pastiche is word-perfect and will appeal to adult mystery fans as well as teenage readers.

Qualey, Marsha. *Revolutions of the Heart.* Houghton, 1993.
In Cory's small Wisconsin town, the Indians generally keep to themselves, so her budding romance with a Cree teen is big news.

Rabinovici, Schoschana. *Thanks to My Mother.* Dial, 1998.
Israeli citizen Schoschana Rabinovici chronicles her experiences of the Holocaust as a child named Susie Weksler, eight years old when the Lithuanian city of Vilnius

falls to the Nazis in 1941 and thirteen when she is liberated (close to death) by the Russians. The extraordinary endurance and resourcefulness with which her mother maneuvers to survive and save her daughter are exhaustively detailed yet riveting.

Rochman, Hazel, and Darlene Z. McCampbell, eds. *Bearing Witness: Stories of the Holocaust.* Kroupa/Orchard, 1995.

An outstanding anthology of short stories emhasizes diversity of tone and voice in selections by Primo Levi, Cynthia Ozick, Hans Richter, and others—all effective in communicating to teenagers the ultimate experience of racism during World War II.

Rosenberg, Maxine B. *Hiding to Survive: Stories of Jewish Children Rescued from the Holocaust.* Clarion, 1994.

Fourteen survivors of the Holocaust describe hiding as children from Nazi persecution in different countries and different circumstances. Each story is harrowing in its bare facts, and each is accompanied by a photograph of the interviewee as child and adult.

Sachar, Louis. *Holes.* Farrar, 1998.

Part mystery and part surrealistic history, partly funny and partly sad, this is the story of a fourteen-year-old who's forced to dig ditches in a juvenile detention center as punishment for something he hasn't done and who, by the end of this compelling story, digs up more than dirt.

Shoup, Barbara. *Stranded in Harmony.* Hyperion, 1997.

Lucas Cantrell, a cheerleader-dating football captain, feels suffocated by the predictability and restricted expectations of life in a small Indiana town.

Soto, Gary. *Buried Onions.* Harcourt, 1997.

Eddie is a sixteen-year-old Mexican American trying to survive Fresno streets torn by gang violence and crime. Readers can only hope that his understanding at the end of the book will lead him to a better life.

Staples, Suzanne Fisher. *Shabanu: Daughter of the Wind.* Knopf, 1989.

Traditions are strong in Shabanu's desert tribe, but her rite of passage into womanhood leads her toward an unexpected marriage and takes readers on an engrossing journey through dust storms and cultural conflicts.

Vande Velde, Vivian. *Companions of the Night.* Harcourt, 1995.

When Kerry runs into some frenzied citizens abducting a young man they claim is a vampire, she aids his escape. But it turns out that he actually *is* a vampire, and her involvement puts her at the center of a battle between the vampires and the vampire-hunters.

Voigt, Cynthia. *The Runner.* Atheneum, 1985.

Bullet Tillerman—angry, rebellious, and alone—runs away from his father's harangues but finds that in the end he must face himself.

Wersba, Barbara. *Fat: A Love Story.* Harper, 1987.

Rita, who is sixteen, weighs two hundred pounds, and is five foot three, takes a while to become confident in who she is, whom she loves, and who loves her. This romantic comedy is by the author of *The Dream Watcher,* a poignant young adult novel published in the 1960s but now out of print.

Werlin, Nancy. *The Killer's Cousin.* Delacorte, 1998.
After being acquitted of the murder of his girlfriend, David moves in with his aunt and uncle only to realize that his young cousin, Lily, harbors even deeper secrets than he does.

Westall, Robert. *The Stones of Muncaster Cathedral.* Farrar, 1993.
A steeplejack who attempts to repair a British cathedral discovers that the rot that afflicts it stems from the evil that still lurks within the stone.

Williams-Garcia, Rita. *Like Sisters on the Homefront.* Lodestar, 1995.
Gayle, a tough-talking black fourteen-year-old who's street-smart but already pregnant for the second time, learns some new lifeways when her mother sends her to stay with straight-arrow relatives in Georgia.

Wolff, Virginia Euwer. *Make Lemonade.* Henry Holt, 1993.
In a book of tough but lyrical free verse, fourteen-year-old LaVaughn babysits for a seventeen-year-old with two children, getting more deeply involved—and seeing more clearly the plight of a young woman without safety nets—as time goes on.

Woodson, Jacqueline. *From the Notebooks of Melanin Sun.* Blue Sky/Scholastic, 1995.
An African-American teenager, named by his mother for the beauty of his black skin, bitterly resents her lesbian relationship with a white woman despite the couple's obvious happiness (and their patience with his rebellion).

Yep, Laurence. *Child of the Owl.* Harper, 1977.
Contemporary kid culture meets—and eventually mixes—with old Chinese traditions when a girl comes to live with her grandmother in San Francisco.

Zindel, Paul. *The Pigman.* Harper, 1968.
Along with *The Outsiders* by S. E. Hinton, *The Pigman* was one of the first young adult novels to favor an entirely—and believably—adolescent point of view. John and Lorraine take turns telling the story of their friendship with the Pigman, a wise and funny old gentleman who keeps a sad secret.

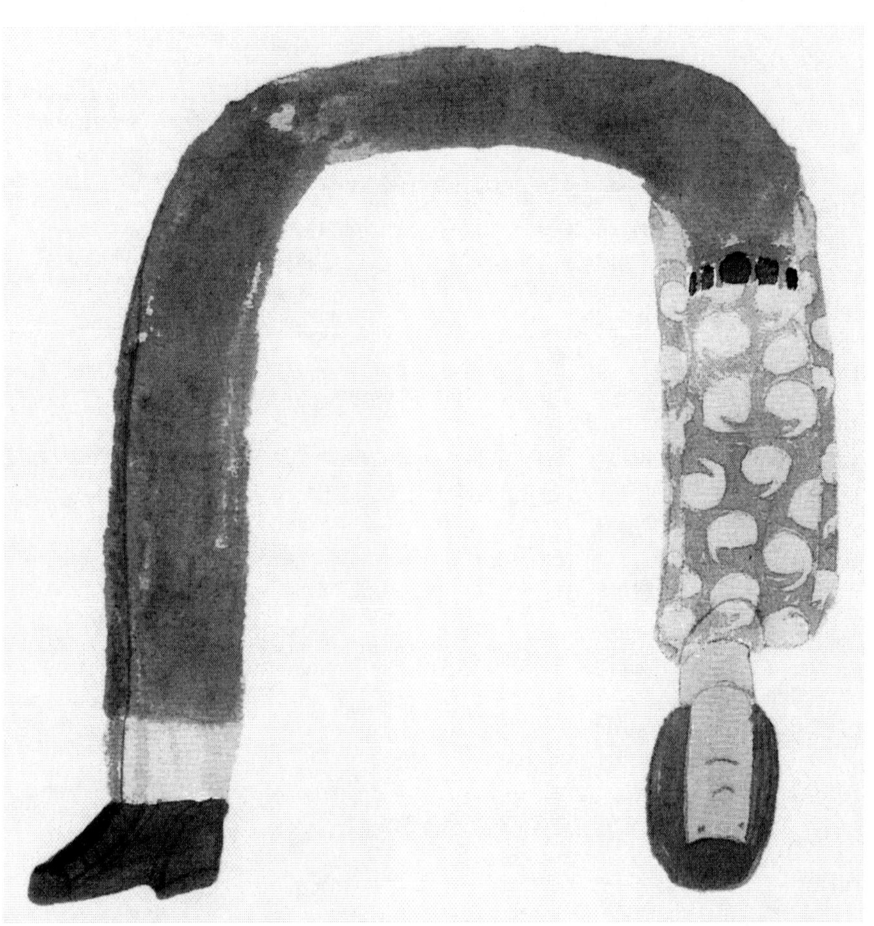

Douglas Florian

7

Poetry for Children

Liar, liar
Pants on fire
Nose as long
As a telephone wire

Kids have probably been chanting that, or something like it, since dinosaurs strolled through the playground. In early childhood, rhyming is as natural as climbing. For some reason a lot of people tune out poetry as they get older, probably because nobody goes around talking in iambic pentameter. Still, it's true that you can't say anything much more briefly than a poem says it, nor catch a fact or feeling much more expressively. Heard over and over, rhymed lyrics are almost unforgettable—witness popular songs and television commercials. Unfortunately, poetry cannot be read quickly and therefore doesn't fit into the modern pace of things. That leaves poetry for those of us who read slowly, either through choice or necessity.

Being a misfit has its own rewards. For me, even newspaper articles require thought, so there are some days I really study the world and some days I don't have the time to consider it even briefly. This makes for an uneven but carefully pondered universe. You can never know everything anyway, so you might as well know something thoroughly. Take this simple fact, stated concisely in an anonymous old rhyme:

For every evil under the sun
There is a remedy, or there is none.
If there be one, try and find it.
If there be none, never mind it.

Such commendable advice is hard to come by, even in prose, and reminds me of the graffiti I used to read on my favorite city jogging route:

Those who know me
know me well.
Those who don't
can go to hell.

The more often I read it, the more it struck me as a succinct article of truth, a truth within easy grasp of either adult or child. It more or less rang in the mind for miles, keeping my heart up no matter how slow my pace may have looked to the public.

This all goes to prove how poetry can boost the humblest activities or objects of daily living. The most common substance can inspire new possibilities. Writes Douglas Florian in "Cake Mistake" from *Bing Bang Boing:*

Mother made a birthday cake
For icing she used glue.
The children sit so quiet now,
And chewandchewandchew.

Or again:

Do commas have mommas
Who teach them to pause,
Who comfort and calm them,
And clean their sharp claws?

Not only can common subjects get heightened attention, but the most grandiose subjects can be humbled, as Constance Levy shows us in "The Color-Eater" from *I'm Going to Pet a Worm Today and Other Poems:*

Sunset mixed this recipe:
Orange and grape and raspberry
. . .

Night came sniffing
Like a pup;
Licked it
Liked it
Lapped it up.

As the critic Northrop Frye wrote in *The Educated Imagination,* "Poetry is not irregular lines in a book, but something very close to dance and song, something to walk down the street keeping time to." Or jog down the trail keeping time to. Or do the dishes by. Or jump rope on the playground with. That rhythmic action of poetry is one of the things that arrests children's attention, satisfying their own restless need for activity. The words of a poem, like children, must *move.* They also play with each other in sound patterns. Listen to the frenetic activity in Marilyn Singer's poem "Beavers in November," from *Turtle in July*—and try saying it faster and faster.

This stick here
That stick there
  Mud, more mud, add mud, good mud
That stick here
This stick there
  Mud, more mud, add mud, good mud
    You pat
    I gnaw
    I pile
    You store
This stick here
That stick there
  Mud, more mud, add mud, good mud
    You guard
    I pack
    I dig
    You stack
That stick here
This stick there
  Mud, more mud, add mud, good mud
    I trim
    You mold
    To keep
    Out cold
This stick here
That stick there
  Mud, more mud, add mud, good mud.

Singer's poem fills the ears like a busy builder and brings to mind an important maxim of poetry that many people overlook: it doesn't have to be serious, it just has to be imaginative. Shel Silverstein has a firm grasp on the efficacy of nonserious poetic statements. There's a swarm of them in *Where the Sidewalk Ends:*

Oh, if you're a bird, be an early bird
And catch the worm for your breakfast plate.
If you're a bird, be an early bird—
But if you're a worm, sleep late.

That's a breakfast poem guaranteed to interfere with any sulk and improve your child's disposition if not his or her appetite. Here's another one, which should be read at sunset, when the day's responsibilities melt away into the freedom of evening:

There is a place where the sidewalk ends
And before the street begins,
And there the grass grows soft and white,
And there the sun burns crimson bright,
And there the moon-bird rests from his flight
To cool in the peppermint wind.

Let us leave this place where the smoke blows black
And the dark street winds and bends.
Past the pits where the asphalt flowers grow
We shall walk with a walk that is measured and slow,
To the place where the sidewalk ends.

Yes, we'll walk with a walk that is measured and slow,
And we'll go where the chalk-white arrows go,
For the children, they mark, and the children, they know
The place where the sidewalk ends.

Unless you can visualize the possibility of a place where the sidewalk ends, it's impossible to appreciate the world of simple everyday phenomena translated into the marvels of verse. Whether the poetry is lyric, narrative, epic, romantic, balladic, humorous, or nonsensical, whether it moves in regular metrical or free verse patterns, whether it rhymes or it doesn't, it must spark something you can imagine. So much meaning can be stored in an image that summons hundreds of unstated associations. The image should be *fresh,* too. "And there the sun burns crimson bright, / . . . / To cool in the peppermint wind." What a swirl of color sensations, compared to a stale cliché like "red as a rose."

Poetry has always been one of the most succulent dishes in the feast of children's books. Nursery rhymes are a springboard to nonsense verses, a tradition inspired by poets from Edward Lear on, and also to what we might call sense verses. Perhaps because of the inimitable Dr. Seuss, picture-book stories in rhyme seem to be a hallmark of children's literature, but in fact such books are extraordinarily difficult to write well. Bill Grossman's *Tommy at the Grocery Store* is one of the genre's effervescent successes: when Tommy's mommy accidentally leaves him behind at the grocery store, the grocer

> . . . thought that Tommy was salami
> And set him on the deli shelf.
> And Tommy sat among salamis
> Softly sobbing to himself.

Tommy is repeatedly purchased by customers who mistake him for a particular food and is returned when they realize that he has a characteristic incompatible with the foodstuff in question. Victoria Chess's illustrations depict the characters as beady-eyed pigs, which keeps the story humorous without lessening the warmth of Tommy's mommy's recovery of her errant son.

The late Roy Gerrard was a particularly gifted practitioner of the story in poetic form whose exaggeratedly compact characters are drolly suited to his rollicking Gilbert-and-Sullivanesque verse. Gerrard's words and illustrations together take readers to prehistoric times (*Mik's Mammoth*), the days of chivalry (*Sir Cedric*), the Roman Empire (*The Roman Twins*), and the Oregon Trail (*Wagons West!*).

More common, of course, are collections of shorter poems. Such contemporary juvenile poetry has been created and championed by a spirited leadership of poets. David McCord is one of the most popular and prolific of these. Most of his poetry has been collected in *One at a Time,* a work of innocent mischief and endless invention. Like all good poets, McCord makes you see things in a new light, and like all good children's poets, he makes you see it in a new light that is accessible from and often descriptive of a child's perspective, as in this verse from "Tooth Trouble":

> When I see the dentist
> I take him all my teeth:
> Some of me's above them,
> But most of me's beneath.

John Ciardi's is another lively voice. My favorite of his collections is *Doodle Soup,* in which he displays characteristic verbal dexterity in versifying funny stories that often proceed by contradiction.

There was a man who went to sea.
He didn't have a ship.
"Once I have learned to swim," said he,
"I'll take a longer trip."

The Canadian poet Dennis Lee is a worthy heir to Ciardi. His *Ice Cream Store* sells itself by the title and makes a natural next step after Mother Goose.

As in other genres, there's a rich range of choice in style and tone of poetry collections for children. Eloise Greenfield's *Honey, I Love* is a warm, lilting celebration of African-American childhood. Ann Turner's *Street Talk* is vibrant free verse in an urban setting, while her collection for older readers, *Grass Songs,* reflects the emotions and experiences of pioneer women crossing the prairie. Lori Carlson's *Cool Salsa: Bilingual Poems on Growing Up Latino in the United States* explores yet another universe of rhythms and images.

Some of these collections are decorated sparely, emphasizing the poetry, but many are accompanied by lavish illustrations in an appealing blend of linguistic and visual art. The 1982 Newbery Medal went to poetry in a picture-book format, Nancy Willard's *Visit to William Blake's Inn: Poems for Innocent and Experienced Travelers.* Alice and Martin Provensen's illustrations are as original and skillful as the poetry. Graphically, the book is designed with Blake's tiger in mind. The dominant hues are tan, gold, and warm brown, generally muted in value, with occasional flashes of intensity, including a stylized yellow sun and some curling flames. Although the illustrations have a dreamlike air, they are anchored by their steady eighteenth-century propriety.

The poetry itself is mystical, in keeping with Blake's own, with that occasional piercing quality of a child's perceptions. It doesn't matter in the least whether children know or care who William Blake is. There are levels here that children enjoy and levels that will elude them until they are older. There are, in fact, some intriguing parallels with Blake's own poetry, but they belong to a longer-winded study. Suffice it to say that Willard has caught her balance between the simplicity and complexity of things in a tone similar to that of Blake's *Songs of Innocence and Experience.*

Charlotte F. Otten's *January Rides the Wind: A Book of Months* is another example of an effective partnership of poetry and art. Each spread offers a free-verse poem of crystalline lyricism, such as:

November swaddles stars,
swims in polar light.
Red foxes dance on stones
lit by the moon.

The verses are accompanied by Todd L. D. Doney's luminescent oil paintings, which bring out the richness of every seasonal hue. The cheerful gravity of Alice Schertle's poetry in *How Now, Brown Cow?* finds a fit match in Amanda Schaffer's vigorous bovine portraits in strong brushstroke textures. Young listeners will be intrigued to hear that the cow who jumped over the moon

> . . . never tried
> to jump again,
> but gazed for hours at the moon.
> They never found the dish and spoon.

Looking for a more conceptually playful poetic outing? J. Patrick Lewis's *Riddle-icious* is an inventive collection of poetic "what am I" riddles in picture-book form. Zany line-and-watercolor illustrations appropriately personify object after object as they quiz readers on identity:

> I
> stand
> in water
> and I needle
> the cat. I get
> spruced up in my
> angel-hat. Tomorrow
> morning there will be
> something for you
> un-
> der-
> neath me.

Another unusual poetry collection won the Newbery Medal in 1989. Paul Fleischman's *Joyful Noise: Poems for Two Voices* includes fourteen poems for choral reading. All the poems focus on insects, their movements, voices, appearance, and metaphoric significance. One of the best is "Digger Wasp," narrated by the female as she digs a protective nest for the young she will never see:

> . . . my young will
> know me well.
> When they care
> for their own children.

There's lots of humor here: a book louse begins, "I was born in a / fine old edition of Schiller." "Whirligig Beetles" has the same frenetic quality as the bugs' movements, which are also captured by pencil drawings swirling around the page. Most of the poems make meaningful use of two voices. In "Honeybees," for instance, there is an amusing back-and-forth between a worker and a queen that ends in a simultaneous chant, "Truly, a bee's is the / worst (best) / of all lives." The poems are of necessity simple on the page, but the sound effects are playful and the dual voice form is a natural for sociable children who want to share the joyful noise of reading aloud.

Many of the best children's poets have doubled as anthologists. Myra Cohn Livingston, who wrote extensively about children's poetry and published numerous anthologies, also had a distinguished career as a poet in her own right, from the brilliant imagery in *Light and Shadow* to the versatile range of forms in *I Never Told and Other Poems.* Her anthology *If the Owl Calls Again* evokes the owl's mythical resonance, and her table of contents forms a rhythmic incantation of its own: "Owls in the Light," "Owls in Flight," "Owls to Delight," "Owls of Night," "Owls to Fright." The poems range from haunting Native American chants ("The owl feathers sing in the air") to funny verses by David McCord, X. J. Kennedy, John Gardner, Jack Prelutsky, Lewis Carroll, and even Sir Walter Scott, who rarely cracked a smile in print. Some of the poems are as hushed as the night, including Livingston's own:

> If you seek answers
> you will find them
> trembling
> on the ground.

Another summons the mouse's point of view ("where the smallest letters / cower in the dark," as Barbara Esbensen writes). Whether the selections are conceptually sophisticated, as is Julia Fields's "Alabama," or simple folk rhymes, they are accessible in style. The subject lends itself to sonorous effects, which are made to order for reading aloud.

X. J. Kennedy, who co-wrote *Knock at a Star: A Child's Introduction to Poetry* with his wife, Dorothy, has authored many volumes of his own. His style is bright, tight, and funny, as in this quatrain from *Brats:*

> On his motorbike Lars stands
> Roaring past us—"Look! no hands!"
> Soon with vacant handle bars
> Back the bike roars. Look, no Lars!

Arnold Adoff, who pioneered anthologies of African-American poetry for children, delights in dancing his words across the page in associated clusters.

His sense of humor sneaks into subjects that lots of readers take seriously, like winning—a natural focus in *Sports Pages,* where he starts one poem with

Dear Horse:
   you want this apple.
   and I
      want that
      competition cup

and ends with the admonition, "Don't / stop." His collection *Love Letters* sticks strictly to the child's-eye view—no romantic slush here:

Please
excuse this printed valentine
but
I really do like at least ten
girls in our grade and maybe
a
few more.

The poet Lee Bennett Hopkins has anthologized everything from holidays to horses, as well as several books of simple, vigorous verse in a beginning-to-read format (*Surprises; More Surprises*). Jack Prelutsky has also popularized poetry in anthologies such as *The Random House Book of Poetry for Children* and *Read-Aloud Rhymes for the Very Young,* but his own verse is perhaps most popular of all: witness the flagrant humor of *The New Kid on the Block.* One of the best ways to sell reluctant readers on poetry is to take advantage of the subject anthologies that zero in on a favorite topic—Hopkins's *Dinosaurs,* for instance—and then lead on to a poet's original collection of verse, in this case Prelutsky's *Tyrannosaurus Was a Beast.*

In selecting an anthology, look for quality and freshness in the selections, generous quantity, variety in tone and style, and sensitivity to the child audience. A seasoned anthologist like Nancy Larrick will organize the poems so that there's an organic linkage in the way they follow one another, leading the reader from one to the next without jarring but never constricting the reader from wandering here and there for a leisurely browse. Look for the anthologist whose tastes reflect your own. Larrick's work always seems to contain a gift selected especially for me. Whenever I need a calming image, I repeat these lines she gave me, by Walter de la Mare, in her anthology *The Night of the Whippoorwill:* "And moveless fish in the water gleam, / By silver reeds in a silver stream." Anthologies can also employ art effectively, as in Nora Panzer's *Celebrate America in Poetry and Art.* This book ingeniously juxtaposes works from the National Museum of American Art with poems about aspects of American life. What could have been merely a gimmicky showcase allows the works to inform one another and explores our nation in a way that facts simply cannot.

Paul Janeczko has enriched young adult literature with anthologies of adult poetry appealing to adolescents, but his mastery of the anthology genre isn't limited to that age group, as he demonstrates in *Home on the Range: Cowboy Poetry.* A collection of his own poetry, *That Sweet Diamond: Baseball Poems,* reflects the sharp empathy of a long-time fan for players (a catcher's "knees sing the blues / They sing 'em when I stoop and bend") and those in the stands (some nuns "settle in a row / behind the first-base dugout / straight as piano keys"). Naomi Shihab Nye is a poet who especially emphasizes international voices in her anthologies, which include *This Same Sky: A Collection of Poems from Around the World* and *What Have You Lost?*

Good poetry makes you slow down and read deeply. It sinks into your mind like a rock dropped in water, sending out rings of meaning. The more time and space you give a poem, the farther the ripples expand your consciousness. "Water looks thin / but weighs thick," writes Constance Levy. Poetry is similarly compressed. Maybe a better image than the stone settling to the bottom of the pond is one of those tightly wadded balls of paper that opens into a flower when you drop it in water. Flowers take time to open, whether they're paper flowers in water or real flowers in spring, and poetry needs time to open as well.

Poetry also begs to be read aloud, to have its sounds savored, which makes it ideal to share with children. When it's read aloud, paradoxically, poetry also makes you see more clearly. Some unusual image, some word surprise is bound to catch you up short and cause a sudden veering off the common course of thought. Listen to Valerie Worth's poem "Toad" from *All the Small Poems* and notice how it sharpens your inner vision.

When the flowers
Turned clever, and
Earned wide
Tender red petals
For themselves,

When the birds
Learned about feathers,
Spread green tails,
Grew cockades
On their heads,

The toad said:
Someone has got
To remember
The mud, and
I'm not proud

The word "earned" is such a surprise, much more exciting than "got" would have been, for instance, and it echoes the sound of "turned" and "learned" without becoming singsong about it. But the best surprise is the toad's crusty self-evaluation, which casts shadows on the pride of others without sounding proud itself—all in a simple but choice comment of eleven final words perfectly suited to the character. The flowers, the birds, and the toad have all been seen in an entirely new way. By sleight of language Worth has let us in on her vision. That's what good poetry does for you—and for your children too.

Poetry for Children

Adoff, Arnold, comp. *I Am the Darker Brother: An Anthology of Modern Poems by African Americans* (11–17). Simon, 1997.
The 1968 edition of this book—one of the earliest young people's anthologies to celebrate African-American poets—was a touchstone, and this revision is enriched beyond the original sixty-four selections to include twenty-one newer poems by stars such as Maya Angelou, Rita Dove, Audre Lorde, Ishmael Reed, and Etheridge Knight. Also, don't miss Adoff's own poetry in collections such as *Sports Pages* and *Love Letters.*

Carlson, Lori M., comp. *Cool Salsa: Bilingual Poems on Growing Up Latino in the United States* (12 and up). Henry Holt, 1995.
Wide-ranging in tone and subject as well as region, these poems—presented in English followed by a Spanish translation or original—have immediate impact on the reader.

Ciardi, John. *Doodle Soup,* illustrated by Merle Nacht (8–10). Houghton, 1985.
A tartly funny mix of narrative poems, poetic jokes, arrant nonsense, and wordplay.

Dunning, Stephen, comp. *Reflections on a Gift of Watermelon Pickle* (12–14). Lothrop, 1966.
This anthology of 114 appealing contemporary poems is illustrated with striking photographs.

Fleischman, Paul. *Joyful Noise: Poems for Two Voices,* illustrated by Eric Beddows (9–12). Harper, 1988.
Playful sound effects for choral reading distinguish this Newbery Medal winner in which all the poems focus on insects, their movements, voices, appearance, and metaphoric significance.

Florian, Douglas. *Bing Bang Boing* (8–11). Harcourt, 1994.

Exuberant rhythms and fresh rhyming distinguish this collection for reading aloud. Also distinguished (and fun) is *On the Wing: Bird Poems and Paintings.*

Gerrard, Roy. *The Roman Twins* (5–8). Farrar, 1998.

In Gerrard's rollicking verse narrative, runaway slave siblings Maximus and Vanilla steal their master's horse and trounce all in the chariot competition.

Greenfield, Eloise. *Honey, I Love: And Other Love Poems,* illustrated by Leo and Diane Dillon (6–8). Harper, 1978.

An African-American child's enthusiasm for life and love for her family form the main themes of this graceful collection.

Grossman, Bill. *Tommy at the Grocery Store,* illustrated by Victoria Chess (4–7). Harper, 1989.

This comic saga in galloping verse tells of a piglet misplaced by his mother at the grocery store and subsequently mistaken for just about every foodstuff the store sells.

Hearne, Betsy. *Polaroid and Other Poems of View* (14 and up). McElderry, 1991.

This collection of forty-seven lyric poems focuses on new angles from which to look inside the human heart and under the surfaces of the world.

Hopkins, Lee B., comp. *Small Talk: A Book of Short Poems,* illustrated by Susan Gaber (6–9). Harcourt, 1995.

Thirty-three very short poems, loosely arranged by season, are varied in tone from gentle reflections to jovial rhymes. Skillful watercolor or colored-pencil drawings illustrate this book by one of the most prolific and skilled anthologists of children's poetry.

Hughes, Ted. *Season Songs,* illustrated by Leonard Baskin (12 and up). Ultramarine, 1975.

Complex but deeply satisfying poetry about the natural world will challenge sensitive readers, who can also feast their eyes on Baskin's sophisticated paintings.

Janeczko, Paul, comp. *Home on the Range: Cowboy Poetry,* illustrated by Bernie Fuchs (9–13). Dial, 1997.

Known for his outstanding poetry anthologies for adolescents, which include *Going Over to Your Place* and *Pocket Poems,* Janeczko here rounds up nineteen robust poems to carry restless preteens from ranch to rodeo.

Kennedy, X. J. *Brats,* illustrated by James Watts (7–9). McElderry, 1986.

Forty-two brief verses, mostly rhymed quatrains, celebrate or denigrate the actions of mischievous children, many of whom meet fearful fates—as do their successors in *Fresh Brats.* Accompanied by slapstick black-and-white drawings, these poems offer high humor by one of the brightest poets writing for children.

Knudson, R. R., and May Swenson, comps. *American Sports Poems* (11 and up). Orchard, 1988.

This all-star lineup of 150 poems about sports has tremendous variety in subject, form, tone, and length.

Larrick, Nancy, comp. *The Night of the Whippoorwill,* illustrated by David Ray (8–11). Philomel, 1992.

With an ear for the mellifluous poetry that has distinguished her other anthologies, Larrick here gathers thirty-four poems to celebrate the night. The illustrations feature teal blues tinged with white or gold for surreal starlit effects, while softly rounded shapes envelop the print.

Lee, Dennis. *The Ice Cream Store,* illustrated by David McPhail (5–8). Scholastic, 1992.

This jolly and generous collection by the Canadian author of *Alligator Pie* and other award-winning poetry offers poems with a natural bounce.

Levy, Constance. *I'm Going to Pet a Worm Today and Other Poems,* illustrated by Ronald Himler (7–10). McElderry, 1991.

With a fresh capacity for attending to nature and for rhyming naturally, Levy leads readers into new perspective on their surroundings, both here and in *A Tree Place.*

Lewis, J. Patrick. *Riddle-icious,* illustrated by Debbie Tilley (7–9). Knopf, 1996.

This playful picture-book collection of riddle poems adds entertaining conceptual gamesmanship to the pleasures of verse.

Livingston, Myra Cohn, comp. *If the Owl Calls Again: A Collection of Owl Poems,* illustrated by Antonio Fransconi (11–14). McElderry, 1992.

Don't shy away from what appears to be a specialized topic. Owls have attracted great poets (of greatly varied cultures) whose range of emotion in capturing these birds with words will surprise many a reader.

McCord, David. *One at a Time,* illustrated by Henry B. Kane (9–12). Little, 1987.

A captivating collection of poems that reflects serious thought and gentle humor by one of America's greatest children's poets.

Merriam, Eve. *The Singing Green: New and Selected Poems for All Seasons,* illustrated by Kathleen Collins Howell (9–11). Morrow, 1992.

The poet plays with words, sounds, twists of meaning, rhythms, and rhymes in this collection, which includes many lively selections from earlier works that are now out of print.

Moore, Lilian. *Poems Have Roots,* illustrated by Tad Hills (9–12). Karl/Atheneum, 1997.

Poems of the environment such as "Snow Dust" and "The Wetter the Better" have a lyrical simplicity that makes them accessible for children relating to their own immediate surroundings with new eyes.

Morrison, Lillian, comp. *Slam Dunk: Basketball Poems,* illustrated by Bill James (10–12). Hyperion, 1995.

All the moves and rhythms that rule the game are played out here on a poetic court.

Myers, Walter Dean. *Harlem,* illustrated by Christopher Myers (9–12). Scholastic, 1997.

Striking multimedia collages illustrate these evocative poems in honor of New York City's historic African-American community: "A journey on the A train / That started on the banks of the Niger / And has not ended. Harlem."

Nye, Naomi Shihab, comp. *This Same Sky: A Collection of Poems from Around the World* (12–17). Macmillan, 1992.

An unusually rich anthology of 161 poems, many in translation, from poets born in countries and regions outside the United States, including Asia, Africa, South America, Canada, Europe, and Australia. Featured here are new writers as well as famous literati such as Octavio Paz, Jean Joubert, and Michael Ondaatje. Nye's brilliant selection of verse for *What Have You Lost?* also emphasizes international voices.

O'Neill, Mary. *Hailstones and Halibut Bones*, illustrated by Leonard Weisgard (8–10). Doubleday, 1973.

Colors take on a new brilliance through the images in this kaleidoscope of poems.

Otten, Charlotte F. *January Rides the Wind: A Book of Months*, illustrated by Todd L. D. Doney (5–8). Lothrop, 1997.

A lyrical cycle of free-verse poems, accompanied by richly textured oil paintings, takes the young audience through the calendar year.

Panzer, Nora, ed. *Celebrate America in Poetry and Art* (10–15). Hyperion, 1994.

This anthology uses images from the National Museum of American Art to illustrate poems offering unusual insight into the American experience.

Prelutsky, Jack. *The New Kid on the Block*, illustrated by James Stevenson (8–11). Greenwillow, 1984.

Most of the hundred-plus poems here are mini-jokes, wordplay, and character sketches, with liberal doses of monsters and meanies as well as common, garden-variety child mischief. Prelutsky is not only a prolific poet but has also produced numerous anthologies, including *The Random House Book of Poetry* and *The Beauty of the Beast.*

Schertle, Alice. *How Now, Brown Cow?*, illustrated by Amanda Schaffer (6–9). Harcourt, 1994.

If you didn't think of cows as poetic before, you will after encountering Schertle's sometimes thoughtful, sometimes droll literary gallery of bovine beauties.

Silverstein, Shel. *Where the Sidewalk Ends: Poems and Drawings* (7–12). Harper, 1974.

Breezy, humorous poems explore the joys and fears of childhood with zany drawings that animate the text. This perennial bestseller was followed by the entertaining collections *A Light in the Attic* and *Falling Up.*

Singer, Marilyn. *Turtle in July*, illustrated by Jerry Pinkney (8–10). Macmillan, 1989.

The great joy of these fifteen nature poems is the pattern of verbal rhythms that reflect the character of each creature, as when the timber rattlesnake sibilantly describes summer and winter with long coiling sounds. The watercolor paintings are also poetic, capturing the essence of each featured fish, fowl, and mammal.

Turner, Ann. *Grass Songs*, illustrated by Barry Moser (12 and up). Harcourt, 1993.

Seventeen free-verse narrative poems based on letters, diaries, and anecdotes of pioneer women match historical and poetic intensity. Turner is equally at home in a city setting and with younger readers, who will also enjoy the fresh flashes and lively effects of *Street Talk.*

Willard, Nancy. *A Visit to William Blake's Inn: Poems for Innocent and Experienced Travelers,* illustrated by Alice and Martin Provensen (7–10). Harcourt, 1981.
Indelible, mystical images mark both poetry and artwork in an exceptional example of bookmaking that won the 1982 Newbery Medal.

Worth, Valerie. *All the Small Poems,* illustrated by Natalie Babbitt (9–11). Farrar, 1987.
Simple language surprisingly used is Worth's way of showing small, everyday things to be important and valuable.

Yolen, Jane. *Animal Fare: Zoological Nonsense Poems,* illustrated by Janet Street (7–10). Harcourt, 1994.
With fresh wordplay that ranges from clever twists to wild wit, Yolen spoofs nonsense itself in these sixteen poems about animals of unknown parts, including the Anteloop, Mustank, Rhinocerworse, Hippopotanoose, Mockit Bird, Grizzly Bare, Blimpanzee, Giraft, Whysel, and Gazealous. The pictures are as skillfully goofy as the poems.

David Wiesner

8

Folklore for Children

Like poetry, a folktale catches fleeting feelings by the tail and holds them just long enough to enjoy them. The two sure ways to quiet a carload of kids are chanting poetry and telling a story. In the early years, all I had to do was say, "Boom, boom, we'll be there soon," which even two-and-a-half-year-old whiners thought was hysterically funny. For my own sake I quickly increased my repertoire so that when the kids picked up and repeated the chant, which they invariably did, I could at least hear a varied replay. If chants cheered them up and diverted them from whacking each other over the head, a folktale or fairy tale really cast a spell of quiet attention over the whole group, broken only by an occasional screech over my driving as I got caught up in the story myself.

There's something breathtakingly clever about that helpless Brer Rabbit fooling a tyrannical Bengal tiger into *begging* to have himself tied up to a tree. There's nothing like watching the little guy win, especially for a child. Such basic themes of the underdog—or underbunny, as the case may be—defeating the overlord reverberate through collection after collection of folktales from every people and place. To count the motifs of folklore is to count the heartbeat of the human race. Scholars have identified more than seven hundred *known* versions of "Cinderella," which probably leaves a good many unknown. These are truly for an all-age audience, stories told for centuries among mixed-generation groups of family and friends until carved down to the most memorable elements.

Folklorists started to write down these tales in the 1700s and 1800s, and over a period of centuries the printed tales continue to reflect changing artistic and social patterns, much as they did in the oral tradition. For ten years I studied the folklore, literature, art, psychological interpretations, and printed history of one story (*Beauty and the Beast: Visions and Revision of an Old Tale*) and then put together an anthology of folktale variants (*Beauties and Beasts*). I found that stories pass back and forth between oral and literary traditions, are told, written down, read, remembered, retold. "Beauty and the Beast" has appeared in poetry, drama, dance, film, and children's books illustrated by Walter Crane (1875), Edmund Dulac (1910), Margaret Tarrant (1920), Arthur Rackham (1933), Gustaf Tenggren (1942), and many others. Today's picture-book versions of the tale are legion, including art by Mercer Mayer, Warwick Hutton, and Winslow Pinney Pels. The story has also been turned into more than one novel for young readers, as mentioned in chapter 6, and has attracted movie makers from Jean Cocteau to Walt Disney.

Books go in and out of print, styles change, but the strong stories stay. In fact, they've been rejuvenated by the growth of children's literature. Now we have selections, collections, translations, and illustrations from every inhabited continent, from a multitude of traditions, in a variety of styles, and for every age group. Just go to the library and you'll rediscover old favorites from your own family traditions, unearth cultural icons you somehow missed, and encounter stories you never knew about, reveling in the narrative diversity the world has to offer.

Folktales have inspired the same kind of endless listening as poetry and the same kind of graphic recreation, from contemporary artists back to the earliest woodcuts for Gutenberg's first book of fables. They've been a part of children's literature from the very beginning, and their contribution continues to increase. Picture-book versions of single tales, which are discussed in chapter 4, are perhaps the best-known examples of folklore for children, but they're really just the start of a long line of possibility. No child ever needs to be without folklore.

Many of us are familiar with the French tales retold in the late seventeenth century by Charles Perrault—"Cinderella," "Sleeping Beauty," etc.—and their variants and companions, such as "Snow White and the Seven Dwarfs" and "Hansel and Gretel," that were collected by the Grimm brothers in the nineteenth century. Other longtime childhood favorites represent a range of nationalities. The "Three Billy Goats Gruff," for instance, is a Scandinavian legacy from folklorist P. C. Asbjørnsen's collection, as is "East of the Sun and West of the Moon." "Henny-Penny" and "Jack and the Beanstalk" are popular selections from Joseph Jacobs's *English Fairy Tales.* These sources remain strong and vigorous contributors to children's literature, but the genre also includes a whole world of other time-honed tales that will enrich young readers and listeners.

In the Americana collections are tall tales from the West, Jack tales from the Southeast, Native American tales from every tribal group. Amy Cohn's *From Sea to Shining Sea: A Treasury of American Folklore and Folk Songs* and Alvin Schwartz's *Cross Your Fingers, Spit in Your Hat* are great places to start, but there's a rainbow of choices waiting for you. John Bierhorst has published well-researched collections of both North and South American Indian mythology and folktales, including the entertaining *Doctor Coyote: A Native American Aesop's Fables* and a fascinating collection called *The Deetkatoo: Native American Stories about Little People.* Virginia Hamilton's words sing in *The People Could Fly: American Black Folktales* or *In the Beginning: Creation Stories from Around the World.*

Brer Rabbit makes an interesting folktale character on which to base comparison of different versions. Van Dyke Parks has adapted the stories for a musical album and theatrical production that eventually found its way back into the books *Jump! The Adventures of Brer Rabbit* and *Jump Again!: More Adventures of Brer Rabbit.* They're both readable (and tellable as well), with moderately colloquial texts that stay on the humorous side without straining ears unfamiliar with the dialect. The portrayals of these folk characters never get cutesy, either in words or graphics. The expression that artist Barry Moser gives to Brer Fox is truly shady; to Brer Wolf, downright spooky.

Of the several recent collections that have included Brer Rabbit stories, Julius Lester's series launched by *The Tales of Uncle Remus: The Adventures of Brer Rabbit* has proved the most complete, well documented, and best adapted for older readers. Although Lester's style is charged with contemporary wit, his interpretation of Brer Rabbit as a universal element of personality ("Whether we are black or white, slave or free, child or adult, Brer Rabbit is us") lends a fine-edged perspective to his narrative. Lester's four volumes represent an enormous storytelling accomplishment. The important structure, tone, and motifs have been respected: "Brer Alligator Learns about Trouble," for instance, even reflects the same pace and rhythm of "Why the Alligator's Back Is Rough" without the impediments of the Gullah dialect.

This is the work of a writer familiar with the methodology of folkloristic and historical research but also with the techniques of flavoring fiction. Lester himself makes wry narrative asides that punctuate but don't intrude on the stories the way the "Uncle Remus" framework does in Joel Chandler Harris's source tales. The animals' dialogue is spontaneously current—adhering, meanwhile, to the bantering tone of the older source and retaining some of the best lines or chants (the rhythmic repartee between Son Riley Rabbit, Riley, and Aunt Mammy-Bammy Big-Money or Biggedy Dicky Big-Bag in "Brer Rabbit's Luck" is a perfect example). Jerry Pinkney's illustrations—black-and-white drawings with occasional double-page spreads in full color—are well drafted, fresh, and funny.

Like most trickster tales, Brer Rabbit's antics are morally ambiguous and raise periodic controversy over whether children should be exposed to them. In her review of Lester's book in the *New York Times Book Review* (May 17, 1987), the novelist June Jordan called Brer Rabbit a "pathological hustler" and accused him of "premeditated violence, compulsive cruelty, exploitation of children, and regular opportunism," along with other "knavery." In his rebuttal, Lester quoted the scholar Karl Kerenyi: "Disorder belongs to the totality of life, and the spirit of disorder is the trickster. His function . . . is to add disorder to order and so make a whole, to render possible, within the fixed bounds of what is permitted, an experience of what is not permitted." Added Lester, "Yes, Brer Rabbit is 'a truly bad rabbit,' because the Trickster is in each of us. He is created in our image. Our task is to receive him and thereby uncover our humanity—if we dare."

Folklore has always been subject to cycles of suspicion from critics who question its value, from nineteenth-century moralists to twentieth-century feminists. There are, for example, a number of collections specifically designed to satisfy contemporary concerns about passive stereotypes of women in folklore: Rosemary Minard's *Womenfolk and Fairy Tales,* Ethel Phelps's *Tatterhood and Other Tales* or *The Maid of the North: Feminist Folk Tales from Around the World,* and Jack Zipes's *Don't Bet on the Prince: Contemporary Feminist Fairy Tales in North America and England.* Despite ongoing objections, however, children delight in folktales as they are continually recreated by new voices.

British folktales have a particularly strong voice in Alan Garner, whose masterful retellings appear in *Alan Garner's Book of British Fairy Tales.* His collection *A Bag of Moonshine* offers entertaining English and Welsh variants of some well-known tales. "The Three Gowks" follows the same pattern as "The Three Sillies"; "Harry-Cap and the Three Brothers" is a variant of "The Lad Who Went to the North Wind"; "Billy Bowker's Mowing Match" is similar to "How Bobtail Beat the Devil." "Hom Bridson" is a changeling tale, and "Belenay of the Lake" is a version of the legend that Susan Cooper adapted in her picture book *The Silver Cow.* The mood varies from humorous to eerie, but almost all the tales are terse, powerful, and rhythmically told, with dialect that is strong but generally accessible. Storytellers will recognize "Mr. Vinegar" and discover some new treasures, such as "The Grey Goat," full of enchanting suspense. The illustrations in color and black-and-white have a nineteenth-century air reminiscent of Arthur Rackham.

Kevin Crossley-Holland's *British Folk Tales: New Versions* is a rich collection, in both range and depth, of fifty-five British folktales adapted from widely varied sources that the author has cited in careful, if idiosyncratic, endnotes. While some of the titles sound familiar, the versions here may not seem so. The satisfyingly rhythmic "Frog Prince" is distinctly different from the Grimms' version. "King of the Cats" appears in monologue form, and "The Small-Tooth Dog," a variant of "Beauty and the Beast," has acquired a modern setting. The author is intimate with this lore, and his innovations render the tales all the more immediate. Crossley-Holland has a strong sense of selection and consistent respect for motif. His most vivid writing adheres closely to the basic shape of the tales. In many cases, as he himself says, "the best thing a reteller can do is 'translate' the dialect into modern English and keep well out of the way." The bookmaking is worthy of the text: handsome print on fine, creamy paper with discreetly miniature, skillful scratch-board drawings opening each chapter. In its revealing and revitalizing of the traditional, this book makes a long-lasting contribution to readers and storytellers alike.

Moving beyond the American and British traditions, you find a dizzying array of possibilities. Want to share some vivid ghost stories? You'll find compelling Chinese versions in Laurence Yep's *Rainbow People.* A youngster who displays a taste for the wise foolishness of *The Stupids* by Harry Allard will probably relish the traditional Jewish tales about the Fools of Chelm, most notably retold by the Nobel Prize–winning author Isaac Bashevis Singer. Harold Courlander's *Cow-Tail Switch and Other Stories of West Africa* is a deservedly enduring classic, and readers who find their appetites thus whetted may want to look up Nina Jaffe's *Voice for the People: The Life and Work of Harold Courlander,* an excellent juvenile biography of the folklorist. Classical myths are still sturdily represented by the D'Aulaires, but kids will also appreciate Marcia Williams's wisecracking comic-strip approach in *Greek Myths for Young Children.*

Ethnic origin isn't the only organizing principle of these collections. Fans of *The Little Mermaid* will enjoy Mary Pope Osborne's *Mermaid Tales from Around the World.* Paul Robert Walker's *Little Folk: Stories from Around the World* stretches, if you'll pardon the pun, from "Rumpelstiltskin" to the Japanese "One Inch Boy." Urban legend–telling kids may already know some of the stories in Alvin Schwartz's *Scary Stories to Tell in the Dark,* but they'll still enjoy using them to scare the bejeebers out of themselves and their friends. Judy Sierra's *Nursery Tales Around the World* is a terrific starter volume that covers the folkloric bases without slipping into the perfunctory, bringing to each story the same freshness a child will bring when hearing it for the first time.

With its inherent structural sturdiness, folklore has been particularly subject to games and creative rewriting. Jon Scieszka's parodic *Stinky Cheese Man and Other Fairly Stupid Tales* is one kind of now-familiar folktale twist, and the sophisticated literary reinterpretations of folktales are another. Sometimes these appear in collections: William Brooke's *Telling of the Tales,* Vivian Vande Velde's *Tales from the Brothers Grimm and the Sisters Weird,* and Priscilla Galloway's *Truly Grim Tales* offer sometimes insightful, sometimes funny, sometimes creepy new takes on old favorites, nudging folklore to the fore for teen readers who thought they'd outgrown it and reestablishing the connections between folklore and fantasy. Some authors, such as Adèle Geras and Donna Jo Napoli, take a full novel to explore a folkloric character. Geras's trilogy of *The Tower Room, Watching the Roses,* and *Pictures of the Night* brings Rapunzel, Sleeping Beauty, and Snow White into postwar Britain and makes them a trio of schoolgirls on the brink of adulthood. Napoli's *Prince of the Pond* is an enjoyably comic retelling, from the frog's point of view, of "The Frog Prince," but her most striking works are her lyrical revisionings of Rapunzel in *Zel* and Hansel and Gretel in *The Magic Circle.* Proof that the narrative powers of literature and folklore can inform one another, her books offer readers a chance to see the force that lies behind images sometimes dulled by familiarity.

Folktales are the epitome of ageless literature. Created, told, and retold to mixed groups of children and adults, they still wear well on every level. They are the bare bones of story. Each archetypal character represents a part of humanity, each action a part of life, each setting a part of existence. When the word "forest" appears, everyone understands it as a symbolic setting for losing one's way, for danger and confusion, for separation from security and those we love. Wolves, giants, kings, woodcutters, fools, beauties, all have distinctly defined roles. That's the secret of folktales' effective functioning in such a small space: they allow each person to imagine the kind of details that modern short stories and fiction must build into the narrative to be believable.

Whatever their style, the best storytellers respect a dynamic tale too much to dumb it down or cuten it up. Naming a hero's fearsome ursine foe Grumbly Bear, for instance, turns an adversary into a toy and deflates the story's tension as well as its dignity. This is an important point because verbal and visual imagery determine the quality of a book. The telling of the tale can either deaden or liven it. In *The Bronze Cauldron: Myths and Legends of the World,* Geraldine McCaughrean catches the music of words and the resonance of their meaning, calling a dragon "green as the mold that grows on graves." She uses simple phrases, but she uses them rhythmically, for complex effects—including suspense: "Three paces from the door, three paces from the window, three paces from where Boy Gwion slept on the floor, stood the witch's bronze cauldron on three bronze legs."

It's important to read a bit from any folklore—aloud, if possible—before you decide to take it home and live with it. A folktale or fairy tale does not have to be watered down for children, either in language or in content. Instead, it needs to be projected with its true power, to be told or read aloud, perhaps graced with some strong illustration, but never cheated of its strength.

Myths, fairy tales, and folktales are every child's rich heritage. They are too deep for a cheap surface treatment. In the right form they'll reach you just as surely as they reach your child because, like poetry, they say so much in so few words that they are easy to carry in the mind. And whether you're old or young, it's important to visit places, at least occasionally, where real terrors lurk but true hearts live happily ever after.

Folklore for Children

Collections of folk and fairy tales have proliferated in the 1990s. The sampling here doesn't include picture-book editions of single tales (those are at the ends of chapters 2 and 3) or even very many collections of tales from one or another country. Instead, I emphasize collections that include stories representing various cultures, classic fairy tales, mythologies, or stories based in the multicultural American tradition with which U.S. children are most familiar. I also take special care to include collections centered on active female characters in order to counteract the typically stereotyped selections that often characterize earlier popular collections.

Bierhorst, John. *Doctor Coyote: A Native American Aesop's Fables* (7–9). Simon, 1987.
Coyote stars in an enticing production that combines Wendy Watson's amusing full-color, current-day cartoon art with twenty fables reworked by Aztec Indians from a Spanish edition of Aesop and reworded again by Bierhorst from a 1628 manuscript. *The Dancing Fox: Arctic Folktales* and *The Deetkatoo: Native American Stories about Little People* are also brilliant examples of folklore adapted with integrity into children's books.

Brooke, William. *A Telling of the Tales: Five Stories,* illustrated by Richard Egielski (9–11). Harper, 1990.
John Henry and Paul Bunyan rub shoulders with fairy tale princes in these stories that use a light touch to reexamine the male roles in folklore.

Cohn, Amy. *From Sea to Shining Sea: A Treasury of American Folklore and Folk Songs* (all ages). Scholastic, 1993.
One of the fullest, richest, and most lavishly illustrated compendia of folklore available for children, this book includes stories and songs generated by various ethnic groups and historical experiences, from Native American creation myths to immigration, the Revolution, Appalachian settlement, seafaring, slavery, building railroads, pioneering, and beyond. There's also a rich array of genres, including trickster tales, nonsense stories, animal stories, tall tales, baseball lore, and ghost stories.

Cole, Joanna. *Best-Loved Folktales of the World* (5 and up). Doubleday, 1982.
Although this prime selection of two hundred tales is not illustrated, it will offer

hours of rich reading aloud, including stories from Western Europe, the British Isles, Scandinavia and Northern Europe, Eastern Europe, the Middle East, the Pacific, Africa, North America, the Caribbean and West Indies, and Central and South America.

Colum, Padraic. *A Treasury of Irish Folklore* (9 and up). 2d ed. Crown, 1967.
A gifted storyteller enriches these adaptations with his own lyrical style, as he did for Greek and Norse myths in *The Golden Fleece* and *Nordic Gods and Heroes.*

Courlander, Harold, and George Herzog. *The Cow-Tail Switch and Other Stories of West Africa,* illustrated by Madye Lee Chastain (8–11). Henry Holt, 1947.
A dynamic folklorist who collected tales from Native Americans, Haitians, and Africans, among others, Courlander focused on honoring cultures as well as adapting their lore in lively collections such as this one, which was a Newbery Honor Book.

Crossley-Holland, Kevin. *British Folk Tales: New Versions* (9 and up). Orchard, 1987.
In both range and depth, this is a rich collection of fifty-five British folktales adapted from widely varied sources cited in careful endnotes.

Curry, Jane Louise. *Back in the Beforetime: Tales of the California Indians,* illustrated by James Watts (9–12). McElderry, 1987.
Drawing from the lore of various California Indian tribes, Curry arranges twenty-two stories into a readable cycle of creation myths featuring the trickster Coyote.

D'Aulaire, Ingri and Parin. *D'Aulaire's Norse Gods and Giants* (9–12). Doubleday, 1967.
Along with *D'Aulaires' Book of Greek Myths,* this is a perennial favorite because of the accessible text and robust illustrations.

Evslin, Bernard. *Greeks Bearing Gifts: The Epics of Achilles and Ulysses,* illustrated by William Hunter (12 and up). Scholastic, 1985.
This vivid account of the Trojan War and Odysseus's subsequent wanderings is typical of Evslin's tautly ironic style, which has graced retellings from *The Green Hero: Early Adventures of Finn McCool* to *Jason and the Argonauts.*

Galloway, Priscilla. *Truly Grim Tales* (12–15). Delacorte, 1995.
Galloway fills out each of these eight stories from somebody else's point of view: that of the giant's wife in "Jack and the Beanstalk," of Rapunzel's original parents, of Cinderella's prince—whose interest in Cinderella springs from his foot fetish.

Garner, Alan. *Alan Garner's Book of British Fairy Tales,* illustrated by Derek Collard (9 and up). Delacorte, 1985.
Garner's adaptations of twenty-one British tales are fluent in the best sense of the oral tradition, rich and varied in style, as effective for reading alone as they are for reading aloud.

Geras, Adèle. *The Tower Room* (12–18). Harcourt, 1992.
In this updated look at the Rapunzel story, Megan's peaceful life at a girls' boarding school gets complicated when, unbeknownst to her guardian, Megan begins an affair with a young man who clambers up the scaffolding to her window. Geras

continues with the story of Megan's friend Alice (Sleeping Beauty) in *Watching the Roses* and Bella (Snow White) in *Pictures of the Night.*

Grimm, Jakob, and Wilhelm Grimm. *Fairy Tales* (5 and up). Various editions.

The German folk and fairy tales collected by these two nineteenth-century scholars and first published in 1812 have become a touchstone of Western culture.

Hamilton, Virginia. *The People Could Fly: American Black Folktales,* illustrated by Leo and Diane Dillon (9 and up). Knopf, 1985.

Brer Rabbit, John de Conquer, and legendary heroes spring to life in Hamilton's cadenced retellings of African-American slave tales, ghost stories, and other lore. *Many Thousand Gone* focuses on stories of slavery and *Her Stories* on African-American women, while Hamilton's many other collections include creation myths and tricksters of the world.

Jaffe, Nina. *A Voice for the People: The Life and Work of Harold Courlander* (12–18). Henry Holt, 1995.

Primary-source research enriches this readable biography of the pioneering folklorist.

Lester, Julius. *The Tales of Uncle Remus: The Adventures of Brer Rabbit,* illustrated by Jerry Pinkney (10 and up). Dial, 1987.

This book and its several successors (*More Tales of Uncle Remus,* etc.) form a wry narrative that includes all the Brer Rabbit stories of Joel Chandler Harris in cleverly updated language.

Levine, Gail Carson. *Ella Enchanted* (10–13). HarperCollins, 1997.

In this novel-length Cinderella story, Ella is a sensible adolescent burdened by a well-meaning fairy's gift of obedience.

Lyons, Mary E. *Raw Head, Bloody Bones: African-American Tales of the Supernatural* (10–14). Scribner's, 1991.

Not for the faint of heart, these fifteen stories include haunting characters such as the Hag, Plat-eye, the Duppy Ghost, the Big Worm, the Night Doctor, and Dead Aaron.

McCaughrean, Geraldine. *The Bronze Cauldron: Myths and Legends of the World,* illustrated by Bee Willey (9–11). McElderry, 1998.

In a series with *The Golden Hoard* and *The Silver Treasure,* this culturally wide-ranging collection employs a style that lends itself to reading aloud.

Minard, Rosemary. *Womenfolk and Fairy Tales,* illustrated by Suzanna Klein (9–11). Houghton, 1975.

Hale and hearty heroines take center stage in this collection of folktales, the first—and still one of the best—to be built on a theme of active women characters.

Napoli, Donna Jo. *The Magic Circle* (12–17). Dutton, 1993.

In this witch's-eye view of "Hansel and Gretel," a midwife and healer develops magical powers that eventually lead to the accusation of witchcraft, which she then espouses in a pact for power to save her daughter. For lighter fare by the same author, try *The Prince of the Pond,* a funny new take on "The Frog Prince."

Norman, Howard. *The Girl Who Dreamed Only Geese and Other Tales of the Far North,* illustrated by Leo and Diane Dillon (9–12). Gulliver/Harcourt, 1997.

Ten dramatic stories, styled with understated humor, reflect Inuit lore as adapted by a collector who knows and respects the tellers' traditions.

Normandin, Christine, ed. *Echoes of the Elders: The Stories and Paintings of Chief Lelooska* (9–11). Callaway/DK Ink, 1997.

A Cherokee adopted into the Kwakiutl tribe, Chief Lelooska retold and illustrated these five haunting Northwest Coast Indian tales before his death in 1996. They've translated well into print, with large traditional figures painted in flat, unlined color patterns against lots of white space.

Opie, Peter, and Iona Opie. *The Classic Fairy Tales* (9 and up). Oxford, 1992.

While this is primarily a book for adult students of folk literature, it contains twenty-four familiar fairy tales that will intrigue young readers as well. The introduction, notes, and illustrations by great artists of the past make the book one to cherish.

Oryx Multicultural Folktale Series (9–12). Oryx Press, 1992, 1993.

The volumes in this series offer readers a collection of folk variants, with commentary, on each of four tale types: *Beauties and Beasts* (Betsy Hearne); *Cinderella* (Judy Sierra); *A Knock at the Door* (George Shannon); and *Tom Thumb* (Margaret MacDonald).

Osborne, Mary Pope. *Mermaid Tales from Around the World,* illustrated by Troy Howell (9–11). Scholastic, 1993.

Enhanced by intriguingly stylized paintings, these stories demonstrate the global allure of the mermaid myth.

Perrault, Charles. *Fairy Tales* (5 and up). Various editions.

Like the Grimms' tales, Perrault's collection of French fairy tales published in 1797 is a story marker for Western culture.

Phelps, Ethel. *The Maid of the North: Feminist Folktales from Around the World,* illustrated by Lloyd Bloom (9–11). Holt, Rinehart and Winston, 1981.

An international collection adds many lesser-known tales to those found in other feminist collections and, in addition, offers some of the most powerful and finely textured drawings to be found in any of them.

Schwartz, Alvin. *Scary Stories to Tell in the Dark,* illustrated by Stephen Gammell (9–12). Harper, 1986.

This book—along with its successors *More Scary Stories* and *Scary Stories 3* and other collections such as *Fat Man in a Fur Coat; Cross Your Fingers, Spit in Your Hat;* and *There Is a Carrot in My Ear and Other Noodle Tales*—is typical of Schwartz's retellings, which have a distinctive flavor of their own without losing touch with folklore.

Scieszka, John. *The Stinky Cheese Man and Other Fairly Stupid Tales,* illustrated by Lane Smith (7–13). Viking, 1992.

The table of contents falls on Chicken Licken's head, the really ugly duckling grows up to be a really ugly duck, and Little Red Running Shorts disappears from her own story in this definitive—and hilarious—postmodern parody of folklore.

Shannon, George. *More Stories to Solve: Fifteen Folktales from Around the World,* illustrated by Peter Sís (7–9). Greenwillow, 1991.

Like its predecessor, *Stories to Solve* (1985), this collection combines the appeal of short, easy-to-read folktales with a riddling quality that turns the stories into solve-it-yourself mysteries.

Sierra, Judy. *Nursery Tales Around the World,* illustrated by Stefano Vitale (3–7). Clarion, 1996.

Featuring strong rhythms and repetition that invite audience participation, this collection of folktales does double duty as a nursery story book for lap-sharing and a sourcebook for parents and professionals. Old favorites are balanced with lesser-known variants on a theme, such as Runaway Cookies or Fooling the Big Bad Wolf, all illustrated with handsome oil-on-wood paintings.

Singer, Isaac Bashevis. *The Fools of Chelm and Their History,* illustrated by Uri Shulevitz (9–11). Farrar, 1973.

Vigorous and funny illustrations enhance the earthy humor and exaggeration of these classic noodlehead tales.

Vande Velde, Vivian. *Tales from the Brothers Grimm and the Sisters Weird* (9–12). Harcourt, 1995.

Short stories lightened with poems offer accessible and provocative slants on some old folktales.

Walker, Robert Paul. *Little Folk: Stories from Around the World,* illustrated by James Bernardin (5–8). Harcourt, 1997.

Ranging in origin from South Africa to the Hawaiian Islands to Europe, these eight tales describe the adventures of leprechauns, nisse, and other legendary petite people.

Williams, Marcia. *Greek Myths for Young Children* (7–11). Candlewick, 1992.

Oversized pages feature zany comic-strip panels that memorably recount the stories of Pandora's box, Orpheus and Eurydice, the twelve labors of Heracles, and others.

Yep, Laurence. *The Rainbow People* (10 and up). Harper, 1989.

Divided into sections entitled "Tricksters," "Fools," "Virtues and Vices," "In Chinese America," and "Love," these twenty richly varied stories are adapted from a 1930s Work Projects Administration oral narrative project that drew on Chinese-American lore.

Yolen, Jane. *Favorite Folktales from Around the World* (9 and up). Pantheon, 1986.

Yolen's wide-ranging, comprehensive collection will please children reading on their own or adults looking for a storytelling source.

Bruce Macmillan

9

Factual Books for Children

I was pushing a stroller along once when suddenly a series of excited noises came out of it. They sounded like "Oh Dee Dee Dee Dee Dee Dee Dee!" A pudgy finger shot out from under the fringed awning and waved frantically toward the sky. All I could see was an airplane.

That's the big difference between the first airplane and the thousandth: that first one always brings a rush of excitement. It's refreshing to be in the company of someone who wonders how that airplane stays up there—or where the thunder and lightning come from and where they go. It restores your sense of balance in varying degrees, depending on how jaded your viewpoint has become and how fresh the child's is.

Because there's so much that children don't know, facts are as miraculous to them as fiction. Everyone knows about the question-and-answer stage: "Where do I come from? What makes the stars white? Why do dogs pee on trees?" Many adults are stumped by such queries. Those who take the time to look things up in the encylopedia—best done with your child—know they'll never get to the end of the cross-examination. As bothersome as this stage may seem, it's the sign of an explosively growing mind. In the matter of education, a child's own curiosity is the greatest tool. It starts long before school does and is a driving force in growing up. And it can be a joy to jaded adults.

Perhaps my favorite sign, next to Big Tomato and the park jogging route graffiti, is the one over the entrance to the Smithsonian Institution: "Knowledge begins in wonder." It does indeed. Educational systems that dampen wonder are taking a chance with passing on knowledge. The habit of discovering things independently can start with the habit of looking through books at a preschool age. Nonfiction for children has mushroomed in quantity and quality to titles on every conceivable subject, from words to World War II. Whatever the child of your choice is interested in, there's bound to be at least one book on the subject. Finding it will probably require a trip to the local public or school library. Some bookstores stock informational books for children, but the range may be limited and you might have to order what you want through the store or over the Internet.

Good juvenile nonfiction serves up information straight from the hip, without patronizing remarks to try to sweeten natural phenomena that are dynamic to begin with. The format will be clean, the illustrations both clear and engaging. The information will be current, well organized, accurate, lucid, and presented with enthusiasm and cited sources of authority. If this sounds familiar, it's because this is exactly the same set of criteria you apply to an adult book of information.

The extra dash of skill required for children's fiction goes for children's nonfiction too: it must be carved down to basics without distortion or oversimplification. The word "stomach," for instance, should never be substituted for the accurate term "womb" in a discussion of reproduction, because to do so would generate multiple misconceptions. Children should learn the right word rather than vaguely associate pregnancy with eating. On the other hand, preschoolers probably don't yet need to know the complications of breech birth or multiple conception. For very young children, there's no better place to start than Joanna Cole's gentle photographic picture book *How You Were Born,* with its clear progression of concepts and color photographs clarifying the basic textual explanations. This is a book that personalizes the facts and makes sure to include some of the emotional as well as the physical aspects of birth.

Too many instructive books for children have generically diagrammed sex and reproduction—or worse, romanticized those subjects. But that's not the case in *It's Perfectly Normal: A Book about Changing Bodies, Growing Up, Sex, and Sexual Health,* where the author, Robie H. Harris, and the illustrator, Michael Emberley, manage to be uncommonly honest without losing their senses of humor. Harris's text—for an older reader than *How You Were Born*—is informal, wide-ranging, and candid; Emberley's pictures are all that and funny too. No fact or image is too embarrassing for them to take on. If you doubt me, just turn to page 23 of *It's Perfectly Normal* and check out the girl looking upside down into a mirror to locate her anus, vagina, and urethra—all conspicuously apparent to the reader. Other pages discuss and portray different-size penises, different possibilities for birth control and safe sex, and different ways a baby can be born.

The pictures show an array of anatomical shapes, ethnic variations, and sexual persuasions. The design is a marvel of coordinated information and illustration. This is cartooning at its best: witty, expressive, and accurately reflective of human antics. Perhaps the closest relative to the bird-and-bee duo who comment throughout the book is the mammoth who chats to the reader in David Macaulay's handbook *The Way Things Work*. In fact, *It's Perfectly Normal* is a kind of human companion to Macaulay's marvel of mechanical explanation.

One of the advantages of *It's Perfectly Normal* is that the cartoon illustrations (there's an example at the beginning of chapter 10, on controversial children's books) extend its appeal to readers in a remarkably broad age range. A younger child can enjoy the art while a parent paraphrases an introduction to the facts of life. An independent reader in the lower grades can seek definitions of both familiar and less-familiar terms in privacy. Preadolescents can test their knowledge against what's so clearly demonstrated here. And adolescents can give a superior smirk while secretly learning what they most need to know about survival in a world threatened by sexually transmitted diseases.

It's important not to be coy or evasive about facts. We don't realize how much information children lack and how literally they take things. A young child logically concludes that coffee cake tastes like coffee or that a nonstop breakfast flight means you eat breakfast nonstop from departure to arrival ("You mean I have to eat breakfast from 9 to 11?" gasped an eight-year-old after studying her ticket). What is this child supposed to make of the statement that Daddy plants a seed in Mommy? Or, moving from biology to history, that Abraham Lincoln was killed while sitting in a box? Or of the account of a slave's childhood that chirps, "For a boy who loved the outdoors as much as Holt did, Plum Ridge was a great place to be"?

These statements have all appeared in juvenile science books or biographies, along with misleading illustrations. One introduction to the human body shows a diagram of huge black sperm without any caption or indication of the actual microscopic size. No wonder kids grow up with fuzzy ideas. Children browsing through a description of Native American medicine may read that "Native Americans preferred to be partially exposed rather than fully clothed, inviting the possibility of parasites and disease," but they'll have a hard time figuring out which of the two possible yet opposite meanings the sentence intends.

Fictionalizing facts is another offender in books of information. Earl the Squirrel's marriage to Mrs. Squirrel, pictured with wedding ring, is not the best introduction to animal habits. Animals that think and feel like people are all right in fantasy, but they violate the truth of science, which is exciting in its own right. So are other truths of nonfiction. Stilted informational dialogue such as "Wow! It's the plumed serpent, Quetzalcóatl" doesn't make an introduction to Mexico livelier but instead suggests the author doesn't trust the subject to be interesting enough on its own. Nor, for that matter, does anyone need recipes that forget to tell youngsters to cook the chicken before cutting it up and putting it in the salad. Nor pictures of a prehistoric mammal with blood spilling luridly from its fangs as it hauls away a cave woman. The natural and manmade world is an infinitely exciting place without being artificially and dishonestly spiced up, covered up, or served up.

It doesn't matter how worthy or meaningful the subject is if nobody can make it through the book. If a text raises questions in your own mind with doubtful statements ("Children who go to museums and read dinosaur books love dinosaurs. But most scientists don't . . ."); if it makes you jump back and forth without getting things quite straightened out; if its cloudy explanations force you back again and again to reread; if it doesn't cite sources or cites statistics that are outdated; if the author has written books about anything and everything rather than focusing on a particular field of interest; if the author skims the surface of fact without delving into what it means; if the information is dumped on the reader in a dull or jumbled heap—well, in each case you have a very good reason to question this as a valid and valuable book for children, whether you're an expert in the given subject or have never heard of it. Those are a lot of "ifs," but the material included in and left out of a book, the skill of presentation, the writing, and the format are all as important as the information itself.

Not that long ago American children learned American history that included little or no mention of African Americans' hard-fought rise in our society from enslaved possessions to free and influential citizens. Before many textbooks began to make tentative revisions by including black leaders and their contributions, Julius Lester wrote *To Be a Slave.* It shares with Milton Meltzer's *Never to Forget: The Jews of the Holocaust* a historical honesty grounded in primary sources and carefully researched facts, all presented from the point of view of an objective but deeply involved writer. Both authors have brought facts to life in the shape of people, to be introduced as "living" information. Both write to be read and experienced, not just to be mentally stuffed away in a file of factual feedback.

Not only do children's and young adult books treat history with new respect, they also offer a range of nuance in treatment and scope. Where Meltzer's book on the Holocaust is strongest on quoting eyewitnesses, for instance, Barbara Rogasky's *Smoke and Ashes: The Story of the Holocaust* is intensely focused on details that include the average caloric content for Jewish food rations in wartime ghettos and realistic reporting on concentration camps, with historical photographs that document the horror more graphically than words can. For young readers who were introduced to the Holocaust in Anne Frank's *Diary of a Young Girl,* Ruud van der Rol and Rian Verhoeven's *Anne Frank: Beyond the Diary* will provide mesmerizing concrete background for the very personal diary entries.

Russell Freedman's nonfiction is distinguished for the balance of background and detail with which he presents his historical subjects. *Indian Chiefs* includes six biographical essays on Native American leaders' resistance to whites who took over their land and lives. The story is a tragic one, and Freedman has written a moving account. Yet he also shows glimpses of the humor with which the victims sometimes regarded the enemy. The Nez Perce, for instance, while fleeing from the army in 1877, "paced themselves to stay two days ahead of Howard. They began to call him 'General Day-After-Tomorrow.'" The perspective in the first and last chapters, framed by Sitting Bull's inauguration as Sioux chief in the 1860s and his murder two weeks before the Wounded Knee Massacre in 1890, gives readers a general context from which the individual stories will emerge to make an unforgettable impression. The writing, selection of historical photographs, bookmaking, and subject are a winning combination that is typical of Freedman's other work as well. *Children of the Wild West, Buffalo Hunt,* and *The Life and Death of Crazy Horse* are notable in examining the other side, underside, and inside of some frontier myths. *Lincoln: A Photobiography* won the Newbery Medal in 1988 for its clarity and selective compression of enormous background research. The first nonfiction book to be so honored since *The Story of Mankind* in 1922, *Lincoln* marks a trend of higher quality in factual books for children and of critics' recognizing it.

History for youth is a particularly rich genre. Albert Marrin, a professor of history, brings to his books a commitment to genuine research and a gift for using original sources to breathe new life into past events and make them understandable; his *Unconditional Surrender: U. S. Grant and the Civil War* and *Virginia's General: Robert E. Lee and the Civil War* are as clear and evocative as Ken Burns's PBS documentary *The Civil War.* Marrin's *Cowboys, Indians, and Gunfighters: The Story of the Cattle Kingdom* conveys both the specific experience and the larger historical changes of life on the frontier without ever becoming dry or textbookish. Vivid writing gives these books a sense of immediacy. In *The Chicago Fire,* Jim Murphy makes readers hear the crackle of flames, but he also explains the process of history-making itself. For a you-are-there feeling from somebody who *was* there, read Willborn Hampton's *Kennedy Assassinated!: The World Mourns: A Reporter's Story,* in which the author tells of that fateful day in Dallas when he was torn between being a cub reporter at a defining moment in history and a grief-stricken witness to a national tragedy.

Another manifestation of this trend toward increasingly higher quality has been a plethora of excellent picture-book biographies for young children. David Adler's *Lou Gehrig: The Luckiest Man,* Demi's *Chingis Khan,* Diane Stanley's *Leonardo da Vinci,* and Jonah Winter's *Diego* are striking examples. Autobiographies and memoirs are another intriguing genre, which has developed almost as explosively in literature for youth as it has in adult literature. Betsy Byars's *Moon and I,* Gary Paulsen's *My Life in Dog Years,* R. L. Stine's *It Came from Ohio!: My Life as a Writer,* and Paul Zindel's *Pigman and Me* are as rewarding as any of the fiction these authors have written.

Current social issues close at hand get full attention in works such as *Dark Harvest: Migrant Farmworkers in America,* one of a series of books by Brent Ashabranner and the photographer Paul Conklin on immigrants and ethnic minorities in the United States. Susan Kuklin's *Irrepressible Spirit* contains the voices of human rights activists worldwide and allows them to explain in their own words what they do and why. Janet Bode balances first-person reports with factual information about phenomena of direct relevance for many teens in books such as *Trust and Betrayal: Real Life Stories of Friends and Enemies.*

Other writers turn their attention to earlier periods in far-flung places, from Patricia Lauber's *Tales Mummies Tell* to Leonard Everett Fisher's *Great Wall of China* and its companion volumes on Toltec pyramids and the Tower of London. David Getz's *Frozen Man* gives an accessible and surprisingly suspenseful account of the forensic analysis of Ötzi, the Bronze Age body found in the Alps.

One of the advantages of reading children's books is being able to impress (if not influence) friends and colleagues with surprising dollops of information. Did you know, for example, that the average life-span of the short-statured ancient Egyptians was about forty years but that King Ramses lived to the age of ninety and was six feet tall? Lila Perl's *Mummies, Tombs, and Treasure: Secrets of Ancient Egypt* explains how X-ray examinations of bone development have documented such findings.

Sound research doesn't necessarily make for heavy reading. Sometimes there's nothing funnier than actual facts. History abounds with the humor that is inevitable wherever human beings are involved. Jean Fritz's series on American leaders such as George Washington, Paul Revere, and John Hancock show their foibles as well as their strengths, a refreshing balance after the adulatory biographies that used to lead children (many of whom maintained such illusions into adulthood) to believe that political figures were the image of perfection. How can you resist a biography of Paul Revere that begins:

> In 1735 there were in Boston 42 streets, 36 lanes, 22 alleys, 1,000 brick houses, 2,000 wooden houses, 12 churches, 4 schools, 418 horses (at last count), and so many dogs that a law was passed prohibiting people from having dogs that were more than 10 inches high. But it was difficult to keep dogs from growing more than 10 inches, and few people cared to part with their 11-and 12-inch dogs, so they paid little attention to the law. In any case, there were too many dogs to count.

Now that's a specific setting for you!

A lively book can make kids think about our most common activities. James Solheim's *It's Disgusting—and We Ate It!: True Food Facts from Around the World—and Throughout History!* provides a cheerfully eclectic look at foods of all cultures, including our own, that are better to eat than to think about. James Giblin is similarly enlightening about dining history in *From Hand to Mouth; or, How We Invented Knives, Forks, Spoons, and Chopsticks and the Table Manners to Go with Them.* The children whose manners you deem less than perfect might be interested in Erasmus's recommendations in 1530, which Giblin quotes alongside an etching by Albrecht Dürer. Perhaps next time your offspring's chin droops dangerously near the mashed potatoes, you'll want to read from Giblin's book for the family's enrichment:

> Take care to cut and clean your fingernails before dining. Otherwise dirt from under the nails may get in the food.
>
> Don't be the first to reach into the pot; only wolves and gluttons do that. And don't put your whole hand into it—use only three fingers at most.

> Take the first piece of meat or fish that you touch, and don't poke around in the pot for a bigger one.
>
> Don't pick your nose while eating and then reach for more food.
>
> Don't throw bones you have chewed back in the pot. Put them on the table or toss them on the floor.
>
> Don't clean your teeth with your knife.
>
> If your fingers become greasy, it is not polite to lick them or wipe them on your coat. Bring a cloth along for this purpose if your host does not provide one. Or else wipe them on the tablecloth.

Maybe you already knew those rules but just didn't have a copy of Erasmus's *On Civility in Children* at hand for ready reference. At any rate, Giblin, who has written on chimney sweeps, scarecrows, skyscrapers, Santa Claus, and other intriguing topics, has already done your work for you in assimilating a lot of history and summarizing it in an interesting way.

If medieval manners don't grab your child's immediate attention, try Lasker's *Tournament of Knights,* which highlights another social ritual of the Middle Ages, and Aliki's lavishly illustrated *Medieval Feast,* which features yet another. Of course, there's also Macaulay's *Castle* . . . Obviously, one book leads to the next, and before you know it, you and your children will have read your way through a whole era of history.

Science is just as well represented in children's books as the social sciences. An amazing number of children are motivated to do scientific research by a fascination for dinosaurs, and the juvenile publishing world has responded with gusto. Aliki's *Dinosaur Bones* and *Dinosaurs Are Different* make good introductions for beginning readers, and that's only the start. *The New Illustrated Dinosaur Dictionary* by Helen Sattler tells a lot more, and a browse through the shelves will reap heaps of books on dinosaurs—including poetry and fiction as well as fact—that you can carry home.

For any subject, it's the creativity of treatment that counts. Laurence Pringle is known for his holistic approach in books such as *The Animal Rights Controversy* and *Coral Reefs: Earth's Undersea Treasures.* His environmental sensitivity has set a standard that we see reflected in books such as Molly McLaughlin's *Earthworms, Dirt, and Rotten Leaves: An Exploration of Ecology,* which emphasizes natural cycles as interconnected rather than isolated phenomena. For a closer look at these cycles, there's Bianca Lavies's *Compost Critters,* which not only explains the natural organisms at work in the compost pile but also uses sharp photographs to give an up-close and personal look at some astonishingly beautiful rot and slime. Even mundane subjects get more sensitive treatment these days, as in Charlotte Wilcox's book

Trash, which makes readers think carefully about recycling their garbage. Another winner is Walter Wick's *Drop of Water,* with its lucid text and mesmerizing photographs that demonstrate both the science and beauty of their watery subject.

The science lessons don't have to be any heavier going than the history lessons. *The Magic School Bus inside the Earth* by Joanna Cole is part of a series of popular hits combining classroom and comic-book humor with a busload of information. Ms. Frizzle's class even takes a field trip inside the human body—without getting cutesy about it. Preschoolers can start mathematics with David Schwartz's effervescent *How Much Is a Million?* Seven whole pages are dedicated to rows of tiny stars with a balloon-load of children floating through them ("If this book had a million tiny stars, they would fill seventy pages. Climb aboard!").

In presenting information graphically, children's science books have become a showcase for photography as well as illustration. Do you suddenly need to find out everything there is to know about raising baby hamsters ("Hey, Mom, didn't we get two females?") Consult *Pet Hamsters* by Jerome Wexler, who's as talented with his camera as he is with shaping facts into an enthusiastic text complete with personal anecdotes. If you think rodents are repulsive but find yourself hosting a multitude because your child's Scout or 4-H project suddenly began to multiply, Wexler's color photos and personal tone may make you a hamster devotee. If nothing else, the book will inspire your child to take full responsibility for hamster care.

Beyond the level of administering a home zoo, Wexler brings you a stunning book of *Everyday Mysteries* that doubles as a guessing game. Closeups of various objects not only surprise you when you find out what they are but also suggest a closer way of looking at the ordinary world. His photographs for Millicent Selsam's books on plants will turn your next walk into an exploration of nature. Their *Maple Tree* marked the first time I ever really understood plant reproduction (even though I had memorized the descriptions offered in the same biology course that included the dead frogs I spoke of earlier), and their book *Cotton* shows the beauty as well as the efficiency of a useful plant.

Seymour Simon is a first-rate science writer who also uses photographs to illustrate his books. If you ever need to comfort a terrified child with the facts of thunder and lightning, you won't find a better book than Simon's *Storms.* Following the format of his stellar series on the sun, stars, and planets, Simon here taps a topic with emotional significance for children who haven't outgrown their early fears. The information itself is inherently dramatic, and the book heightens the drama with bold color photos of cumulonimbus clouds (including a diagram to show air movements), storm cells, squall lines, hailstorms, gust fronts, lightning play, tornadoes, and hurricanes. The display is awesome, and the text respects it. Explanations are clear but never condescending, the science of radar, satellite, and computer tracking as astounding as the ancient theory of Thor's chariot striking clouds. Children seeking material for reports will find the real power of facts in *Storms.*

Natural history is also a beneficiary of some terrific photography. The aforementioned Bianca Lavies, a dauntless provider of amazing images, takes readers into a world thickly laced with elegant green snakes in *A Gathering of Garter Snakes.* Herpetophiles will also want to slither over to Mary Ling and Mary Atkinson's *Snake Book,* whose oversized double-page spreads, literally wall-to-wall snake, reveal the gleaming scales and intricate patterns in a way that real life seldom does. Those who prefer their animals less snaky will appreciate Bruce McMillan's *Nights of the Pufflings,* which details the unusual but true story of Icelandic children's annual rescue and release to the sea of baby puffins that have gone astray. McMillan's photography gives the puffins as much character as the children.

Nonfiction can be bibliotherapeutic as well as informative and entertaining. Mister Rogers gives kids a preview of scary experiences so their fears can be defused by reassuring discussions beforehand. His *Going to the Hospital* should be a prerequisite for preschoolers, just as *The Hospital Book* by James Howe will prepare older kids in case of an emergency or even a routine visit. Photographs of instruments and procedures offer a chance for questions. Just voicing the apprehension helps to alleviate it, and clear explanations can further ease fears. Bibliotherapy is a complex, even controversial process, but where the adult connection is sensitive and where books are considered friends, we know it sometimes works.

Whether children suffer from major problems or not, they all suffer occasionally from having nothing to do. Did I say *they* suffer? Their families are the real victims. The popular hobby book answers that old familiar whine, "I'm bored!" Steven Caney's *Kids' America* is a handy kind of answer. It will consume hours of attention, of making, doing, playing, and finding out. You can either grab it and give it to the whiner for some peace and quiet or join in the fun yourself. It's the ultimately practical craft–whole earth catalog for all ages.

Over the years we've been blessed with specialized titles on everything from carving pumpkins to cutting out puppets. Want to spend an aerodynamically experimental and very entertaining afternoon with your youngster? Have a look at Florence Temko's *Planes and Other Flying Things,* which provides sound instructions and clear step-by-step illustrations for nearly two dozen paper aircraft. As long as you've got the paper out, what about dipping into Joan Irvine's *How to Make Holiday Pop-Ups,* which offers easy-to-follow directions, achievable results, and projects suited to celebrations from all over the world? Adults who find themselves secretly drawn toward the model plane, train, and car counters should take note: the juvenile craft-book shelves are a hobbyist's field day. Children have the good sense not to be embarrassed by such interests. Take advantage of the situation and exploit it for your own sake. Two of my middle-aged friends spend their weekends on their knees, running model trains—and they don't even have children. But they do have the latest children's books on model trains.

If you get hold of the right book, you may even learn how to beat your kid at chess. In games, art, crafts, and cooking, children's books can be a real boon. Does your heart sink when you learn that not only are you supposed to produce your child's class play costume but your child begged to be a pterodactyl? Go to the library. If there's not a children's book on how to make pterodactyl costumes (there wasn't when I looked, but there may be one by now) at least there will be books with clear illustrations of pterodactyls. Or have a look at Angela Wilkes's *Dazzling Disguises and Clever Costumes,* which offers ingenious tips on creating crazy costumes that will turn out okay in spite of the most uncoordinated pair of hands.

Before I got my hands on a good basic juvenile (i.e., clear and simple) introduction to knitting, my practice sweaters looked like they might fit a boa constrictor. Whatever your craft problem, it can be solved by the kind of illustrated, step-by-step approach used in a well-planned children's book. You can pick up a new skill yourself at the same time your child is learning how to do it. Making mistakes together is always more fun than making them alone.

Whatever the situation, books help you meet the tried and true Boy Scout requirement: Be prepared. Anybody stuck with a raft of youngsters on a rainy day will have crayons handy, so maybe you'd like to get hold of a book called *How Is a Crayon Made?* by Oz Charles. The color photography is positively radiant and the manufacturing equipment mesmerizing. That double-page spread with rows and rows of new, tightly packed crayons will inspire kids to sharpen their own. Kids who prefer verbal craft will relish riddle books. One of the most popular genres of all, they go over well during that age when the entire conversation seems to consist of fourth-grade jokes. Try Katy Hall and Lisa Eisenberg's *Creepy Riddles* for its combined appeals of wordplay and faux-horror.

If you've got an athlete on layup or a youngster who's beginning to think that a particular sport looks like a lot of fun, there's probably a book to help. Books on sports are everywhere, ranging from biographies (some of stars that everybody knows, some of figures kids may be fascinated to learn about) to manuals on gymnastics, baseball, and in-line skating to more personal examinations of a child attending ballet classes or karate lessons or getting close to the action, as in Joan Anderson's photoessay *Batboy: An Inside Look at Spring Training.*

There's plenty for children to learn and plenty of books from which to learn. And it's surprising how many tidbits an adult can pick up along the way. Stay open to the kind of ongoing exploration kids come by naturally. For an introduction to an unknown subject—worms, wizards, willow trees, or electric motors—you won't do better than a good children's book. So the next time those nagging questions start up, join in the search for an answer. The process may start with a book and lead to a new awareness—and for your child, a lifelong habit of active thought.

Getting the Facts

Adler, David A. *Lou Gehrig: The Luckiest Man,* illustrated by Terry Widener (8–10). Gulliver/Harcourt, 1997.

Illustrated with acrylic paintings that capture the monumental feeling of this baseball star's popularity and written with admiration that never crosses into adulation, Adler's beginning biography traces Gehrig's youth in an immigrant neighborhood, his career with the New York Yankees, and his terminal illness.

Aliki. *Medieval Feast* (6–8). Crowell, 1983.

This picture book with illustrations composed in the style of a medieval manuscript describes the elaborate preparations for and exciting celebration of a king's visit to an English manor in about A.D. 1400.

Anderson, Joan. *Batboy: An Inside Look at Spring Training,* photographs by Matthew Cavanaugh (8–10). Lodestar, 1996.

Anderson's engaging photoessay follows a San Francisco Giants batboy through a typical fourteen-hour workday during spring training.

Arnold, Caroline. *Trapped in Tar: Fossils from the Ice Age* (9–11). Clarion, 1987.

The enthusiastic text, accompanied by black-and-white photographs of models and reconstructed skeletons from the George C. Page Museum of La Brea Discoveries, describes the kinds of fossils found in southern California tar pits.

Ashabranner, Brent. *Dark Harvest: Migrant Farmworkers in America,* photographs by Paul Conklin (12 and up). Dodd, 1985.

An outstanding combination of coherent narrative and sensitive photography will take readers into the fields with migrant workers who, in many cases, tell their own stories of what life is like following the crops.

Avi. *Finding Providence: The Story of Roger Williams,* illustrated by James Watling (8–10). HarperCollins, 1997.

This exciting first taste of colonial history introduces a man who defied Puritan leaders to defend religious liberty but then had to escape and survive in the wilderness.

Bishop, Nic. *The Secrets of Animal Flight* (8–11). Houghton, 1997.

In clear prose, this book tells—and shows, with crisp photos and detailed diagrams—exactly how different animals fly and just why humans can't (a 150-pound person would need a wingspan of 120 feet!).

Bode, Janet. *Trust and Betrayal: Real Life Stories of Friends and Enemies* (12–18). Delacorte, 1995.

Using interviews and feedback from peers and professionals, Bode's book combines the allure of a soap opera made real with the opportunity for genuine insight into a crucial but underexamined aspect of life.

Brown, Marc. *Dinosaurs' Divorce: A Guide for Changing Families* (6–9). Little, 1988.

An openly prescriptive text is relieved by a simple, smooth delivery in comic-strip format, with ridiculously funny green reptile children expressing their way through the vicissitudes of divorce.

Byars, Betsy. *The Moon and I* (9–12). Messner, 1992.

With an informal style that will recruit young readers into an immediate I-thou relationship, Byars serves up real-life characters and incidents with all the aplomb of fiction, including dialogue and dramatic details.

Charles, Oz. *How Is a Crayon Made?* (3–6). Simon, 1988.

From the cover photograph of an orderly field of Crayolas through the clean design of the pages, this book shows exactly what it is that kids love about a box of crayons.

Cole, Joanna. *The Magic School Bus inside the Human Body,* illustrated by Bruce Degen (7–9). Scholastic, 1989.

Like Ms. Frizzle's class trips to the waterworks, inside the earth, and back to the time of the dinosaurs, this jaunt uses humorous action and cleverly cartooned graphics to uncover a world of scientific information, including a rough ride through the digestive system, a narrow escape from some white blood cells determined to engulf germy intruders, then on to the brain, down the spinal cord, through the nervous system, along some muscles, and out . . . the nose. Some ride!

Colman, Penny. *Rosie the Riveter: Women Working on the Home Front in World War II* (10–14). Crown, 1995.

Numerous historical black-and-white photographs illustrate this smoothly written account of women's participation in a labor force depleted by male workers gone off to war. Colman has focused on other female-driven social movements in *Mother Jones and the March of the Mill Children* and *Fannie Lou Hamer and the Fight for the Vote.*

Cooper, Ilene. *The Dead Sea Scrolls,* illustrated by John Thompson (9–12). Morrow, 1997.
This riveting account of the history, discovery, acquisition, and restoration of the Dead Sea Scrolls reads like an Indiana Jones adventure, from the discovery of the first seven scrolls by Bedouin shepherds to the scrolls' computer-generated recreation.

Davidson, Rosemary. *Take a Look: An Introduction to the Experience of Art* (10–14). Viking, 1994.
Generously illustrated with reproductions in color and black and white, this comprehensive discussion involves readers in looking, thinking about what they see, and looking again.

Davies, Nicola. *Big Blue Whale,* illustrated by Nick Maland (5–8). Candlewick, 1997.
With fluid, descriptive prose that's well matched to the graceful watercolor illustrations, Davies discusses the life cycle of the biggest creature on earth, comparing it to familiar objects (the skin feels like a hardboiled egg, but it's slippery like wet soap) and explaining how it eats, migrates, communicates, and cares for its young.

Demi. *Chingis Khan* (5–8). Henry Holt, 1991.
From history and legend, Demi has selected a few of the most dramatic scenes in Chingis Khan's life and portrayed them with a fine sense of sweeping landscape in which the tiny human figures appear dwarfed by the vast steppes where they ride, fight, and die.

dePaola, Tomie. *The Quicksand Book* (7–9). Holiday, 1977.
In a rare combination of fun and fact, dePaola incorporates a scientific description of quicksand with a tongue-in-cheek tale about rescuing Jungle Girl, who is getting some firsthand experience with the mucky stuff. Jocular drawings broaden the humor.

Fisher, Leonard Everett. *The Great Wall of China* (8–10). Macmillan, 1986.
Fisher has fitted the dramatic history of Emperor Ch'in Shih Huang Ti's great wall, built with forced labor to keep out Mongol invaders, to primary-level students' grasp of time and place, channeling the real impact through monumentally scaled, boldly textured paintings in shades of black, white, and gray.

Fleischman, Sid. *The Abracadabra Kid* (11–15). Greenwillow, 1996.
A magician by training and trade, this author of ten McBroom tall tales and a Newbery Medal winner (for *The Whipping Boy*), among other books, talks about the comic adventures in his own life, complete with cliffhangers.

Freedman, Russell. *Children of the Wild West* (10–13). Clarion, 1983.
A smooth narrative and numerous historical photographs are combined for an

intriguing look at how children fared in pioneer times. Widely cited for the collective biography *Indian Chiefs* and winner of the Newbery Medal for *Lincoln: A Photobiography,* Freedman has added to his laurels with other biographies, including *Eleanor Roosevelt* and *Martha Graham.*

Fritz, Jean. *And Then What Happened, Paul Revere?* illustrated by Margot Tomes (8 and up). Putnam, 1973.

Lightened with humorous moments and expanded by Tomes's expressive drawings, Fritz's portrayal of the colonial minuteman is scrupulously authentic in every detail, as are others in this lively series that includes *What's the Big Idea, Ben Franklin?, Why Don't You Get a Horse, Sam Adams?* and *Where Was Patrick Henry on the 29th of May?*

Getz, David. *Frozen Man,* illustrated by Peter McCarty (8–10). Henry Holt, 1994.

This account of the discovery of Austria's mummified Stone-Age corpse eschews gory photography for an emphasis on the forensic side of things and may well stimulate the interest of young readers who didn't think they liked science.

Giblin, James. *From Hand to Mouth; or, How We Invented Knives, Forks, and Spoons and the Table Manners to Go with Them* (9–11). Crowell, 1987.

The title says it all in this ingeniously conceived social history of eating utensils. Both the anecdotes and the illustrations will whet young readers' appetites.

Greenberg, Jan, and Sandra Jordan. *The American Eye: Eleven Artists of the Twentieth Century* (11–17). Delacorte, 1995.

Like *The Painter's Eye* and *The Sculptor's Eye,* this is a clear, friendly, liberally illustrated text that examines varied artists in terms of style, technique, and effect.

Hall, Katy, and Lisa Eisenberg. *Creepy Riddles,* illustrated by S. D. Schindler (6–9). Dial, 1998.

The inhabitants of these riddles may be ghastly, but they're bound to elicit howls of laughter from new readers looking for a hair-raising good time.

Hampton, Wilborn. *Kennedy Assassinated!: The World Mourns: A Reporter's Story* (10–15). Candlewick, 1997.

This blow-by-blow account of a young reporter's on-the-spot experience brings home the drama of one of the nation's greatest tragedies.

Harris, Robie H. *It's Perfectly Normal: A Book about Changing Bodies, Growing Up, Sex, and Sexual Health,* illustrated by Michael Emberley (9–14). Candlewick, 1994.

This frank, cheerful, and clearly organized discussion of sexuality in its many manifestations gets a boost from detailed cartoons that lighten the mood but also clarify the information and feature all kinds of bodies: young, old, fat, thin, white, black, brown, and tan—and all perfectly normal.

Howe, James. *The Hospital Book,* photographs by Mal Warshaw (9–11). Crown, 1981.

A realistic but supportive look at a hospital stay includes photos and descriptions of admission, routine daily care, common tests, and surgical procedures.

Irvine, Joan. *How to Make Holiday Pop-ups,* illustrated by Linda Hendry (8–11). Morrow, 1996.
With the instructions and diagrams here, kids will be able to turn out three-dimensional designs suitable for all occasions.

Kimmel, Eric, ad. *Be Not Far from Me: The Oldest Love Story,* illustrated by David Diaz (11–14). Simon, 1998.
With rich gravity Kimmel retells stories of Old Testament heroes and heroines in their relationship to a majestic and demanding God. The lustrous illustrations and book design also project a deeply respectful tone.

King-Smith, Dick. *I Love Guinea Pigs,* illustrated by Anita Jeram (4–7). Candlewick, 1995.
A chatty, personal text includes information and anecdotes about these perennial pets, depicted in expressive pen-and-wash illustrations.

Krementz, Jill. *How It Feels When a Parent Dies* (10–14). Knopf, 1981.
Young readers will feel less alone and adults will better understand how to help children through a hard time thanks to the honest opinions expressed by the eighteen young people interviewed and photographed here. Also available in similar format are *How It Feels to be Adopted* and *How It Feels When Parents Divorce.* On a lighter note, check out *A Very Young Skater.*

Krull, Kathleen. *Wilma Unlimited: How Wilma Rudolph Became the World's Fastest Woman,* illustrated by David Diaz (6–9). Harcourt, 1996.
She weighed only four pounds at birth, she was black and poor in a racist southern town during the 1940s, and she was crippled with polio as a child. Simply told, her story is riveting, as are the multimedia collage illustrations in which intense colors, thick outlines, and organic shapes sweep us into the driving motion of the subject.

Kuklin, Susan. *From Head to Toe: How a Doll Is Made* (7–9). Hyperion, 1994.
An engaging photoessay introduces us to the craftspeople along the doll-making line who do the design, molding, eye-setting, hairdressing, and costuming. Older readers exploring their social consciences will appreciate Kuklin's *Irrepressible Spirit: Conversations with Human Rights Activists* (1996).

Lasker, Joe. *Tournament of Knights* (6–9). Crowell, 1986.
Bright, action-packed watercolors portray a medieval tournament, from the pronouncement and tent raisings to the gathering of knights and testing of noble-born youths in melee and joust. This is as well illustrated as Lasker's glowing *Merry Ever After: The Story of Two Medieval Weddings,* but is perhaps of more general interest to children.

Lasky, Kathryn. *Monarchs,* photographs by Christopher Knight (9–11). Harcourt, 1993.
Expanding on a scientific subject that has inherent aesthetic appeal, Lasky's vivid descriptions join with Knight's dramatic full-color photographs to document the life cycle of monarch butterflies, which migrate from the coast of Maine to the mountains of Mexico.

Lauber, Patricia. *Volcano: The Eruption and Healing of Mt. St. Helens* (9–12). Bradbury, 1986.

With a smoothly energetic style that makes the facts flow cohesively, this book recounts the sequence of developments in Mount St. Helens's eruption. Diagrams, maps, and high-quality color photographs add dynamically to the ecological concepts presented.

Lavies, Bianca. *A Gathering of Garter Snakes* (8–10). Dutton, 1993.

Curiosity led the author to document, with a personable text and arresting color photographs, the thousands of garter snakes that spend the winter in Manitoba, where they hibernate, mate, eat, shed their skins, and interact with local residents.

Lester, Helen. *Author: A True Story* (5–8). Lorraine/Houghton, 1997.

Illustrated with humor-filled cartoons and kid-pleasing anecdotes, this is a breezy autobiography about the trials and tribulations of becoming a published author.

Lester, Julius. *To Be a Slave,* illustrated by Tom Feelings (12 and up). Dial, 1968.

This powerful chronicle of slavery in the United States draws on moving, firsthand accounts that are skillfully set into historical context.

Ling, Mary, and Mary Atkinson. *The Snake Book,* illustrated by Frank Greenaway and Dave King (8–12). DK Ink, 1997.

Striking oversized color photographs reveal snakes in all sizes and shapes, often sporting beautiful body patterns and creating sinuous designs with their long supple bodies.

Macaulay, David. *The Way Things Work* (10 and up). Houghton, 1988.

After his landmark series showing the step-by-step engineering of major historical constructions (*Castle, Cathedral, City, Pyramid),* Macaulay undertakes to explain everything else, from zippers to transmitters, in a giant, inventively illustrated reference/browsing book that explores the workings of modern technology (with the help of a diverting woolly mammoth). Updated in 1998 as *The New Way Things Work.*

Mark, Jan, ad. *God's Story,* illustrated by David Parkins (11–14). Candlewick, 1998.

This memorable retelling of Biblical stories, from creation to the promise of a Messiah, is elegantly restrained in both writing and illustration.

Marrin, Albert. *Cowboys, Indians, and Gunfighters: The Story of the Cattle Kingdom* (11–17). Atheneum, 1993.

Picking his way carefully through legends and skeletons, Marrin creates a detailed and vivid picture of the U.S. conversion of the Plains from grassy buffalo habitat to cattle-feeding, money-making (and -losing) property. Generously illustrated with period photographs and art, this is one of the author's many well-researched, well-written books, which include *Unconditional Surrender: U. S. Grant and the Civil War* and *Virginia's General: Robert E. Lee and the Civil War.*

McLaughlin, Molly. *Earthworms, Dirt, and Rotten Leaves: An Exploration in Ecology,* illustrated by Robert Shetterly (9–11). Atheneum, 1996.

This friendly guide uses the common earthworm to teach observation, experimentation, and documentation and stresses respect for the creature and its natural environment.

McMillan, Bruce. *Nights of the Pufflings* (5–10). Houghton, 1995.
On a small island two hundred miles south of the Arctic Circle, Icelandic children help young puffins survive by finding—and releasing at the seashore—those confused by village lights and endangered by cars or predators. The heartwarming process is brilliantly described and photographed.

Meltzer, Milton. *Never to Forget: The Jews of the Holocaust* (12 and up). Harper, 1976.
Meltzer's compact, intensely human, carefully authenticated history of the Nazi extermination of Jews relies on eloquent quotations from survivors' eyewitness accounts and excerpts from the journals of those who died.

Murphy, Jim. *The Great Fire* (9–12). Scholastic, 1995.
Illustrated with period photographs and engravings, this account of the 1871 Chicago Fire conveys the human drama and historical background with intriguing details of how the blaze started, raged, and gutted the city.

Patent, Dorothy Hinshaw. *Back to the Wild,* photographs by William Muñoz (7–9). Gulliver Green/Harcourt, 1997.
As usual with this author-photographer team, the information is objective but deftly interwoven with personal anecdote. Here they focus words and camera on endangered species (including the red wolf) that have been bred in captivity and then released into the wild.

Paulsen, Gary. *My Life in Dog Years,* illustrated by Ruth Wright Paulsen (11–15). Delacorte, 1998.
Fans of Paulsen's gripping young adult novels can relax here and enjoy eight brief chapters that lovingly portray the dogs who helped raise and save him, including his lead sled dog in the Iditarod and a border collie that borders on genius. An earlier book, *Woodsong,* contains more intensely dramatic autobiographical stories.

Perl, Lila. *Mummies, Tombs, and Treasure: Secrets of Ancient Egypt,* illustrated by Erika Weihs (10–13). Clarion, 1987.
With the help of well-formatted photographs, maps, and drawings, Perl incorporates a good deal of information on burial customs, religious beliefs, and historical background, along with specifics of the mummification process and the archaeological finds that have kept the study of the dead a dynamic one. The subject of mummies fascinates children, who will also enjoy Patricia Lauber's *Tales Mummies Tell* and Eileen Pace's *Wrapped for Eternity.*

Pringle, Laurence. *Elephant Woman: Cynthia Moss Explores the World of Elephants,* photographs by Cynthia Moss (9–12). Atheneum, 1997.
As he has so often done in the past, Pringle brings a holistic perspective, this time to a Kenyan elephant research project directed by a woman with twenty-five years of experience, some of it captured in this vivid portrayal of her efforts to balance

human and animal needs. *Animals at Play, The Animal Rights Controversy,* and many other titles attest to Pringle's skill in nosing out interesting and telling details.

Rogasky, Barbara. *Smoke and Ashes: The Story of the Holocaust* (12 and up). Holiday, 1988.

This carefully researched history of the Holocaust details the Nazi operations calculated to solve the "Jewish Problem" with slave labor and death camps. Historical photographs document the horror more graphically than words.

Rogers, Fred. *Let's Talk about It: Stepfamilies,* photographs by Jim Judkis (5–8). Putnam, 1997.

As he has done in the past, Rogers deals calmly with situations that may be emotionally charged for young listeners and viewers, who can look at the photographs of these new stepfamilies for the same reassurance they find in Mr. Rogers' Neighborhood.

Sattler, Helen. *The New Illustrated Dinosaur Dictionary,* illustrated by Joyce Powzyk (10–14). Morrow, 1990.

The author of many books on dinosaurs, including *Baby Dinosaurs* and *Dinosaurs of North America,* offers here a readable, comprehensive dictionary that includes history and evolution as well as descriptions of more than three hundred species, with fine pen-and-ink drawings.

Schwartz, David M. *How Much Is a Million?* illustrated by Steven Kellogg (5–8). Lothrop, 1985.

Kids (and adults!) who have a hard time imagining concepts like a million, billion, or trillion will get lots of help from these ingenious explanations and expansive watercolor pictures, some of which offer page after page after page (seven in all) of 100,000 stars for the restless young reader to count. When you finish this one, try *If You Made a Million.*

Selsam, Millicent. *Cotton,* photographs by Jerome Wexler (8–10). Morrow, 1982.

Lucid explanations and unusual, magnified full-color photographs follow an amazing plant's growth and processing.

Simon, Seymour. *The Sun* (8–10). Morrow, 1986.

One in a series of stunning photoessays about stars and planets, *The Sun* simplifies a complex subject without distorting or diminishing it.

Solheim, James. *It's Disgusting—and We Ate It!: True Food Facts from Around the World—and Throughout History!* illustrated by Eric Brace (8–11). Simon, 1998.

Solheim's flavorful look at culinary culture offers a bounty of information about foodstuffs past and present, alien and familiar. Lively formatting and a sassy cast of new-wavy critters make this book easy on the eye if not on the tummy.

Stanley, Diane. *Leonardo da Vinci* (8–11). Morrow, 1996.

In an intelligently selective text, the biographer of figures as complex as Peter the Great and Cleopatra here depicts an enigmatic Renaissance genius amid his unsettled times. Her illustrations seem amazingly comfortable alongside da Vinci's art.

Stine, R. L. *It Came from Ohio!: My Life as a Writer,* as told to Joe Arthur (8–12). Parachute/Scholastic, 1997.
Fans of the junior horror series Goosebumps will be surprised to discover the mild-mannered man beneath the supersonically prolific author, who seems to enjoy his writing as much as kids do.

Sutton, Roger. *Hearing Us Out: Voices from the Gay and Lesbian Community,* photographs by Lisa Ebright (12–17). Little, 1994.
In fifteen engaging interviews, gays and lesbians—some teens, some older—talk about their lives and about issues such as coming out, lesbian parenting, military policy, equal rights work, and homosexuality and religion.

Temko, Florence. *Planes and Other Flying Things* (7–11). Millbrook, 1996.
Notebook paper will never be the same after its users take hold of this compact compendium of paper-airplane designs.

Tripp, Nathaniel. *Thunderstorm!,* illustrated by Juan Wijngaard (8–10). Dial, 1994.
Kids drawn in by Wijngaard's alluringly ominous cover painting of a towering thunderhead will find inside a natural suspense story, as the inhabitants of a small farm await a change in weather that the text explains in factual but dramatic detail. Kids afraid of thunder and lightning can learn to understand them instead.

van der Rol, Ruud, and Rian Verhoeven. *Anne Frank, Beyond the Diary: A Photographic Remembrance* (11–14). Viking, 1993.
Photographs of the Frank family, relevant documents, even the diary itself bring the life of Anne Frank into new and startling focus.

Wallace, Karen. *Think of an Eel,* illustrated by Mike Bostock (4–7). Candlewick, 1993.
From endpapers depicting developmental stages of eel growth in eye-catching watercolors, through pages filled with long slender shapes, the life cycle that organizes this information is reflected in rhythmic graphic patterns of blue and green—a symbiosis of poetic facts and visual figures.

Westray, Kathleen. *A Color Sampler* (7–9). Ticknor & Fields, 1993.
Westray's fresh approach to presenting colors and their myriad combinations also plays with shapes, as each page of information is dedicated to a traditional quilt pattern stylized into precise designs.

Wexler, Jerome. *Everyday Mysteries* (7–9). Dutton, 1995.
A veteran photographer who has produced many simple—and simply beautiful—books about plants and animals (*Pet Hamsters, Sundew Stranglers: Plants That Eat Insects*) here demonstrates once again that natural facts are in fact a miraculous mystery, as in the closeups of a cantaloupe and a potato chip!

Wick, Walter. *A Drop of Water* (8–11). Scholastic, 1997.
Illustrating fifteen simple science experiments, Wick's magical color photography reveals the beauty of water in liquid, crystalline, and vaporous forms.

Wilkes, Angela. *Dazzling Disguises and Clever Costumes* (7–11). DK, 1996.
Cogent instructions, reasonable expectations, and an imaginative approach combine to bring some terrific costumes within youthful reach.

Winter, Jonah. *Diego,* illustrated by Jeanette Winter; Spanish text by Amy Prince (5–8). Knopf, 1991.
Although it has no more than a few sentences per page, this picture-book biography of Diego Rivera is rich and rewarding because the subject led such an unusual and creative life, the text (printed in both English and Spanish) is never condescending, and the miniature paintings are involving and reflective of Rivera's work.

Zindel, Paul. *The Pigman and Me* (12–17). Zolotow/HarperCollins, 1992.
A landmark author of young adult books reveals the sources of his storytelling in a chaotic childhood with one guiding light, a wise old Italian who reveals the secrets of life, such as: "In every fat book, there's a little thin book trying to get out"; and "A closed mouth gathers no feet."

Michael Emberley

10

Controversial Children's Books

We want the best of all possible worlds for our children. That's understandable, but it demands an impossible idealism from their books. It amounts to asking that children hear no evil, see no evil, speak no evil, taste no evil. Yet those requirements contradict the very existence of literature, because literature is a mirror of the world. Children know there is evil as well as good in the world. The trick is learning to cope with it. To do that, a child needs to learn how to recognize it, how to sort it out.

One of the complicating factors is that everyone defines evil in a different way. Is it sex, obscenity, violence, simplistic politics, heretical religion, bad writing, clumsy art, or taking a bite out of your friend? And who's to say what's evil for someone else's children? In fact, who's to say for your children? They're separate human beings who will make their own choices—with or without parental agreement—as they establish their independence.

That can be a rude surprise, but there's a way to prepare for it. We can't—and don't want to—keep children from thinking. But we *can* take a position of leadership in their thought by opening up issues and discussing them. It's a lot more effective to join in reading what children are reading and to express reasoned opinions of what they're reading than to hide or confiscate their books. Partners can discuss books; dictators forbid them. Partnership breeds respect; dictatorship breeds rebellion. An open-book policy isn't just about the theoretical rights of the child, it's what works best.

There's an inordinate attraction to things forbidden. For every book taken off the shelf by a committee objecting to some sinful passage, five avid readers rise from the ranks to examine that very passage. Remember hiding whatever book, magazine, or comic it was you hid under your mattress? Anyone's natural curiosity is aroused by having to peek through the keyhole or pry open the lock instead of walking right through the open door. Then, of course, curiosity is blissfully satisfied by discovering that the forbidden book deals exactly with what is most interesting, from sex to social problems.

This works on a community level as well as on an individual level. Wichita Falls, Texas, provides a case in point. In 1998 a minister there protested two books about gay parents, Leslea Newman's *Heather Has Two Mommies* and Michael Willhoite's *Daddy's Roommate,* by paying for the books but refusing to return them to the library. After the incident was publicized, so many people wanted to read the books that the librarian had to put holds on them and, consequently and according to policy, order more copies than the library originally had—in addition to the fifteen copies donated by sympathetic patrons.

It's particularly ironic to censor a book that is relevant to young people's needs. Here's a typical letter of objection to a junior novel, Norma Fox Mazer's *Saturday, the Twelfth of October,* and my (equally) typical reply:

> [Letter]: Your review does not mention that one of the main themes was the symbolic use of a lack of menstruating as a dominant fear of a girl. If you know seventh and eighth graders you will know what a carnival they would have with this. Ours are no different than other junior high people, I'm sure, and anything dealing with a sexual theme or profanity is grist for their mill. Because of this, even though I found it a well-developed novel, I did not feel that I could put it on our shelves.

> [Reply]: Menstruation should not be signaled or warned against or classified with profanity. It should be included in junior high students' books exactly because it *is* "grist for their mill"—in other words, of significant and natural interest to them in their stage of development. As long as it is treated with dignity and ease, as it is here, I would hate to think that a descriptive plot summary would keep librarians from ordering it. You yourself found it a well-developed novel and did not mention exactly why the symbol of menstruation was in poor taste; it seems to me that young people's dominant fears should be discussed in their literature.

Judy Blume's *Forever* has been a prime target for censorship because it details a young couple's first sexual intercourse. The pages where "it" happens are always well thumbed. The topic of sexuality, treated in fiction or in nonfiction for young people, is one of the scariest things for adults and most likely to create controversy. *It's Perfectly Normal,* discussed in chapter 9 as a good example of nonfiction, with an illustration at the beginning of this chapter, is a popular target for challenges.

Now here's the big surprise: kids want to know about sex. Really, exactly, how it happens. *All kids are curious about sex.* Let it be emblazoned above the doorway of every institution. We cannot stop this curiosity any more than we can stop time from marching on. But here's another surprise: just because they read about it doesn't necessarily mean they're going to do it—at least not right now. Eventually they will, but not because of this or any other book. Thoughts and actions are not synonymous, which is something we usually struggle hard to impress on our children. We tell a two-year-old that it's okay to be angry but it's not okay to bite the person who makes you angry. Thinking about biting a person and actually biting that person are two different things. We all think about all kinds of illicit things that we never do. Thinking is neither bad nor illegal. In fact, the unthoughtful, the unsuspecting, are more often surprised by their own and others' actions than are those who have been educated about what to expect. *Forever* is not an advertisement for running out to lose one's virginity. So read it and discuss it with your preteens or adolescents if they're so inclined, or let them read it in the privacy only books can provide.

There's no question that today's teenagers are going to have sex education. But is it going to be from the media, from peers, or from a responsible adult? There's no question that they'll eventually experience sex, one way or another. There *is* a question of when and how. The more they've had time to think and talk about sex in the sheltered and loving environment of their homes, the better prepared they'll be to make choices and not be victims of circumstance, as are so many teenagers who are surprised when they become pregnant. Most adults want children eventually to find sex comfortable, not guilty or furtive or destructive. The right attitude can be formulated a lot better over a book than in the back seat of a car.

"Language" is as likely to draw fire as sex. Over two decades ago there was an outcry over fourteen swear words in Johanna Reiss's novel *The Upstairs Room,* which deals with the hardships visited on two children by Hitler's drive to exterminate the Jews during World War II. People did a lot worse than swear on the Western Front, but they *did* swear. In 1994,

James Lincoln Collier and Christopher Collier's novel of the Revolutionary War, *My Brother Sam Is Dead,* received two challenges, one successful, from parents objecting to swear words. To recreate the reality of some characters, scenes, and settings, literature has to include profanity, obscenity, or street language; this is nothing young readers don't know and can't keep in context. This doesn't mean that swearing is proof of a book's merit, but neither is its absence. Those fourteen damns that somebody took the trouble to count in *The Upstairs Room* seem pretty mild in light of the traumatic experiences and burning issues of war, as portrayed in a well-written, realistic but not violent novel about an unavoidable past. The question is, Should we lie and say these words don't exist or should we teach children how to deal with them?

Hardly a week goes by without a juvenile or young adult book being censored somewhere. The American Library Association regularly updates a publication called *Banned Books Resource Guide* in which are listed all the books challenged or banned—along with the location, date, and reason—during the most recent year. You'd be startled to find out what appears in the hundred-odd pages of that alphabetic listing: from "Alexander, Lloyd. *The Wizard in the Tree* . . . because a character in the story uses the words 'slut' and 'damn'" to "Zindel, Paul. *The Pigman* . . . because the novel features 'liars, cheaters and stealers.'"

There is certainly a valid place for concern about the horrors to which children can be exposed, but many controversies seem to have nothing to do with real horrors. The books that focus attention rarely involve violence to the human spirit or body. The throwing overboard of babies from a slave ship, the brutal killing of a gang member, the abuse of a child have all appeared in children's books without causing a ripple of concern. Most objections center around occasional profanity or mild sexuality, which are regular parts of a child's real world. It seems to be the puritanical taboos of our society that raise eyebrows, not the harm that may be done to children's psyches. It's what we ourselves have trouble dealing with, not what *children* have trouble dealing with. Because times are changing so fast, it's not easy to stay in touch with children whose world differs so much from our own childhoods. Some pressures and problems will always be the same, but others are profoundly new and different.

Because of this, writers and publishers are now taking greater moral risks with more children's books than ever before. They're dealing with more problems of significance in our society, and they're heading further and further into controversy. One of the most courageous examples is Lothrop, Lee &

Shepard's publication of *Hiroshima No Pika* by Toshi Maruki. In the format of a picture book, this is really for older children and junior high or high school readers who must face a world at risk. Like most effective works of art, *Hiroshima No Pika* tells a story instead of preaching a sermon. The point is more than made by the details of seven-year-old Mii's experiences on August 6, 1945, the day the atomic bomb fell on Hiroshima, the day her mother dragged her and her wounded father through the city and across three rivers to a beach, where they lay unaided for days. The writing shifts clearly between her personal view and a background explanation of what happened generally. The balance between small examples—a swallow hopping by because its wings were too burnt to fly—and historical description of a city laid waste is perfectly maintained.

The text tells only half the story, though. Full-page paintings involve the reader in a journey that is indescribable beyond a certain number of words. The artist has walked a fine line between literal and expressionistic presentation. There's enough realistic detail to see and feel what's happening, with enough distance of things simply suggested to keep children from being overwhelmed by horror—again, that masterful selection of particulars. Color and movement sustain what detail there is and expand the impact of Mii's limited vision. We feel the trauma through identification with one child, but the tragedy is multiplied by a swirl of bodies flung all around. Most lines are horizontal, shapes of the dead or dying, those fleeing across the pages. A burning red rivets the attention among black, gray, or dark green masses, with an occasional flash of intense blue in remnants of tattered clothing from a tranquil past.

I wish no child had reason to read such a book. Certainly, the artist-author and editor wished there had been no reason to create or publish it. But the fact that the events happened and should never happen again makes this important to every child at some stage when he or she can understand and deal with it, whether at the age of nine with guidance from an adult or at the age of thirteen during a study of documentaries from World War II. A few other books—Eleanor Coerr's *Sadako and the Thousand Paper Cranes,* Tatsuharu Kodama's *Shin's Tricycle,* and Junko Morimoto's *My Hiroshima*—turn atomic destruction from an abstraction to immediate reality. The scarcity of such books is a surprising fact considering the many literary reminders of the Holocaust.

Those who have never experienced a nuclear attack may find it unimaginable. Even those in rural Japan were not sympathetic to the suffering of the survivor whose story is told here. It is a story that is hard to tell, hard to believe, hard to listen to. But it is even harder *not* to pay attention to it. Our children need to laugh, but they also need to cry over other peoples' fates and develop concern for the fate of their own world. The flight of the swallow will be in their hands.

A number of young adult books, including Robert O'Brien's *Z for Zachariah* and Caroline Stevermer's *River Rats,* are set in a post–nuclear war world, providing older kids with a natural forum for thought and discussion. Although both of these books are futuristic, there are many more books that delve into aspects of past wars, especially the Holocaust.

Gudrun Pausewang's *Final Journey* is a shockingly realistic novel set in a boxcar carrying the eleven-year-old protagonist to the "showers" of Auschwitz. Between the first and last moments, we come to know a community of individuals bonded by emergency and witnessed through the eyes of a young girl whose rite of passage, unbeknownst to her, leads to death. The suspense of the journey is heightened by the death of the girl's grandfather, the birth of a baby boy, and the murder of a young man attempting to escape but most of all by the relentless spread of feces from a designated "toilet" corner, an image that vividly represents the degradation of the group. Although this fiction honestly reflects historical facts, it never falls into a representative mode of generic docudrama. The individuals we learn to care about are the ones we lose: many men, most women, and all the babies, children, and preadolescents . . . all of them. The book offers no intrinsic hope—and many people have distinguished children's literature from adults' by the hope offered in the former—but only the implied hope that readers will feel this story so deeply that they will never participate in the kind of hatred or indifference that allowed the Holocaust to happen.

Even more difficult to consider realistically is the genocide of the African slave trade that was an integral part of U.S. history. Tom Feelings spent many years creating his book *The Middle Passage: White Ships, Black Cargo.* Following a description of his own quest for his African past comes a historical overview of the slave trade, printed on gray paper, and then sixty-four pages of wordless graphic narrative depicting the horrors of capture and subjugation, from home village to distant shores. The book's large size and black endpapers signal a dramatic tone that is sustained throughout the artist's inventively formatted gallery of black-and-white images. The opening spread of a brilliantly sunlit landscape quickly gives way to scenes of terror as African people are attacked, beaten during a forced march to seaside fortresses, branded, and loaded in cramped tiers aboard ship. Scenes of rape and murder gather power from chiaroscuro—the contrast of ghostly whites and their precisely delineated dark victims. Rhythmically repeated lines and shapes are softened by mottled textures or fuzzy backgrounds, yet the viewer is constantly taken by surprise, a reflection of the human cargo's experience of shock.

It's risky to produce a beautiful book about an ugly subject, and the book is all the more politically charged by the prominence of some graphically rhetorical posterlike scenes such as that of a baby supended between two spears. Like the Holocaust, however, slavery evokes emotional response as well as intellectual understanding, and Feelings has justifiably imbued history with agony. He is probably best known for illustrating picture books (*Moja Means One: Swahili Counting Book* and *Jambo Means Hello* were both Caldecott Honor Books), but this book appears in its publisher's young adult category. Appropriated steadily and effectively for junior high and high school students studying U.S. history, *The Middle Passage: White Ships, Black Cargo* will find buyers and users in adult departments as well as in collections for young people.

It is almost a platitude that children's books are a controversial item these days, with frankness in subject and language that was never dreamed of years ago and that raises more and more hackles as time goes on. "Sweetness and light" is an order long past in children's literature. It never was a reality in most children's lives. Today, children are confronted both in the media and in their everyday reality with situations involving drug addiction, alcoholism, irresponsible sex, extramarital pregnancy, abortion, child abuse, rape, insanity, murder, suicide, prostitution, gang violence, death (by war, accident, and disease), personal conflicts, physical and mental disabilities, hostile divorces, senility, poverty, abandonment, and racism, together with all the sociopolitical -isms that abound. Sometimes several of the above crowd into a single life, and therefore into a single story. Trouble never seems to come in ones.

That's not so much a conscious decision on the writer's part as a reflection through the writer of what our society is, of what we're all going through. It's true that too many problems can overload a plot in terms of focus and narrative development; in fiction as in nonfiction, a worthy subject does not guarantee a good book. But writers and artists of integrity shouldn't be attacked for artistic honesty about what is going on around them, nor children for their need to know and understand. A troubled society provokes troubling books. As one character says to his readers in Paul Zindel's *Confessions of a Teenage Baboon:*

> The last thing I've got to tell you is there are things that are done to me in this story that aren't very nice—but I'm going to tell you anyway because

> maybe some of you will learn something from them. Maybe there are some of you who are as ashamed and mixed up as I was and don't know how to handle the problems of being alive that people don't warn you about. And that's the main reason I'm writing this confession—because I don't think we should go on keeping quiet about these things. All the lying has to stop somewhere.

The important thing to remember in sorting out thoughts about literature that deals with challenging or sensational themes is not to view the books in isolation. These books reflect basic changes in our times. Books for children have always been a mirror of society's threats as well as its ideals. Early children's books were haunted by the fire and brimstone of hell, along with the religious rewards or punishments of those who had or had not sinned. To the modern reader, that's every bit as shocking as the sex and obscenity that outrage some parents today. It's not the authors who are to blame, or the publishers, but our own society. Most writers are simply being honest about what they see, and most children, just like adults, would prefer not to be lied to. They know, for instance, that child abuse is a ubiquitous problem. Heartwrenching details of individual cases permeate the daily news, and these don't all get wrapped up with happy endings. Children would—and should—expect to read about it in their literature. It's there, from physical abuse in books such as Willo Davis Roberts's *Don't Hurt Laurie,* Michelle Magorian's *Goodnight Mr. Tom,* and Gillian Cross's *Pictures in the Dark* to sexual abuse in Cynthia Grant's *Uncle Vampire,* Jacqueline Woodson's *I Hadn't Meant to Tell You This,* Brock Cole's *Facts Speak for Themselves,* and many other works of fiction and nonfiction.

In one year there were nine novels for grade school readers involving child abuse. One story had a young girl used as a police lure for a psychotic rapist-killer, while in another a girl was almost killed by her insane mother. A historical novel included a sexual scene between mother and son. A southern period piece had an unbalanced preacher assaulting a child. Many kids know these things go on. Should they pretend not to? It may have happened in their family or to a friend or some acquaintance in school. Is it enough to know and look away? There are no easy answers in reacting to books like these. In the old days they would have seemed like soap operas. Now they sound like the six o'clock news. The number of juvenile books about child abuse almost doubled during every five-year period from 1965 to 1989 (the battered child syndrome was identified around 1962 and surfaced to social consciousness in the succeeding years); in the last ten years, physical abuse has subsided as a pivotal plot theme, to be eclipsed by books treating sexual abuse or books that depict physical abuse as part of a larger dysfunction. As time passes, new topics settle into the landscape of literature—just like the case of books about child abuse—and no longer represent trends but simply "blends," part of the scenery we expect because it represents the reality of our own awareness.

The same thing happened with books on AIDS. The disease was identified, publicized, and incorporated into fiction and nonfiction, with children's books a part of the cycle (usually trailing about two years behind adult books). M. E. Kerr's *Night Kites* and Theresa Nelson's *Earthshine* are two of many books centering on characters who must deal with a fatally infected family member. Is there anyone who *wouldn't* want to protect their kids from AIDS?

Here's a case where crucial information necessarily involves frankness about sexuality, and most people, whatever their political persuasion, acknowledge the fact that information on this subject is necessary—in one form or another—for young people. Yet information is only the beginning. What about the emotional repercussions of children dealing with friends and loved ones dying of the disease, of schools embroiled in controversy about enrolling students with AIDS? There's no way that children's books can be untouched by problems haunting the society in which children live.

In the best books, such problems appear not as case studies but as story portraits so vividly realized that they touch the reader with the bond of identification. The fact is, kids need some well-written books about what's going on in their world; otherwise literature will seem at best irrelevant and at worst hypocritical. Fantasy and science fiction can offer popular escape routes into other worlds, but realistic fiction must travel this one as honestly as possible. Even fantasy and science fiction must, as Jillsy Sloper said in *The World According to Garp,* "feel true." And kids do want to read enticing books, as evidenced by the titles they pilfer from the adult shelves: *Jaws* and *Flowers in the Attic* in the recent past, *Forever Amber* and *From Here to Eternity* in the distant past, and many other "questionable" selections from the ever-changing adult best-seller list. It's ironic that the adult books kids covet are often less-sensitive, less-intelligent, less-thoughtful treatments of challenging subject matter than the books written expressly for young people. There's one element that worried or outraged adults should take into consideration before censoring controversial children's books: while skill obviously varies, it's rare to find a writer in the world of juvenile literature who doesn't care deeply about childhood—the pain and pleasure of growing up, about children—and who doesn't shape the resulting material with that care.

Factual books banned from the open shelves are often the books that contain the very facts children need most—on reproduction and birth control, for instance. And there are still places where children cannot find out about evolution or communism from a school or library book on that subject. In each case, the information is considered a threat and so is kept hidden away. Ironically, some of the most liberal organizations in the country have spearheaded the most conservative tactics in banning anything considered politically or socially unacceptable. A picture of a black woman shown doing the dishes has been decried as racist and sexist—a double whammy—no matter what the context. Depicting an old man in a rocking chair is interpreted as being ageist because such a portrayal shows no respect for the liveliness of people over sixty-five.

Margot Zemach's picture book *Jake and Honeybunch Go to Heaven* was the focus of enormous controversy because it depicts an African-American man named Jake who goes to his reward and finds that God and the heavenly multitude, all black, are rejoicing with jazz and a barbecue. One critic, Denise Wilms, summarized the issues in *Booklist,* a review journal published by the American Library Association:

> Is its picture of Depression-era (or pre-Depression?) working-class black culture celebratory, or does it perpetuate offensive stereotypes? Is a ribs-and-chicken dinner and a dance band in heaven legitimate humor/comedy, or is it an unfortunate furthering of the myth of black shallowness? If these elements are interpreted as stereotypes, are they offset by such positive elements as a black God and the fact that Jake is redeemed and has restored order to his heavenly home? In addition, its lighthearted view of heaven may be an affront to some groups who see heaven in a more somber light.

The unquestionably high quality of the storytelling and watercolor art, the fact that the author is white, and the fact that the text included no information about folkloric sources made this book the subject of an especially complex set of questions. However, it's not an isolated example. In 1998, a teacher who read Carolivia Herron's poetic picture book *Nappy Hair* aloud to her third grade class in Brooklyn found herself confronted by a group of violently angry parents. The teacher was white, the parents were African American, and the subject was a sensitive one: a little girl's tight black curls, depicted in riotous profusion ("One nap of her hair is the only perfect circle in nature"). The book suggested to some parents a stereotype to which they did not want their children exposed. It did not seem to help that the author was African American and that the book had been recommended by an African-American children's literature specialist from Teachers College, Columbia University. Because anger precluded discussion, everyone lost—especially the children, whose young and enthusiastic teacher left the school.

Writers and artists must be socially sensitive, but writing cannot be sociologically dictated. All kinds of ideas and ideals are imposed as standards on children's books in a way they never are on adult books because children are seen as impressionable, to be molded in the right form. The writer's charge of observing life acutely is often sacrificed in an attempt to send messages to the child. The question of how to protect our children from harm is an important one. They start out so small, defenseless, and trusting that we never want a blow to fall. In order to protect them, we control them. But control and protection are two different things. It's important to *keep* love as a part of the control and *keep out* the fear and insecurity that lead to overcontrol, or to a wish to force children into thinking the way we want them to. That amounts to power, not protection. Sometimes it's hard to sort out the two.

Being permissive is certainly not the answer. Permissiveness doesn't work any better than force, because children need direction and want limits set to keep them safe. The key seems to be a realistic, responsible involvement in a child's knowledge and activities. It takes time and energy, and books make one of the best meeting grounds for an exchange of opinion. No one can deny feelings and physiology in the long run; they'll come out one way or the other. It's best for adult and child to pull up the shades together and take a good look at what's going on.

Reading, in fact, can be the least harmful first encounter with any controversial problem. Of course, powerful writing can twist anyone's dreams into nightmares; even cheap pulp can have unpredictable effects. But both of these are one step removed from experience and give the inexperienced scope for thinking without having to react. Melvin Burgess's *Smack*, winner of the Carnegie Medal and Guardian Prize for fiction in Great Britain, depicts a fourteen-year-old running away from an abusive home with his girlfriend and getting hooked on heroin, but the book certainly doesn't recommend either course. Instead, it shows with authentic realism what can happen to addicted kids—for whom there are not very many, or very certain, happy endings.

Although a few controversial books present genuinely overwhelming problems, sometimes what captures public indignation seems funny, especially in picture books. People have objected to Raymond Briggs's *Father Christmas* because Santa squats on the toilet (and later enjoys a sip of cognac thoughtfully left for him by an understanding father). John Steptoe's *My Special Best Words* also has drawn some fire because it shows a child sitting on the toilet. Many small children spend a good deal of their time on the toilet, and surely it doesn't hurt them to see somebody else achieving success too.

It's hard to predict what will provoke criticism. Margaret Mahy's *Boy Who Was Followed Home* raised alarm because the boy swallowed a pill to get rid of the hippopotami accumulating on his lawn; Walter Dean Myers's *Young Martin's Promise,* because Martin Luther King Jr. was a "leftist hoodlum"; Mary Rayner's *Mr. and Mrs. Pig's Evening Out,* because the baby-sitter was a wolf; *Some Swell Pup,* because Maurice Sendak's pictures illustrate a dog peeing; *Wind Rose* by Crescent Dragonwagon, because it shows a child's parents discreetly wrapped in a blanket together in bed; *The Bear and the Fly* by Paula Winter, because so much furniture is destroyed while the bear is chasing the fly; *Ben's Trumpet* by Rachel Isadora, because an African-American boy's father is shown elbow-deep in a poker game; and *Rapunzel,* because, in some versions, the long-haired heroine has twins before she and the prince have a chance to marry and live happily ever after. The most alarming thing about any of these picture books, really, would be if a child missed out on them.

One of the biggest waves of objection has been to the appearance of anything supernatural in children's books. Eve Bunting's *Scary, Scary Halloween* is a good example. Tailored for nursery and preschool holiday read-aloud sessions, this is a slightly spooky picture book with bright graphics on a black background showing costumed creepies prancing through the night, all watched by four pairs of green eyes hiding under a porch. The devils, monsters, and goblins turn out to be children, of course, and the eyes belong to a cat and her three kittens, but the faces on the creatures, pumpkins, and even trees will inspire shivers of delight in any darkened room. Not everybody agrees. One letter in response to my positive review of the book termed such literature "intellectually diseased." Books like this not only frighten but corrupt readers, the letter writer claimed, and may lead to "young people's depraved, criminal, or even suicidal behavior."

Yet even books that take witchcraft seriously are often intent on delving into human truths rather than supernatural powers. Donna Jo Napoli turns in her young adult novel *The Magic Circle* to a dark tone and highly charged plot developed as a kind of prequel to "Hansel and Gretel." It is in many ways a groundbreaking book, treating demonic evil seriously and flying in the face of politically correct revisionist history about women falsely accused of witchcraft. Although the community does react with conventional ignorance and hatred toward this social outcast, it's the narrator's own pride that proves her downfall. The scene where she breaks the magic circle to retrieve a coveted ring is gripping enough to make a reader want to stop reading so she won't do it. When she and her daughter are tied to the stake—where she makes a demonic pact to save her daughter from the flames—we perceive the sinister underside of magic, which is really the dark side of human nature. Witchcraft is used in this book not to advance any "intellectually diseased" position but to explore humanity more fully.

Ironically, the same people who object to "evil" in books may allow television to baby-sit their children or entertain their teenagers for hours every day; and television, while more graphically detailed, does not allow the same scope for thinking. Whereas the ability to read a book guarantees certain levels of intellectual activity and development, television can barrage the brain of the youngest child via visual and aural reception. The child may be unprepared mentally, emotionally, and experientially.

Thinking involves getting a message, processing it, and reacting to it. Watching television all day long can slow down intellectual development by curtailing a critical thought process. If children can learn to respond to television, it can be used constructively, but they must learn to act as critics, not gullible receptacles of the message delivered. By contrast, reading both depends on and furthers a more individually varied, active, and deeper range of experience. It is a gentle but strong step toward knowledge for the unexposed child.

There have been enough words written about television and its effects on society to sink the *Titanic.* Television is constantly dragged into competition with books, but it doesn't really belong there. It's distracting to compare the two. Books and television (or movies) can and do stimulate each other, as was evident with the popular TV series "Little House on the Prairie" and with films such as *Mary Poppins* and *Babe.* However, television must be watched selectively rather than continuously. Given the nature of most television programs today, a children's book is likely to be more stimulating to a child's independent thought and imagination.

The Internet is another contemporary influence that provokes questions and concerns, all the more so because of the difficulty of knowing exactly what—and who—is out there in the millions of Web sites, chat rooms, newsgroups, and listservs. As with television, there is good and bad, supportive and troubling; as with television, selectivity is the name of the game. Wonderful as the Internet can be, there's a specific kind of stable narrative imagination and physical experience that books alone offer.

For all media, it's important to ask the same questions: What's honest and what's exploitative? What's fad and what's for keeps? What's open-minded and what's mindless? For me, personally, violence is the thing that most often raises these questions. Obscenity seems harmless by comparison, and sex shouldn't necessarily be lumped together with problems in the first place. But a book or television program must be very moving and meaningful for me to feel it's worth a violent scene that will intrude on my mind and dreams. When my children were young, I felt the same way about the books and programs to which they were exposed. As strongly as I react to violence as a violation, however, and as much as I would have liked to keep violence away from my children's sight and experience, I knew I couldn't. Violence has been part of their world. I hate it, I have trouble dealing with it, I wish it would go away, but there it is. They didn't grow up without hearing of rape, murder, and war through adult conversations, in newspapers, on television, or by rumor.

I often felt the impulse to keep them away from books that dealt with violence, but I thought it was better that my children and I learned to deal with it while they still had the security of my home and the benefit of my experience. We were able to read and talk together about what's good, what's bad, what's upsetting, what's moving, what's cruel, what's worthwhile, what must be faced, what should be turned off or objected to.

Each of us must answer individually the questions regarding any troublesome element in our child's world. First, should such a problem appear at all in children's books? My conscience answers yes because the problem exists and must be prepared for. Second, how should it be treated if it does appear? My own standard demands a combination of skill, care, and imagination. Third, who decides what's a problem in the first place? I believe it must be you and your child, deciding for yourselves. Finally, who enforces that decision, and on whom? This is perhaps the trickiest question of all.

What I consider a problem may not alarm someone else. I would hate to have had a school principal decide that a book must come off the shelf—out of my child's reach—because another child's parent demanded it removed; or out of another child's reach because I demanded it removed. No one should *have* to read a book, but everyone should have the *right* to. Censorship is a private decision. When it goes public, somebody's rights are going to get stepped on.

My own experience is that children don't need censorship; what they need is adult involvement. It's easier to say "Get rid of it" than to say "Let's face it together." *Sam, Bangs, and Moonshine,* a picture book by Evaline Ness that won the Caldecott Medal in 1967, is the story of a young girl who can't tell the difference between fantasy and a lie—and because of that she sends a playmate on a chase that almost kills him. Samantha finally learns that, although she needn't give up her dragons and magic carpets, she must perceive and communicate clearly what is real and what isn't. We must all learn the same thing. Giving children any less than our best perception of reality is a costly mistake.

Controversial Children's Books

Anonymous. *Go Ask Alice* (12 and up). Prentice-Hall, 1971.
A diary details the tragedy of a teenage girl's introduction to the drug culture—and the horrors she finds there.

Blume, Judy. *Forever* (12 and up). Bradbury, 1975.
For high school seniors Katherine and Michael, first love brings intense emotional and sexual responses that are specifically detailed here.

Bunting, Eve. *Scary, Scary Halloween* (3–6). Clarion, 1986.
A sprightly picture book with bright graphics on a black background shows four pairs of green eyes (which turn out to be kittens) watching costumed creepies (trick-or-treating children) prancing through the night.

Burgess, Melvin. *Smack* (14–17). Henry Holt, 1998.
An abused fourteen-year-old and his girlfriend find refuge and new friends—along with a heroin habit—in the abandoned building where he seeks shelter from life on the streets.

Cole, Brock. *The Facts Speak for Themselves* (13–18). Front Street, 1997.
Fourteen-year-old Linda's life of disorganized squalor takes a dramatic turn when her stepfather shoots her adult lover.

Cormier, Robert. *The Chocolate War* (12 and up). Pantheon, 1974.
The one teenage boy who refuses to participate in a high school fund-raising campaign faces terrifying consequences at the hands of the system.

Feelings, Tom. *The Middle Passage: White Ships, Black Cargo* (12 and up). Dial, 1995.
A wordless graphic narrative depicts the terrible journey of Africans captured for slavery—from their home village to distant shores—with superimposed images that will imprint viewers with the agony of history.

Grant, Cynthia. *Uncle Vampire* (12–17). Atheneum, 1993.
A victim of incest creates a fantasy world that finally breaks down in this suspenseful novel that ends if not happily then at least with possibilities of help and hope.

Herron, Carolivia. *Nappy Hair,* illustrated by Joe Cepeda (4–8). Knopf, 1997.
Sitting around a picnic table set on fresh green grass, Brenda's African-American family celebrates their togetherness—and her wild black curly hair. Brenda her-

self energetically races through the pages in a neon-green dress with a yellow ruffle and black-and-white high tops, joyfully heading for her obviously sublime destiny. A bright palette for an exuberant story.

Holland, Isabelle. *The Man without a Face* (12 and up). Lippincott, 1971.
Lonely fourteen-year-old Charles turns to his aloof tutor for friendship and learns that love can have many faces.

Kerr, M. E. *Night Kites* (13–17). Harper, 1986.
Already caught up in some seriously problematic dynamics with friends and girlfriends, seventeen-year-old Erick suddenly must deal with a homosexual brother who has come home with AIDS. Kerr has always tackled adolescent problems head-on, as in her book *Dinky Hocker Shoots Smack!*—not about a drug addict but a food addict whose problem doesn't seem serious enough to attract her parents' attention.

Klein, Norma. *Mom, the Wolfman, and Me* (10 and up). Pantheon, 1972.
Brett and her mom have a terrific relationship, but is there room in their unconventional lifestyle for a third party?

Maruki, Toshi. *Hiroshima No Pika* (8 and up). Lothrop, 1982.
Dramatic artwork and simple narrative convey a child's horrifying experiences in Hiroshima the day the atomic bomb was dropped, concluding with a picture of the lanterns released annually along the city's seven rivers in honor of the dead.

Nelson, Theresa. *Earthshine* (10–13). Jackson/Orchard, 1994.
With her father dying of AIDS, Slim gets involved with a church youth group for kids close to people with the disease. The group's pilgrimage introduces a comedic note into this touching and inevitably tragic story.

Pausewang, Gudrun. *The Final Journey* (13–17), translated by Patricia Crampton. Viking, 1996.
Pausewang's courageous and devastating novel, showing the viewpoint of a doomed eleven-year-old girl in a railway boxcar filled with Jews being transported to Auschwitz, will help readers understand what happened to victims of the Holocaust.

Reiss, Johanna. *The Upstairs Room* (9–12). Crowell, 1972.
Hidden by a Dutch farm family, a Jewish girl and her sister survive the Nazi occupation during World War II.

Sendak, Maurice. *In the Night Kitchen* (4–8). Harper, 1970.
In an amazing dream, Mickey flies out of his clothes, into a cake, and through the air in a plane made of batter.

Weik, Mary. *The Jazz Man* (8–10). Atheneum, 1966.
Striking woodcuts and a stark text portray a deserted child who turns to music and memories for consolation.

Zemach, Margot. *Jake and Honeybunch Go to Heaven* (5–8). Farrar, 1982.
With ebullient watercolor paintings depicting an all-black cast of characters (in-

cluding God and the angels), Zemach tells the story of how a man and his contrary mule find a place in heaven.

Zindel, Paul. *Pardon Me, You're Stepping on My Eyeball* (12 and up). Harper, 1976. The offbeat story of two teenagers, "Marsh" Mellow and Edna Shinglebox, who meet in group therapy and help each other out of their confusion. Several of Zindel's other books, including *My Darling, My Hamburger,* have also been controversial.

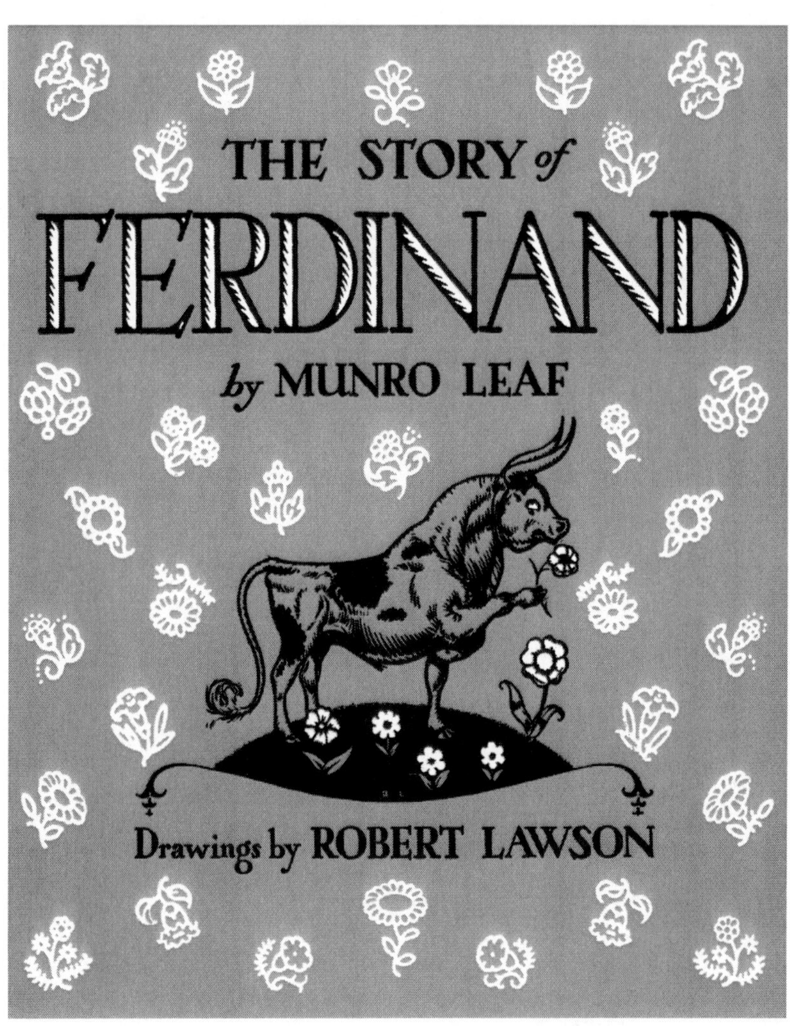

Robert Lawson

11

Live Classics

I remember walking down the block with one of my children, feeling the old familiar tooth-grinding impatience, when she stopped in the middle of the sidewalk to look at a worm. I thought about how late we were and urged her to hurry and finally grabbed her hand and pulled her along with a gentle but determined insistence. She cried. I worried.

I've forgotten what we were late for, but I'll never forget that worm. It was an interesting worm, and I don't know why I didn't try watching the worm the way *she* did instead of watching her watch the worm the way *I* did. I could have learned a lot. I could have seen something of importance about the worm, the child, and myself. Appointments do have to be kept, but worms also have to be watched. It's unfortunate that it seems easier for adults to make appointments than to take the time to watch worms, though the former may be no more important or interesting or informative than the latter.

By the same token, it seems easy to send a kid off to a surefire distraction like "Sesame Street" or Archie comics. There's nothing wrong with that; in fact, we all need to do it sometimes. However, if that's all we do then we miss a lot. Child and adult need each other. Every adult has been a child, and if the child inside the adult dies, something important to adulthood is lost.

Children and children's books give voice to the inner child. I still have some of my childhood books. They're valuable not only because they're old and beautiful but because I can never read anything again as a child. They summon a wealth of childhood feelings and associations, yet I can still appreciate them as an adult.

I feel the same way about my worn leather mitt and baseball. They were sewn strong and are still good. It's important now to use them both with a child—mine or someone else's. What's vital is making the connection between the child I was and the child that is. This is a kind of immortality, passing on the mitt, the baseball, the book. Today's child and tomorrow's child need to add their own new books, too. That's what keeps us all fresh.

The children's books you want to keep will have to be enduring. They'll live long and wear well. They won't be the first thing you grab off the rack at the checkout counter to silence your squirming grocery-cart rider. They'll be books that you love enough to pass on. For the child, they may represent the heart of family or an escape from it. I loved it when my parents took turns reading to me and my siblings, and I loved turning to the privacy of reading alone. Any household can be chaotic, from broken toilets to birthday party disasters, but in print there's a structured world. Books may resemble life, but unlike life they've been ordered out of chaos. A children's book is a dream of other things. It's a chance to see through the cracks of life into distant realms. The child or adult who wishes for more can find it. Like the important people in life, books that have grown with you stay with you.

The booklist for this chapter consists of pre-1950 standards that still live and breathe and are widely available. (A few old favorites also appear in the picture book and fiction lists at the ends of chapters 2, 3, and 5.) Books do have a life of their own. These classics are vital enough to have befriended generations of readers and to continue inducting newcomers into the companionship of story.

Live Classics

Aesop. *Aesop's Fables* (7–11). Various editions.
These brief, highly structured animal tales usually disguise ironic points about human nature, generating discussion and creative writing projects for home or classroom.

Alcott, Louisa May. *Little Women* (10 and up). Various editions.
Meg, Jo, Beth, and Amy are four very different sisters who share good times and bad in this memorable family classic set in Civil War–era America.

Andersen, Hans Christian. *The Fairy Tales of Hans Christian Andersen* (7–11). Various editions.
Andersen's haunting fairy tales portray both the vulnerable and the ridiculous in human nature.

Barrie, J. M. *Peter Pan* (9–11). Various editions.
The story is carried beyond the action of the play as Mrs. Darling is disposed of in a sentence and Wendy grows up, marries, and has a daughter who takes care of Peter's spring house cleaning now that Wendy has become caught up in the earthbound disenchantment of adulthood.

Baum, L. Frank. *The Wizard of Oz* (9–11). Various editions.
Children are most likely to be familiar with the film classic about Dorothy's adventures outside of Kansas, but they'll find the book just as enchanting.

Burnett, Frances H. *The Secret Garden* (10 and up). Various editions.
A self-centered girl and a pampered invalid boy learn compassion within the walls of an abandoned garden.

Carroll, Lewis. *Alice in Wonderland* (10 and up). Various editions.
A white rabbit, a mad hatter, and a grinning Cheshire cat—they're all here in this much-loved fantasy about a young girl's extraordinary journey down the rabbit hole.

Collodi, Carlo. *Pinocchio* (9–11). Various editions.
Pinocchio's adventures have perennial appeal for children who are thankful, each time they hear or see the story, that their own noses don't grow with every lie.

Defoe, Daniel. *Robinson Crusoe* (12 and up). Various editions.
Survival on a deserted island makes for a story that satisfies any youngster who dreams of creating a new world with total independence.

Du Bois, William Pène. *The Twenty-one Balloons* (9–11). Viking, 1947.
The amazing voyage of Professor William W. Sherman, who started out from San Francisco in one balloon and was picked up three weeks later in the Atlantic with twenty. A traveler's tale par excellence, with subtle black-and-white drawings.

Estes, Eleanor. *The Moffats,* illustrated by Louis Slobodkin (9–11). Harcourt, 1941.
Still a family favorite, this book chronicles the everyday activities of four children who get in and out of trouble at a lively pace.

Farley, Walter. *The Black Stallion,* illustrated by Keith Ward (9–12). Random, 1944.
The first in a series that has hooked readers for decades, Farley's book will satisfy horse lovers with the adventures of a boy and the black stallion he tames, loves, and races.

Forbes, Esther. *Johnny Tremain,* illustrated by Lynd Ward (10–12). Houghton, 1943.
A historical novel with such vivid characterizations and plot that readers seem to find themselves back in Boston at the outset of the Revolutionary War.

Grahame, Kenneth. *The Wind in the Willows* (8 and up). Various editions.
A romantic water rat, a peaceful mole, and a majestic badger conspire to keep their

boastful friend Toad out of trouble in this cozy, exuberant story of life in the Wild Wood.

Henry, Marguerite. *Misty of Chincoteague,* illustrated by Wesley Dennis (9–11). Rand, 1947.
Interwoven with the fast-paced story of two children's love for the wild ponies of Chincoteague is the flavor of life on the small island, reflected in well-drafted illustrations.

Kipling, Rudyard. *The Jungle Book* (8 and up). Various editions.
The gripping story of Mowgli, a boy raised in the jungle by animals that are both wild and wise.

Lang, Andrew. *The Blue Fairy Book* (7–12). Various editions.
This collection, the first in a series with entries titled in various hues, benefits from a nineteenth-century folklorist's witty adaptations.

Lawson, Robert. *Rabbit Hill* (9–11). Viking, 1944.
Sly drawings portray the animals who worry about what kind of people may take over their terrain.

Lear, Edward. *The Complete Nonsense of Edward Lear* (9–12). Various editions.
Uproarious line drawings by the author illustrate a collection of inspired silliness.

Lofting, Hugh. *The Story of Dr. Dolittle,* illustrated by Michael Hague (9–11). Rev. ed. Morrow, 1997.
Updated versions of this classic retain the action and exaggerated humor of animals guiding misguided people but have been revised to omit the sometimes racist attitudes of the original books.

MacDonald, George. *The Princess and the Goblin* (9–11). Various editions.
Underground goblins endanger a princess's life in this absorbing nineteenth-century fantasy.

McCloskey, Robert. *Homer Price* (9–11). Viking, 1943.
Homer doesn't really mean to get into trouble—it just comes naturally in McCloskey's small-town book of every-child episodes.

Nesbit, E. *Five Children and It* (10–12). Unwin, 1902.
"It" is a Sand-fairy, or Psammead, who grants one wish a day to the children of a vacationing family. Each wish brings a new adventure, and each adventure brings new woes in this enduring fantasy first published at the turn of the century.

Pyle, Howard. *The Merry Adventures of Robin Hood* (9–11). Various editions.
Pyle's powerful artwork, medieval in flavor, distinguishes an elaborately styled text celebrating one of England's most popular heroes. *The Story of King Arthur and His Knights* is another eye-catching epic cycle.

Spyri, Johanna. *Heidi* (9–12). Various editions.
Heidi's companionship helps cure a crippled child in the mountains of Switzerland.

Stevenson, Robert Louis. *A Child's Garden of Verses* (6 and up). Various editions.
Imaginative poems create a rich picture of childhood feelings and dreams. For older siblings, don't forget the swashbuckling adventures in *Treasure Island.*

Tolkien, J. R. R. *The Hobbit* (8 and up). Houghton, 1938.
Elves, trolls, and goblins engage in battles and quests in this compelling, enduring fantasy saga.

Travers, P. L. *Mary Poppins* (9–12). Rev. ed. Voyager/Harcourt, 1985.
What readers wouldn't want a nanny to take them on fantasy flights with a flick of her magic umbrella—the way Mary Poppins does for the Banks children?

Twain, Mark. *Tom Sawyer* and *Huckleberry Finn* (10 and up). Various editions.
Exciting books of mystery, dramatic escapades, and comic misadventures chronicle the lives of two boys growing up on the Mississippi River in the mid-nineteenth century.

Wilder, Laura Ingalls. *Little House in the Big Woods* (8–12). Harper, 1953.
Laura's story of family life in the forests of Wisconsin captures the adventure and drama of everyday pioneer life.

David Macaulay

12

Tracking Down Good Books

Having a head full of ideas and titles can make the search for children's books challenging. Or frustrating. The local bookstore may offer little more than a row of popular series and a handful of classics. You may have no idea where to start on the Internet. The public library may be unfamiliar territory or understaffed. Your children's classroom experience may be limited to textbooks, and the school library may be nonexistent. It's hard to find high-quality items among the mass market book products that are available in grocery and variety stories. And last but not least, you and your child may disagree about which books are good books.

Such situations are typical, but don't give up, because there's gold at the end of the rainbow. It's all in knowing how to look for it. The key is persistence. One strike is worth a lot of digging. The best place to start is the closest public library. Your tax dollars already support it, so you might as well take advantage of it. The library can be a gold mine of information about books and other resources. The librarian will probably be familiar with the titles mentioned throughout this book and should be able to pull them off the shelves, get them from other libraries, or suggest similar titles that are available.

You may also discover story hours, film programs, and book clubs at your local library. Parenting and toddler programs are a valuable, popular addition in many systems. On afternoons when everyone needs to get out and the park is cold or crowded or just visited once too often, try the library. If you're a working parent, don't despair: evening and weekend hours at most libraries mean you and your children don't have to miss out on the fun. A bridge of books is an ideal way to span the gap between a parent and a child's separate worlds, and a weekly visit to the library can solidly structure a bridge that will survive floods of tension from childhood dependency through adolescent rebellion.

The American Library Association publishes a helpful list of "Notable Children's Books" and "Best Books for Young Adults" every year. The list is available at local libraries and on the ALA Web site at http://www.ala.org/, or a print version can be ordered directly from the American Library Association, 50 East Huron, Chicago, IL 60611. Almost all libraries feature national and state award books—if you can't find them, just ask. Most children's librarians have something of a missionary's zeal about converting people to children's books, and the bewildered adult is a prime candidate for conversion!

If you find yourself signing out the same books over and over again, maybe they're worth owning. Prepare for a trip to the bookstore, and if you don't find something you're looking for, *ask for it.* Books not in stock can easily be ordered, as long as they're still in print. You can even ask specifically about paperback editions, which may allow you to buy several books instead of one. These days, even picture books are beautifully reproduced in paperback and are surprisingly sturdy. Your enthusiastic recommendation of a title might well persuade a store to keep it in stock. When bookstore owners sense a new interest among their clientele, they'll often reevaluate their stock, so it's worth establishing a personal relationship through visits and conversations with sales clerks. Many bookstores are also responding to the booming interest in children's literature with storytimes, visits by authors, and other child-centered events you and your children might enjoy. It's a competitive time for bookstores, and especially if you're not blessed with a nearby or well-stocked, well-staffed library, it makes sense to patronize the stores offering services that suit your needs.

Used bookstores may also have sections of children's books. Although the luxury of choice is diminished, plenty of good books have been popular enough to be readily available, and some stores also offer shelves of mass market series titles at prices you may find very tolerable. Another trick to book shopping is learning to spot high quality even on supermarket racks, where distributors often pile up a lot of junk. There are good Golden Books and bad ones; there are interesting Disney titles and dull ones; there are beautiful pop-up and "gadget" books mixed in with ugly, cluttered ones; there are funny comics and violent ones. Make comparisons and trust your own taste. Look especially for imaginative artistic design and skillful writing, no matter where you find the book.

The drawback to buying books over the Internet is that you can't browse them first. If you already know what you're looking for, however, online bookstores can be an effective way to acquire a book, and they can be a real boon if you live in a bookstore desert. The bookstores offering online ordering include chains such as Barnes and Noble, which many buyers know already; some capable online services have allowed local stores to go national or international (Oregon's Powell's Books is now a popular source far beyond the Pacific Northwest) or to exist only online, such as Amazon.com. If you're looking for an out-of-print favorite, the Internet may be your best friend. Search sites such as BookFinder.com and Acses will allow you to search a multitude of store and dealer listings simultaneously, and many specialized children's book dealers who don't have their inventory searchable online will still have Web sites and will be happy to answer e-mail inquiries about titles. Most stores will allow you to arrange payment over the telephone or by mail if you prefer not to place the actual order over the Internet.

It's important while combing the racks—whether real or virtual—to discuss what you see with your kids. Their reactions are crucial. It's no failure if a good book isn't a mutual hit. Adults and kids are bound to have different tastes. One way to cope with fad influences is to say, "Why don't you get that with your allowance and I'll buy something we *both* like." It's important to offer your own judgment as balance, not as something forced on your children but as an additional boost to their own interest and independence.

Early on I had to learn to contain my enthusiasm because it threatened my children's independence. They would bring home a school mail-order listing of books and ask me which ones I'd choose, and then they'd quickly settle on something else. It was a stage they had to go through before we reached a point of mutual respect for each others' tastes, which led to interesting exchanges of opinion as they learned to articulate their own reactions. Some parents have formalized this process through mother-daughter or father-son or simply parent-child book clubs that select a book to be the focus of discussion at each meeting.

The influence of school peers is enormous and often accounts for a book's overnight success. It will pass from hand to hand like lightning when it achieves "group status." Judy Blume's books flourished by word of mouth long before critics or paperback promotion gave them a boost. Teachers and parents should be quick to spot this peer popularity phenomenon as a good starting point and *read what's popular,* whatever it is. The teacher can find out from the class, and you can find out from the teacher and from your own kids.

The school situation is fertile for exploration, but it needs parent involvement. Teachers are often so pressed by administrative and curriculum demands that they don't have time for books. It may sound strange to teach reading and literature without books, but that's just what happens. Textbooks, worksheets, and vocabulary lists are substituted for more motivating stories because the results can be easily measured and tested. In spite of curricular pressures, though, many teachers do read out loud and are responsive to parent interest and suggestions.

The school library or media center may be another gold mine, or it may need your assistance. Your informed interest will establish a link that leads to a helpful relationship with the person in charge. If there's a good school library, your children should feel at home in it, and your encouragement in the form of a visit can set the precedent as well as turn the school librarian into another personal resource for books and information. Some school libraries thrive on parent and child volunteers. PTA involvement often leads to book fairs at school, with organizational support from local bookstores.

There are other organizations to turn to outside your locality. The Children's Book Council at 568 Broadway, Suite 404, New York, NY 10012 has pamphlets on selecting children's books. The International Reading Association puts out an annual list of "Children's Choices" that is available on the Children's Book Council Web site (listed with other resources at the end of the chapter). Newspapers and magazines run roundup reviews, especially before Christmas, when bookstores stock up.

Even if you're not interested in using the Internet as a buying tool, you might want to make use of the information it offers, which ranges from publishers' promotions of children's titles to lists of award-winning books past and present to sites for and even by kids about popular series. The Children's Literature Web Guide is the daddy of them all, providing a wealth of material of its own as well as links to most established children's literature sites on the World Wide Web. While it's important to remember that nothing is authoritative merely because it appears on the Internet (or in print!), the multitude of valuable facts and informed opinions you can find online is well worth exploring.

Tracking Down Good Books

Allison, Christine. *I'll Tell You a Story, I'll Sing You a Song: A Parent's Guide to the Fairy Tales, Fables, Songs, and Rhymes of Childhood.* Delacorte, 1987.

More an anthology than a guide, Allison's book brings together some of the best known nursery rhymes and folktales, with one- or two-page lists of suggestions that serve as introduction to each section.

The Black Experience in Children's Books. New York Public Library, 1994.

This annotated bibliography, organized by age and subject matter and updated every six to seven years, suggests books about African Americans and black Caribbeans, Africans, and Britains.

Blake, Barbara. *A Guide to Children's Books about Asian Americans.* Scolar, 1995.

A useful source for those interested in exploring the way this growing population is reflected in children's literature.

Books for You. National Council of Teachers of English, 1995.

Recommended books for high school students in various categories such as love stories, mysteries, and fantasy. For more information contact NCTE, 1111 West Kenyon Road, Urbana, IL 61801-1096.

Butler, Dorothea. *Babies Need Books: Sharing the Joy of Books with Children from Birth to Six,* illustrated by Shirley Hughes. Rev. ed. Heinemann, 1998.

A year-by-year guide to sharing books aloud, this source emphasizes British publications, but the suggestions for imprinting literature are global.

Carter, Betty. *Best Books for Young Adults: The Selections, the History, the Romance.* American Library Association, 1994.

A compilation of annual lists of Best Books for Young Adults from 1966 to 1993.

Chambers, Aidan. *The Reading Environment: How Adults Help Children Enjoy Books* and *Tell Me: Children, Reading, and Talk.* Stenhouse, 1996.

An experienced author, editor, and children's literature advocate gives anecdotal tips on how to connect children and books.

Dreyer, Sharon, ed. *The Bookfinder: A Guide to Children's Literature about the Needs and Problems of Youth Aged 2–15.* American Guidance Service, 1989.

A useful resource cross-references problems such as divorce and illness to books that contain such problems as their dominant themes.

Egoff, Sheila, et al., eds. *Only Connect: Readings on Children's Literature,* 3d ed. Oxford, 1996.

A thought-provoking collection of essays written by authors, illustrators, and critics on the many facets of children and their reading. Egoff is also the author of *Thursday's Child: Trends and Patterns in Contemporary Children's Literature.*

Gillespie, John T., and Corinne J. Naden, eds. *Best Books for Children: Preschool through the Middle Grades,* 5th ed. Bowker, 1994.

Thousands of books for children, from preschool to grade six, are briefly described and listed by subject.

Gose, Elliott. *Mere Creatures: A Study of Modern Fantasy Tales for Children.* Toronto, 1988.

Adults with a scholarly bent will enjoy this study of ten twentieth-century fantasy classics. Gose connects them to folklore and suggests psychological interpretations related to animal tricksters.

Hazard, Paul. *Books, Children, and Men,* 5th ed. Horn Book, 1983.

Classic commentary on children's books in several countries from a French scholar of comparative literature.

Hearne, Betsy. *Sharing Picture Books with Young Children* and *Picture Books: Elements of Illustration and Story.* Videocassettes, color, VHS, Beta. American Library Association, 1986, 1987.

The first of these two tapes informally introduces books for the earlier stages of childhood development; the second closely examines the art and narrative of two picture books.

Hearne, Betsy, ed. *The Zena Sutherland Lectures, 1983–1992.* Clarion, 1993.

Each of ten outstanding authors and illustrators delves into a special area of interest in a series of lectures delivered in honor of Zena Sutherland, who was the editor of the *Bulletin of the Center for Children's Books* for twenty-seven years.

Hopkins, Lee Bennett. *Pass the Poetry, Please!* Rev. ed. HarperCollins, 1998.

"From Mother Goose to Dr. Seuss—and beyond," Hopkins discusses ways to incorporate poetry into children's lives, with good advice on which poets to rely on.

Horning, Kathleen T. *From Cover to Cover: Evaluating and Reviewing Children's Books.* HarperCollins, 1997.

An up-to-date, intelligent discussion of criteria by which to evaluate children's books of all kinds, with clear and copious examples.

Huck, Charlotte. *Children's Literature in the Elementary School,* 5th rev. ed. Holt, Rinehart and Winston, 1994.

A textbook that emphasizes child development and the research that reflects the growing importance of literature for a child's language growth and reading achievement.

Hunt, Peter, ed. *Children's Literature: An Illustrated History.* Oxford, 1995.

Abundant, well-reproduced art and a straightforward text by several well-known scholarly authorities make this a prime choice for deeper background on children's books from the sixteenth through the twentieth centuries.

Lewis, Valerie V., and Walter M. Mayes. *Valerie and Walter's Best Books for Children: A Lively, Opinionated Guide.* Avon, 1998.

This 700-page compendium offers annotations for a multitude of children's books arranged by reading level.

Lipson, Eden Ross. *The New York Times Parent's Guide to the Best Books for Children.* Rev. ed. Random, 1988.

With a spacious layout and handy cross-references, this sourcebook enables parents to pick from more than a thousand titles suggested and described by the discerning children's book editor of *The New York Times Book Review.*

Lukens, Rebecca. *A Critical Handbook of Children's Literature,* 6th ed. Longman, 1999.
Lukens's literary analysis explores concepts of theme, plot, style, and tone in children's books.

McGovern, Edythe M., and Helen D. Muller. *They're Never Too Young for Books: A Guide to Children's Books for Ages 1 to 8.* Rev. ed. Prometheus Books, 1994.
Emphasizing titles published for children since 1980, when this book was first published, McGovern and Muller outline the uses of literature with young children and provide briefly annotated lists organized by theme and genre. Criteria for evaluation and tips for reading aloud are also included.

Notable Children's Books and *Best Books for Young Adults.*
These pamphlets, with booklists selected by American Library Association committees, are available annually from the Association for Library Service to Children and from the Young Adult Services Association, respectively, 50 East Huron, Chicago, IL 60611. They're also available on the ALA Web sites listed below.

Perrin, Noel. *A Child's Delight.* Dartmouth/New England, 1997.
Chatty essays about books the author recommends for children represent personal picks rather than a systematic professional overview, but the tone is friendly and informal.

Phelan, Patricia, ed. *High Interest–Easy Reading: An Annotated Booklist for Middle School and Senior High School,* 7th ed. National Council of Teachers of English, 1996.
Organized by subject and theme, this bibliography suggests a wide range of books with reading levels accessible to teens.

Reed, Arthea. *Comics to Classics: A Parent's Guide to Books for Teens and Preteens.* Rev. ed. Penguin, 1994.
A summary approach to the reading interests of adolescents, including fiction, nonfiction, reference books they need for school, and tips to tie in with TV, video, and computer technology.

Richardson, Selma. *Magazines for Children: A Guide for Parents, Teachers, and Librarians,* 2d ed. American Library Association, 1991.
Children and young adults who won't read books will often read magazines, which are less intimidating and more browsable. Richardson uses consistent criteria to evaluate what's available.

Rochman, Hazel. *Against Borders: Promoting Books for a Multicultural World.* American Library Association/Booklist, 1993.
Crossing cultural boundaries in print is the first step toward a more global perspective, according to the author of *Tales of Love and Terror: Booktalking the Classics Old and New,* and here she suggests many of the books that support this humanitarian goal.

Schon, Isabel. *The Best of the Latino Heritage: A Guide to the Best Juvenile Books about Latino People and Cultures.* Scarecrow, 1997.
From a long-recognized authority in the field, this annotated bibliography is organized by country and region.

Smith, Lillian H. *The Unreluctant Years: A Critical Approach to Children's Literature.* American Library Association, 1991.
An early and contagiously enthusiastic look at the literary aspects of children's books.

Sutherland, Zena. *Children and Books,* 9th ed. Longman, 1997.
The best and most widely used textbook on children's literature, this is a regularly updated resource that reads well and contains a wealth of information, including lists of award winners, adult books about children's literature, and useful bibliographies.

Sutherland, Zena, et al. *The Best in Children's Books: The University of Chicago Guide to Children's Literature, 1985–1990.* Chicago, 1991.
A collection of reviews from *The Bulletin of the Center for Children's Books* makes an excellent guide to good reading.

Sutton, Wendy K., ed. *Adventuring with Books: A Booklist for Pre-K–Grade 6.* National Council of Teachers of English, 1997.
A periodically updated, selective subject guide to good titles with popular appeal.

Tomlinson, Carl M., ed. *Children's Books from Other Countries.* Scarecrow, 1998.
Sponsored by the United States Board on Books for Young People, this annotated bibliography will connect American readers not only with other countries but also with different cultures within the United States.

Townsend, John Rowe. *Written for Children: An Outline of English-Language Children's Literature,* 6th ed. Scarecrow, 1996.
An eminent British critic and novelist traces the development of children's literature in England, the Commonwealth, and the United States.

Trelease, Jim. *The Readaloud Handbook.* 4th ed. Viking/Penguin, 1995.
Trelease's best-selling guide underscores the rationale for reading aloud, along with "do's and don'ts" and plenty of books to include in every family's personal library.

Wolf, Shelby Anne, and Shirley Brice Heath. *The Braid of Literature: Children's Worlds of Reading.* Harvard, 1992.
This book reports on a fascinating nine-year study of two girls raised with reading from birth: what books they loved, how they incorporated books into their lives, and what those books ultimately meant to their development.

Your Reading. National Council of Teachers of English, 1995–96.
An annotated list of books for middle school and junior high school students in categories such as "Family," "Home," and "Staying Alive."

Journals to Keep Current

Booklist

A professional review journal published twice a month by the American Library Association includes sections on current children's books and books for young adult reading, in addition to information on new adult books, reference books, and nonprint materials.
Web site: http://www.ala.org/booklist

The Bulletin of the Center for Children's Books

Published monthly (except in August) by the University of Illinois Press for the Graduate School of Library and Information Science at the University of Illinois at Urbana-Champaign, this is the only major journal devoted entirely to reviews of children's books, with timely, critical evaluations by a committee of professionals who have worked with children.
Web site: http://edfu.lis.uiuc.edu/puboff/bccb

The Horn Book

This venerable journal, issued every two months, contains articles on children's literature as well as regular columns and selective reviews.
Web site: http://www.hbook.com

Kirkus Reviews

Bookstore owners often rely on the prepublication reviews in *Kirkus,* which covers books for children and young adults as well as adults.

The New Advocate

This quarterly journal contains a "Book Review Sampler" as well as articles on children's literature.

The New York Times Book Review

Although the number of reviews in this weekly supplement is limited, the viewpoints are interesting and lively.

Riverbank Review of Books for Young Readers

This accessible, generously illustrated quarterly features articles and reviews of interest to parents as well as professionals.

SLJ/School Library Journal

This monthly journal contains articles on children's librarianship and literature, as well as reviews written by librarians in the field.
Web site: http://www.slj.com

VOYA: Voice of Youth Advocates

A bimonthly journal devoted to reviewing books for or of interest to young adults.

Web Sites

URLs can change (and Web sites can disappear, just as books go out of print), so if an address doesn't work, try using a search engine to find the site name.

Acses
http://www.acses.com
The Acses site searches and provides price comparisons for new and used books from nearly two dozen stores and services worldwide.

American Library Association/Association for Library Service to Children (ALSC)
http://www.ala.org/alsc
American Library Association/Young Adult Library Services Association (YALSA)
http://www.ala.org/yalsa
These two excellent Web sites contain, among many other items of information, lists of notable and award-winning books for children (ALSC) and young adults (YALSA).

BookFinder.com
http://www.bookfinder.com
The original book-search site on the World Wide Web, BookFinder.com allows you to search in one pass through the inventory of several worldwide consortia and large new and used bookstores.

Children's Book Council (CBC)
http://www.cbcbooks.org
This is a rich Web site with information about children's trade book publishers and publishing, along with lists such as "Children's Choices," an annual bibliography compiled in coordination with the International Reading Association. You can print the list off the Web site for free or write for a paper copy to IRA, Attn: Dept AG, 800 Barksdale Road, P.O. Box 8139, Newark, DE 19714–8139. Other handy resources available on the CBC site are "Notable Children's Trade Books in the Field of Social Studies," "Outstanding Science Trade Books for Children," "Not Just for Children Anymore," "75 Authors and Illustrators Everyone Should Know," and "Choosing a Child's Book."

Children's Literature Web Guide
http://www.acs.ucalgary.ca/~dkbrown
Between discussion boards, reference lists, and links to just about every relevant site on the Internet, this is the quintessential electronic source of children's literature information.

Cooperative Children's Book Center, University of Wisconsin at Madison (CCBC)
http://www.soemadison.wisc.edu/ccbc/
This is a valuable selection site that pays special attention to books of multicultural, intergenerational, and gender-conscious themes in children's books. The annual publication *CCBC Choices* is especially helpful.

Kay Vandergrift's Special Interest Page
http://www.scils.rutgers.edu/special/kay/kayhp2.html
This lively Web site offers a scholarly approach to information on and discussions of children's literature.

Parents' Choice

http://www.ctw.org/parents/choice

Along with brief, accessible articles on child development and family life, this site offers review roundups of books, videos, and toy products.

Trina Schart Hyman

Afterword

Since the first edition of this book was published in 1981, literacy has become a battle cry in the United States and throughout the world. Without a broadly literate public, our technological advances can be more dangerous than beneficial. We've also begun to recognize the role of children's books in verbal, visual, scientific, and cultural literacy. Trends in juvenile literature have reflected a new awareness that literacy begins at birth. An entire genre of board books for infants has boomed since 1980. Parents who occasionally made, sewed, or laminated a book if they wanted to read aloud to very young children now have a wide range of high-quality, ready-made choices at the bookstore or library. But your children don't have to be babies to turn a new page. They also don't have to be gifted, environmentally supercharged, vitamin fed, or privately educated. All children are latently literate. Whatever their stage of development, the principle is the same. Mastery depends on motivation.

Babies don't learn language because they're supposed to, or even because they have to, but because they're surrounded by it. Similarly, children don't learn how to read because they're supposed to but because they're surrounded by people who read and things that must be read. Literature is the road to literacy. More and more studies in early childhood development and education show how significant the quality of literature is to the child's reading experience. Teachers who read aloud from good children's books and who support sustained silent reading time provide the foundation for a future reading public. We've seen evidence of a reawakening to this fact on many levels.

P.S. 192 in New York City became a model of what children's books can do for a public school. In 1987, 92 percent of the students in P.S. 192 were from non-English-speaking families who lived below the poverty line. Injected with the energetic commitment of the American Reading Council, the teaching staff, and gift books from publishers—as well as a program called PARP, Parents As Reading Partners—P.S. 192 was turned into a reading center. There are now PARP programs all over the country, and the injection of parents into not just the administrative process but the actual reading process can only bring reading closer to children.

One of my kids once stopped in the middle of reading an assigned textbook passage and pounded her fist on the table. "Boring, boring, boring," she shouted. "It's just one word after another." Isaac Bashevis Singer said that unknown words are not prohibitive, but boring stories are. Our traditional reliance on unimaginative textbooks (and there *are* some imaginative ones) is perhaps best summarized by a cartoon that appeared in *Commentary* (Nov. 6, 1986). Under a picture of children filing out of a school is the caption, "An idea drill, actually. Any time an idea breaks out in a textbook, the alarm rings and the children exit immediately in single file and wait 50 yards from the building until the 'all clear' sounds."

Before the Chicago Public Schools committed to literacy through literature, the skills-and-drills-worksheet system of reading instruction had resulted in some children not holding a book in their hands until fourth grade. The education of children must clearly include instruction of teachers in the importance of children's books, the criteria for evaluating them, and the techniques for using them. In addition, teachers need administrative support to prioritize time for books.

Because it's central to literacy, children's literature can affect the quality of life and work for coming generations. Several public policy statements cite children's books as vital to reading programs (in place of or in addition to textbooks, worksheets, skills drills, etc.) and specifically refer to the poor preparation teachers receive in training programs that require no background courses in juvenile literature. *On Becoming a Nation of Readers: The Report of the Commission on Reading* (issued in 1984 by the National Institute of Education/U.S. Department of Education) states it loud and clear: "The single most important activity for building the knowledge required for eventual success in reading is reading aloud to children" (23). This process should start at birth or shortly thereafter. As for curriculum priorities, "there is no substitute for a teacher who reads children good stories. It whets the appetite of children for reading, and provides a model of skillful oral reading. It is a practice that should continue throughout the grades" (51).

Among the recommendations of the report are that children's reading should include more "classic and modern works of fiction and nonfiction that represent the core of our cultural heritage" and that "access to interesting and informative books is one of the keys to a successful reading program. As important as an adequate collection of books is a librarian who encourages wide reading and helps match books to children" (119).

In spite of much lip service to—and genuine interest in—the important role of family services, children's services, and literacy, government and state funding for work in those areas is often the first to be cut. Yet the quality of our children's imaginations will determine the future. The literature, art, and information to which children are exposed deserve our most astute, committed attention. Historically, children's literature has been a publishing niche fostered and protected by librarians. With the 1970s came a drying up of federal funds, a general tightening of library and school budgets, and, at the same time, a consciousness-raising about the importance of parental involvement in the reading process. Publishers relied less on institutional distribution and more on bookstore sales. That meant eye-catching graphics that would hook a consumer's attention from the display shelf—lots of toy books, television and movie spin-offs, lavishly illustrated fairy tales, sumptuous editions of classics. The flashy or the familiar sometimes won out with a public uneducated about children's books and unsure of how to choose them.

Where there's a market, there's the danger of a mass-market mentality. Editors often lose their power to accountants as conglomerates take over publishing companies. It's commonplace for a huge corporation to own many imprints that were once independent. The membership of the Children's Book Council, an organization of juvenile trade publishers, shows how few independent publishers are left. In 1966, the total number of CBC regular members not affiliated with any other CBC member was seventy-two; in 1976, forty-six; in 1986, sixteen. By 1996 it had leveled off at seventeen, but a new phenomenon had developed: the growth of associate members, "small" independent publishers with fewer than forty-five books in print and fewer than twelve titles in the preceding calendar year. Twenty-two of these small, independent children's book publishers were members of the CBC as of 1998, certainly a hopeful sign for publishing diversity. We're also on the verge of a revolution in electronic publishing—books on the World Wide Web—that may allow individuals and small concerns to reach as many (if not more) readers as the large publishers.

Big corporations go for big production and bigger profits, which means that quality may suffer because it costs time and money. Titles can drop out of print with breathtaking swiftness, especially since changes in tax laws have eliminated publishers' deductions on storing backlist books. Series are cheap, and they sell quickly. Animorphs and other mass-market series have glutted the market. Celebrities sell, too. In the last twenty years, children's books have become an industry, with the expectable quantity of slick, gimmicky products packaged for fad effects. That development hasn't killed quality, though. Some publishers still take chances on innovative voices. New writers have been found, encouraged, and published, with a subtle balance of art and story. Parents simply have a more commercialized array of books—and more extremes of quality and variety—from which to choose. The challenge to distinguish the extraordinary from the ordinary is greater than ever. But the search for voice, vision, detail, and enduring quality will not go unrewarded.

Many of the changes recently affecting juvenile publishing are inherent in a literature that has finally come of age. The bad multiplies with the good, but consumers can affect the maturation of children's literature by recognizing, valuing, and buying the best. Be guided by quality, not guilt. Parents and teachers are besieged with direct-mail ads and school book club ordering forms that offer more stickers, stuffed toys, and posters than good books. Don't be afraid to resist this kind of commercialized pressure. You can offer children more with a weekly trip to the library or a special-occasion browse at a bookstore. Patronize bookstores that provide personalized service. Children's bookstores have multiplied, and children's departments in chain and independent stores have expanded as well; many offer storytimes and other child-centered events. If a bookstore stocks only best-sellers, ask the manager to make special orders rather than accepting something you don't want just because it's available on the shelves. If there's resistance, shop elsewhere, including via mail order or the Internet. Ask your librarian to keep you posted on state and local as well as national children's book awards.

Most important, be inventive in relating your children's enthusiasms to books. Video and computer games often feature graphic and story motifs that figure in literature. Children who love to play the Nintendo version of "Wizards and Warriors" or "Myst" on CD-ROM will revel in J. R. R. Tolkien's world of wizards and warriors. Each child is drawn to different books for different reasons. That's why the individual link is so crucial. You may think you don't know as much as a professional, but the truth is that you know more because *you* know your child. With practice, you can also get to know the books. In time, you'll trust yourself to make the connection better than any best-seller list or computer-generated bibliography. Remember that parents and teachers serve the same function as storytellers in the oral tradition: they stimulate the imagination and cultivate verbal, visual, and cultural literacy by connecting book and child.

If we each sat down to make a list of the fifty best books since 1950, we'd all come up with different lists. Yet a few books would surface repeatedly. We can study those books for their elements of endurance. The books about which we differ will yield lively discussion on the dynamics of reader response, public reception, and the vagaries of stardom and obscurity. The subject of children's literature has drawn together professionals with an interest in the relationship of the child to narrative, art, and information. Literature for children and young adults, along with the role of fairy tales and storytelling in both cognitive and affective areas of development, has opened up a rich field of academic study with interdisciplinary connections to education, psychology, literature, art, and history. The impact of story on reading motivation, the elements of folklore and mythology that have survived in contemporary literature for children, the cultural and social history reflected in children's books, the issues of censorship and moral education versus aesthetic freedom, the impact of technology on printing and graphics, and the economics of publishing and distribution—these are subjects to challenge any inquirer.

Stimulating books provoke stimulating questions: What is the real difference between literature for children and literature for adults? What is the effect of compression on the development of fiction, nonfiction, and poetry? Can form be simple and content be complex, or does simple form determine simple content? What devices can be used to abbreviate literature without sacrificing its integrity? Does simplicity lead to oversimplification? Can oversimplification ever be effective in children's literature, as it is in archetypes, caricatures, and spoofs? Does brevity imply shortcuts of craft? Are brevity and complexity compatible?

Children's books have made me think hard about the long and short of story. For the last three decades I've seen and evaluated many of the children's books published every year. There's a moment at the beginning of Hannah Green's *I Never Promised You a Rose Garden* when a therapist debates with herself about which new patient she'll take on for therapy. I often think of that moment during weekly book review meetings for *The Bulletin of the Center for Children's Books,* where I'm a consulting editor. Of the approximately five thousand books the Center receives each year, about a third will be selected for further consideration and approximately one-fifth of those will eventually be reviewed in the journal. Which ones and why are questions constantly and carefully considered in looking over newly arrived books. The challenge of selection can be as overwhelming to the editors of *The Bulletin* as it is to a new parent entering a bookstore.

Thirty-five years ago, when I walked into my first job as a children's librarian, I thought I could read everything. Five years later, when I started my first job as a children's book reviewer, I thought I was lucky to get the chance to. In the thirty years I have been a book reviewer, myriad children's books have come to my attention. The more I see, the fewer I realize I can do justice to. But I also realize that not all books deserve equal attention.

Stephen Roxburgh, for many years the children's book editor at Farrar, Straus and Giroux, and later the founder of Front Street Books, thoughtfully defined his job as one of giving each manuscript a "just and patient hearing." But that's not how children read. Children play with books. So I try to balance children's lighter sense with an understanding of how precious time and literature are. My youngest child—another resistant reader—gravitated toward the choose-your-own-ending adventure series that make most grown-ups groan. She gobbled them up like popcorn, but she still looked forward to my reading aloud the kind of literature that lives forever.

When my close-up vision gets blurred by too many books, I try to take a longer, deeper look at one book. The great books are there. We need training to criticize them, but a primary appreciation cannot come without fresh perspective. The Irish poet Seamus Heaney said, in describing his childhood, "I think I spent a lot of my time just standing looking, gazing with my eyes open, timorously. The inner place of your first being is a large solitary gaze out at the world." We should all read with those eyes.

Author-Illustrator Index

Note: Italics denote an illustrator only. An asterisk indicates more than one book by the author is discussed on that page.

Subject Index

❁ Betsy Hearne teaches children's literature and storytelling in the Graduate School of Library and Information Science at the University of Illinois at Urbana-Champaign. The former children's book editor of *Booklist* and *The Bulletin of the Center for Children's Books,* she has reviewed books for thirty years and contributes regularly to the *New York Times Book Review.* Hearne is the author of *Beauty and the Beast: Visions and Revisions of an Old Tale,* as well as the editor of several collections of essays and folktales and (with Roger Sutton) of *Evaluating Children's Books: A Critical Look.* In addition, she has published five novels for children, two collections of poetry for young adults, and the picture book *Seven Brave Women,* for which she received the Jane Addams Children's Book Award.

❁ Deborah Stevenson has been on the staff of *The Bulletin of the Center for Children's Books* since 1989 and has been associate editor since 1998. She has taught children's literature in the Graduate School of Library and Information Science at the University of Illinois at Urbana-Champaign, at Indiana University Northwest, and in the continuing education programs at the University of Chicago and the University of Illinois at Urbana-Champaign. Her articles have appeared in *The Horn Book Magazine, Children's Literature Association Quarterly,* and *The Lion and the Unicorn.*

Typeset in 10.5/13 Adobe Minion
with Novarese Medium Italic display
Designed by Cope Cumpston
Composed by Celia Shapland
for the University of Illinois Press

University of Illinois Press
1325 South Oak Street
Champaign, IL 61820-6903
www.press.uillinois.edu